The Rising Price
of Objectivity

The Rising Price of Objectivity

Philanthropy, Government, and the Future of Education Research

Michael J. Feuer

To Sabrine —
A great ally in the
fight for evidence!

Best!
Michael.

Harvard Education Press
Cambridge, Massachusetts

Paperback ISBN 978-1-61250-957-0
Library Edition ISBN 978-1-61250-958-7

Library of Congress Cataloging-in-Publication Data

Names: Feuer, Michael J., author.
Title: The rising price of objectivity : philanthropy, government, and the future of education research / Michael J. Feuer.
Description: Cambridge, Massachusetts : Harvard Education Press, [2016] | Includes bibliographical references and index.
Identifiers: LCCN 2016022046| ISBN 9781612509570 (pbk.) | ISBN 9781612509587 (library edition)
Subjects: LCSH: Education—Research—United States. | Endowment of research—United States. | Education and state—United States.
Classification: LCC LB1028.25.U6 F48 2016 | DDC 370.72—dc23 LC record available at https://lccn.loc.gov/2016022046

Published by Harvard Education Press,
an imprint of the Harvard Education Publishing Group

Harvard Education Press
8 Story Street
Cambridge, MA 02138

Cover Design: Ciano Design
Cover Photo: RuslanDashinsky/Getty Images
The typefaces used in this book are Minion Pro and ITC Legacy Sans

To my family
And in memory of Bill Taylor and Bob Linn

Contents

Foreword by Ellen Condliffe Lagemann ix

INTRODUCTION 1

CHAPTER 1 WHITHER ALTRUISM? 15
Philanthropy and Its Discontents

CHAPTER 2 GOOD GOVERNMENT PAYS 47
The (Social) Science of Education Research

CHAPTER 3 LIGHTS UNTO THE NATION 73
The Rise and Decline of the American Advice
Industry

CHAPTER 4 A POLICY GRAMMAR 109
The Present Is Tense, the Future Imperfect

Notes 149

Acknowledgments 181

About the Author 183

Index 185

Foreword

A S I READ Michael Feuer's *The Rising Price of Objectivity: Philanthropy, Government, and the Future of Education Research*, I was reminded of two experiences, both of which pertain to this timely and wise book.

The first experience occurred some years ago, when, as president of the Spencer Foundation, I was invited to brief a group of congressmen and senators about the needs of the education research community. After listening to my plea for more funding to study fundamental problems of teaching, learning, leadership, and organization, one then prominent member of the House commented that we did not need more research since we knew what was needed to improve education. All we needed, he said, was "better teachers" and that did not necessitate research. I countered by saying, that, yes, we did need better teachers—we always need better teachers—but that research would help us understand how to prepare and help those teachers. That did not please my friend the congressman, who replied: "You professors are all alike. You make things too complicated." Having delivered that message, he then turned on his heels and left the meeting.

I thought of that exchange as I read *The Rising Price of Objectivity* because the book poses a rightly complicated and very important question: are current conditions in the philanthropic world, and among government research funders and private think-tank and research policy organizations, likely to erode possibilities for informing education policy with evidence culled from careful, disinterested, balanced research? In addressing that question, Michael raises a number of concerns about philanthropy, having to do with issues of accountability and the potential for special influence among today's super rich. In doing so, he calls out those critics of the best-known large foundations, notably Gates, Broad, and Walton, for being unduly harsh and simplistic and balances the charges that have been leveled against those organizations with historic comparisons as well as with carefully crunched data about the grant making of a wide range of funders.

In framing his worries about the nation's capacity to base its education policies on solid, warranted knowledge, Michael does not limit his discussion to philanthropy. He analyzes the full array of factors that shapes what policy makers know as they set the course for our schools and colleges. As I read Michael's discussion, I wished I could say, "Sorry, Mr. Congressman, this is, indeed, a complex matter and it needs a complicated story." Here, all in one short and eminently readable volume, one is asked to contemplate any number of matters relevant to the production, distribution, and use of education research. In all cases, one is also invited to consider both sides of the issue. For example, it is generally considered to be a good thing that an increasing number of people have been trained in research methods and are engaged in studying education. But an increased supply of researchers also intensifies the struggle to win funding, which may encourage researchers to tell funders what they want to hear, rather than what they need to hear. Here's another example. To be accountable, foundations must be open to assessments of their giving, more open than has traditionally been the case. But is it possible to have fully "objective" assessments when anyone engaged in such an exercise is likely to want to please the foundation he or she is studying in order to be eligible for future assignments or even a grant? *The Rising Price of Objectivity* offers a comprehensive, scholarly account of the many dilemmas involved in funding and making sense of research relevant to the making of sound education policy. Just for that it is a must-read book, but it offers even more.

To explain, let me turn to my second experience. Shortly before I met my favorite congressman, I was invited to serve on a National Research Council committee that was impaneled to generate advice for Congress concerning the meaning of "scientific research" in education. When we gathered for our first meeting and went around the table introducing ourselves to one another, I was dismayed to find that the committee included a number of people who had taken positions on matters of education policy with which I vehemently disagreed. Over twelve months of fairly intense work on our report, we all got to know one another quite well and learned to talk frankly about the evidence we were reviewing. The political labels we had brought to our work—ranging from conservative to liberal or, in my case, "overly soft Deweyite"—quickly became meaningless. What mattered were the rationales we articulated for the positions we espoused.

The work of that committee and many others like it explains not only the topic of this book, but also the tone of its argument. Through a long and distinguished career at the Office of Technology Assessment and the National Research Council, Michael Feuer has been schooled in civil discourse aimed at achieving consensus based on reliable data. He brings the beliefs, values, habits of mind, and style of argumentation he acquired working at those organizations to the concerns he describes here. He has seen the way groups of people, coming from very different backgrounds and positions, can talk across difference in a common quest to understand a controversial problem. He has witnessed their capacity to approach, through open discussion, their best approximation of a full and true clarification of what is involved in that problem. His experience has convinced him that, however imperfect it may be, knowledge generated in this way provides a good basis for policy making in a democratic society such as ours. It's a reasonable, enlightened position, presented with passionate, yet tempered, care; and its appeal in this era of anti-intellectualism and high partisanship should be great.

The Rising Price of Objectivity closes with a number of concrete proposals for improving the processes by which research funding is distributed, public and private funders are held accountable, and the findings of research are aggregated and disseminated. Whether any of his recommendations actually gain traction—and, as Michael suggests, their merits would depend on how they were worked out in practice—they underscore the importance of this book. *The Rising Price of Objectivity* is a commentary on the way we have set the direction and rules for collective, public action since at least the time of the Civil War. That approach—especially as it relates to the increasingly complex environment of philanthropic and government support for education research—may need some adjustment today. At the same time, to abandon it through indifference, without due deliberation, would be an unfortunate mistake. That is Michael Feuer's message in this compelling new book, and as concerned citizens we should take note.

Ellen Condliffe Lagemann
Levy Institute Research Professor, Bard College
Distinguished Fellow, Bard Prison Initiative

Introduction

A FEW YEARS AGO, at a gathering to celebrate the retirement of a distinguished colleague, an education researcher who had also held many high-level policy positions, I went on a little fishing expedition. I wondered aloud if anyone else was worried about the role of large private foundations in school reform, about the extent to which their influence is subject to any form of public accountability, whether their connections to the federal government are a problem, and what all of this might mean for education research and the uses of social science to inform public policy.

Lots of bait there, and I was glad to be in friendly waters—or so I thought.

My question was mild compared to the rather more potent rhetoric that was seeping into the public discourse. One of the harshest examples appeared earlier that year in Diane Ravitch's book slamming the high-stakes accountability and reform strategies of the Bush and Obama administrations.[1] Her chapter on the changing role of big philanthropy includes the now familiar trope about the "the billionaire boys club," which has endured as a recurrent motif in her frequent and fierce blogging. Ravitch summarized her basic argument in an interview with *Democracy Now!* in March 2010:

> We have never in the history of the United States had foundations with the wealth of the Gates Foundation and some of the other billionaire foundations—the Walton Family Foundation, The Broad Foundation. And these three . . . are committed now to charter schools and to evaluating teachers by test scores. And that's now the policy of the US Department of Education. *We have never seen anything like this, where*

foundations had the ambition to direct national educational policy, and in fact are succeeding. [italics added][2]

Note the several arguments woven there: the magnitude of current foundation giving allegedly unique in history, the commitment to a particular (and questionable) reform agenda, and the influence of foundations on national policy. Other commentators have amplified the theme in even more shrill tones, as in this excerpt from an article by Joanne Barkan in 2011:

A few billion dollars in private foundation money, strategically invested every year for a decade, has sufficed to *define the national debate* on education; sustain a crusade for a set of mostly ill-conceived reforms; and *determine public policy* at the local, state, and national levels. In the domain of venture philanthropy—where *donors decide* what social transformation they want to engineer and then design and fund projects to implement their vision—investing in education yields great bang for the buck. [italics added][3]

In contrast, my query was mild, inquisitive more than assertive. Still, one listener didn't like where I was heading. "Michael," he quipped, "you're starting to sound more and more like Richard Nixon." Ouch! I offered my friend the knife from my heart, we had a few laughs, and we turned our attention to other pressing issues such as whether the Washington Nationals would make it to the playoffs. I recall that it was fun thinking that Richard Nixon—no friend of foundations when they tried to assert a progressive influence in education and other social policy areas—and Diane Ravitch may have had more in common than either of them would likely want to admit, an irony made juicier given Ravitch's journey from her role in a Republican administration that was suspiciously and punitively critical of public education, circa 1988, to her exalted status as a left-leaning defender of teachers and teacher unions today.[4]

In any case, being likened to Richard Nixon is not something you forget easily, and in the years since I have continued to smart from the suggestion. Though I am even more worried today about trends in funding of education research (and the social sciences generally), I have come to believe that outsized attacks on the role of big foundations are not helpful, and that the real challenges to the production of useful and credible evidence to advise policy makers will not be solved if we succumb to extreme rhetoric. Ravitch's claim that "we have never seen anything like this" is surprising coming from a historian with a substantial record of publications and public service. Yes, the scale is different—Mike McPherson, a prominent foundation head and education leader, once quipped that Gates is the only foundation you can see from outer space. But there *is* precedent worth remembering.

For example, in its day, the Carnegie Corporation of New York, now the twenty-first-largest foundation in the United States (as of the end of 2014), was considered a pioneering behemoth of private largesse.[5] The distinguished Bard College education historian Ellen Condliffe Lagemann, former president of the Spencer Foundation and former dean of the Harvard Graduate School of Education, quotes Henry Pritchett, who had led the Carnegie Foundation for the Advancement of Teaching (founded in 1905) and then became a key architect of the new corporation: "[Andrew] Carnegie had established the greatest endowment ever given to a group of men for the promotion and diffusion of knowledge and understanding amongst the people of a nation."[6]

Historical data of this sort is helpful—I should say mandatory—in weighing claims and counterclaims about the size and influence of philanthropic organizations. We also need to view in historical perspective allegations that, in today's environment, there is too much alignment between foundations and the government. We need a wide lens to look into these matters, one capable of three- and four-dimensional views: changes in the scope and power of philanthropy and connections between the private foundation sector and the federal government are not taking place in a policy vacuum, but rather during a period of recurrent turbulence in the world of research generally and the behavioral, social, and education sciences specifically.

Which is why the query to my colleagues included reference to the changing federal role. In my mind was the nagging feeling, borne of my own increasingly difficult attempts to obtain grants from agencies such as the US Department of Education, the National Science Foundation (NSF), and the National Institutes of Health (NIH). Maybe my pile of unfunded proposals was the symptom of a deeper and more systemic pathology? To paraphrase the joke attributed to Freud, sometimes those sour grapes might really be sour.

Here, too, it can be tempting to overstate current trends and ignore the longer history. Periodically in our past, the idea of public funding of science has suffered the ups and downs of economically driven budget cycles, and has been subjected to intense public and political scrutiny. Indeed, our remarkable progress in science and technology, largely the result of decisions taken after World War II (which, for example, led to the establishment of the NSF), would not have been possible without that kind of introspection. Today, again, we confront political challenges to research, bordering, in some cases, on intrusions that have the scientific community quite rightly rattled; and although neither reduced budgets nor edginess about government "waste" are new phenomena on the American scene, that's not a reason to ignore current trends.[7]

Consider, for example, the rising supply of qualified scientists (in many fields), which I happily take as an indicator of the robustness of our university-based training programs. These researchers seek varying levels of externally sponsored financial support, depending on the nature of their work and the need for expensive laboratory equipment or data collections; and without proportional increases in available funding, increased demand for research dollars inevitably leads to increased competition, which may not always result in better-quality proposals or projects. If the squeeze on federal resources pushes new scholars to the private sector, that is, the corporate or nonprofit foundation world, those organizations may find themselves in even more powerful and influential roles, but operating without the customary constraints and traditions that ensure quality control, protection of human and other subjects, sharing of data, and transparency in dissemination of results. Will reduced federal support lead to even more anxiety about the disproportionate role of foundations? It is this type of convergence, a kind of financial pincer, even more than the apparent synchronization of public and philanthropic strategic preferences, that worries me.

I believe that, on balance, the American approach to funding of science, which has always involved some degree of private and public partnership, has done more good than harm, recurrent fluctuations in quantity and political enthusiasm notwithstanding.[8] The question now is whether today's trends portend a more gloomy future, and whether and how education and education research specifically might suffer. Add to this question yet another aspect of our ecology of research, namely, the role of organizations that exist to provide independent and "objective" scientific advice to inform policy, and the picture becomes more complicated and, in a sense, even more troubling.

The common complaint that American culture (political culture especially) is anti-intellectual is hard to square with our history of a robust appetite for independent, credible, and, in many cases, quantitative information to inform and advise those in charge of designing and implementing public policy. Americans may flirt with stupidity, but they buy knowledge. Nothing more effectively grabs the public psyche than international comparative statistics on student achievement, the latest findings from epidemiological studies of smoking or obesity, new data on economic and educational inequality, evidence of decline in life expectancy, or the average salaries earned by corporate moguls. Although less obviously relevant to public policy, sports statistics fill pages of newspapers and websites. At the federal level, especially, there is substantial demand for independent and credible data on a wide range of social and economic and educational issues: by some estimates, we spend upward of $5 billion per year on data collections, studies, evaluations, and research ostensibly aimed at bringing hard evidence to the table where complex policy questions are debated and political decisions are ultimately negotiated.[9]

How the findings from all that research actually make their way into policy remains murky—as it must, given the tensions and complexities etched into the system. Part of the American governance experiment, now in its third century, is reconciling a craving for data with a distrust of experts, in managing a system that thrives on numbers but makes decisions by politics, in wanting nationally representative and reliable advice but still privileging locally inspired decisions. We never liked the idea of "philosopher-kings," or "scientist-kings" for that matter; on the other hand, we have always wanted input from men (and, more recently, women) in their lab coats, even if their recommendations are not easily or quickly incorporated into policy and practice. There is more than a hint of "approach-avoidance conflict" in our historical relationship to scientific knowledge.

In this peculiar ecology of politics and governance, we have cultivated a special niche for organizations that aspire to intellectual and scientific neutrality, offering nonpartisan analyses of social and economic problems and advice based on ostensibly objective research and deliberation. Of course, universities play a dominant role here, though, by and large, the knowledge they produce comes from individual researchers (faculty and students) and doesn't usually carry their institution's imprimatur explicitly. The popular press often cites scholars' work with reference to where they work or to the institution that publishes the journal in which they are publishing. When the headline reads "Harvard Gun-control Study Destroys Gun-control Agenda," the university is clearly not responsible for the opinions or findings expressed in the cited report.[10] Most importantly, university-based research may have an impact on policy, but that's not its principal raison d'être.

The think tank, on the other hand, in its various forms, is a different invention that responds explicitly to the demand for evidence to support policy decisions, and is neither as enriched nor as burdened by standards of academic inquiry and freedom as universities and the scholars who do research and teach in them. I focus on this segment of what I shall be calling the "advice industry" in chapter 3. Some think tanks operate as holding companies for individual scholars and policy analysts and, in that sense, bear a resemblance to the way research is organized in universities. Frequently, the staff are given license to pursue their own studies and apply varying evidentiary standards within the norms and cultures of their respective fields and disciplines; increasingly, they are encouraged to articulate personal opinions that may precede or follow from their analyses.

In some cases, there is a greater institutional role in such matters as review and publication, with strict rules about what gets released, to whom, and following what kind of scrutiny. The RAND Corporation, for example, which is a combination think tank and contract research and evaluation organization, has a long and honored tradition of rigorous peer review and resistance to meddling by funders when it designs studies or reports results. Other organizations—the National Academy of Sciences (NAS), the National Academy of Education (NAEd), the Office of Technology Assessment (OTA)—have (or had) their own special features, in terms of their institutional affiliations, funding sources, honorific and service responsibilities, and review mechanisms. Indeed, because these organizations are (or, in the case of OTA, were) founded and structured with quite stringent definitions of their respective public responsibilities and legal overlays, they occupy an important niche in the advice industry; and as I will argue in chapters 3 and 4, some of their main features are worth considering as we explore mechanisms and policy options aimed at reinforcing the role of research to inform policy generally and education specifically.

It pays to expand this discussion, as it relates to a central question of this book, namely, whether the aspiration for political and financial neutrality in social science research, so necessary for the sake of assuring the credibility of evidence, is at risk because of the confluence of market forces and the increasingly strident partisanship of public and political discourse. One way research organizations strive to avoid the appearance or reality of external influence affecting the tone, substance, and credibility of advice, especially when it may include critiques of government activity, is to avoid taking any federal funding. Unlike the NAS and NAEd, which receive substantial funding from the government (the NAS operates under special legally binding arrangements designed to protect scientific integrity), and OTA, which was an arm of Congress and operated under a federal budget line item, major think tanks such as the Carnegie Endowment for International Peace (founded in 1910) still adhere to the policy of refusing government money. On the other hand, the Brookings Institution (founded in 1916) gets a small fraction of its total program budget from government grants and contracts.[11] RAND, and American Institutes for Research, on the other hand, two of the largest and most respected private contract research and evaluation shops, obtain the lion's share of their funding from government, which makes their processes of review and dissemination all the more important. Smaller organizations, for example, the Center on Education Policy (founded in 1995 as an independent nonprofit and now part of the George Washington University), began with a self-imposed rejection of federal support, but are now rethinking their attitudes, given the changing nature of private and corporate philanthropy and the awareness that federal funds have long been an essential source of support for scientific research.

My point here is that the structure and governance of think tanks and their norms of inquiry and communication (discussed in greater detail in chapter 3) are important factors in understanding their role in policy making. The additional issue I address in this book is whether and to what extent changes in the style and substance of private-sector philanthropy, which has been a traditional patron of many such research organizations (including those that do accept public funds), coupled with changes in the scope and magnitude of the federal role brought about by fiscal and political constraints, affect their capacity to produce and diffuse credible and objective research.

I will suggest that three concurrent and overlapping sets of forces may together be compromising the principle of research oriented to the improvement of policy and practice. It is a motif that keeps deans of social science and education and other citizens who care about *evidence-informed advice* awake at night.[12] The book explores the convergence of (1) the rise of "strategic" philanthropy in an increasingly crowded field of corporate and family foundations, (2) budget constraints and recurrent government reluctance to fund objective and independent research applied to understanding and solving social and educational problems, and (3) a financially pinched advice industry that may be less and less able to steer clear of partisan and commercial influence. Although I usually try to "worry efficiently," I do wonder if the ideal of independent and objective scientific advice is essentially doomed.[13] In more theoretical language, are there natural (or what economists might refer to as "tragic") outcomes that are predictable given the collision of individual researchers' interests (their legitimate need to raise external support for their work and their desire to advance professionally) and the public good (objective inquiry that challenges mainstream views, even those promulgated by the biggest public and private funders)?

In chapter 1, I start with trends in the foundation world, which has become something of a bête noire in the contemporary discourse on education reform. I consider economic and political aspects of the American approach to charitable giving, and implications for the provision of public goods generally and education specifically. I review recent data on spending patterns among foundations of different sizes, along with selected narratives those foundations use to describe their missions.[14]

The upshot of my analysis is a pair of complementary arguments. First, much of the rhetoric about the dangers of excessive private investment in social reforms—especially but not limited to education—is exaggerated.

There may be something vaguely satisfying in scapegoating people or organizations with massive wealth; after all, even liberals enjoy some schadenfreude now and then. But ultimately little good comes from attacks that play loose with logic and facts and undermine a tradition, rooted in the core principles of American democracy, which, on balance, has done more good than harm.

At the same time, this defense should not be read as an apologia for the status quo. My second argument is that the sensationalist rhetoric notwithstanding, trends toward advocacy-driven philanthropy and concentration of private wealth need careful monitoring. The drift among some of the largest foundations away from traditional norms of knowledge production and diffusion and toward the selective gathering of data to support programs based on partisan ideology, rather than sound empirical inquiry, threatens the value of research applied to the improvement of governance and advancement of the public good.

In chapter 2, I turn to trends in federally funded scientific research, with a focus on the agencies principally responsible for education and the education sciences. I rely mostly on publicly accessible data from the NSF, the US Department of Education, and the NIH, which have websites permitting detailed compilations of statistics on funding, grants, and related information. Again, I am concerned here with a problematic convergence of patterns. The good news is evidence of growth in the supply of well-trained education researchers seeking to orient their scholarship to improvement of education and other public goods. Enrollments in graduate programs in social science generally and education specifically have been stable (and, in some areas, growing), and I would argue that the rising supply of doctoral-level social scientists reflects a healthy and abiding commitment to research as a tool for understanding and solving social and economic problems.[15]

The less good news is about the funding environment. Growth in the supply of scientists seeking research grants would naturally lead to increased competition and reduced odds of obtaining needed funds even if federal research and development (R&D) budgets were stable; but when those budgets are strapped, which is the case today in the wake of the Great Recession of 2008–2009 and the sequestration of federal funds, the likelihood of securing needed funding has dropped further. Perhaps even more important than these economic constraints are the motivations of politicians who are unable or unwilling to fathom the long-term benefits of research—especially when the findings might interfere with ideology and religion—and the result is a toxic brew that threatens the scientific research enterprise generally and its role in education reform and improvement specifically.

Chapter 3 is about the advice industry, the increasingly dense constellation of think tanks, research-intensive universities, and nonprofit as well as for-profit research and evaluation companies that are deservedly hailed as bastions of objectivity and independence but have lately become more vulnerable to the forces of competition and the influence of private and public sponsors of their work. I focus on trends outside the university sector, where dramatic growth in the number of research organizations and think tanks, especially those that, for good reason, have not sought federal financial support for fear of appearing beholden to political agendas, has led to substantially heightened competition for limited private (philanthropic) resources.

The predicament that all think tanks and other players in the advice industry face, and one that is of obvious concern to a general public awaiting credible evidence, is this: Does accepting financial support from corporate and nonprofit foundations, from foreign governments with geopolitical or economic interests, or from other interested parties compromise the objectivity and credibility of the studies these research organizations are asked to conduct? Do researchers working in think tanks (and other such organizations) feel explicit or tacit pressure to tailor their studies (and findings) for fear of losing the needed financial support? How different would the perception and reality of institutional objectivity be if think tanks more readily accepted support from government agencies charged with promoting scientific research?

On the surface, it might appear that more competition should result in more rigorous and credible advice: in general, competition is said to drive up quality. But what if think tanks pursue market share by offering a tailored product line—studies and evaluations with findings more finely tuned to the perceived needs or preferences of their prospective clients—even at the expense of scientific standards of evidence? Do they face incentives to cut corners on basic methodological principles? In these times of heightened cynicism, it would perhaps not be surprising, but would still be painful to acknowledge, if norms of inquiry in think tanks and other advice-giving institutions were compromised for the sake of producing results more favorable to existing or anticipated funders, many of whom, as I have already suggested, give the impression of starting with strong and preconceived views about what the problems are and how to fix them. Anecdotal evidence as reported in the mainstream media, based largely on conversations with researchers in even the most prominent think tanks, does not clinch this argument about threats to objectivity, but it does ring an alarm.[16]

Whether universities faced with declining enrollments and other fiscal pressures are vulnerable to these forces further complicates the picture. Early-career faculty with impeccable research training need extramural support of their research, which is of course a key component in their quest for academic advancement and tenure. Moreover, many university-employed academics have secondary affiliations at major think tanks, further muddying the waters of institutional type as a determinant of research scope and style. There is sufficient reason to worry that scholars, wherever they work, find themselves steered toward funding sources that expect certain kinds of results. Once again, the convergence of forces perpetuates a vicious cycle: increased competition may cause erosion of evidentiary standards, leading to loss of faith in science as an input to governance, which in turn may further reduce public confidence even in our world-class university system and public willingness to pay for it, which in turn adds fuel to the fire of research budget cuts, which creates more competition. Intercepting this fast-moving train without injuring all the passengers is a complex policy challenge.

Which is the focus of chapter 4, where I summarize the key arguments and weave in four potential policy interventions, aimed at reducing the potential damage from these trends. I focus on education, but hope my proposals may spur discussions of whether and how the issues I'm raising affect other fields of research applied to policy and governance. My recommendations, framed as policy options to generate a broader debate, derive from an underlying set of assumptions (or hopes): that objective research is valued as a public good, that the system through which credible and useful education research is pumped into the policy discourse may not be sustainable without collective action to assure its viability, and that we have the political will and institutional creativity to design and implement corrective and protective policies. Cynics who deny the validity of any or all of these assumptions might as well put the book down now.

A NOTE ON LANGUAGE

In the book's title and scattered throughout, I use "objective" or "objectivity," which sets off alarm bells for some readers, especially philosophers who have actually struggled to make meaning of such words. I am grateful to anonymous reviewers for alerting me to the distracting effect this word might have. For example, one reviewer noted that "objectivity" is sometimes used to "dismiss disciplinary research (history, anthropology, philosophy, law, and qualitative sociology) in favor of quantitative studies," and asked, "What would important research look like in education if the research questions, methods, and write-up weren't influenced by researchers' values and beliefs?" So I want to try to clarify first, and then offer a compromise.

I do not mean by "objectivity" a preference for a particular type of research, for example, quantitative and experimental studies, over research of a more qualitative or ethnographic nature. In fact, I have written elsewhere and align myself with those who argue that qualitative inquiry has a long and established tradition, that its scientific features are (or should be) debated no more and no less than so-called quantitative studies, and that, in the community of scholars who define themselves as "qualitative," there are many who apply relevant and rigorous evidentiary standards as regularly as do their colleagues in political science, econometrics, psychometrics, and quantitative sociology.[17]

I have also written on the need to acknowledge, invite, and even celebrate the role of personal values and experience in the construction of research designs. Simply put, my argument is not only an ethical one—that the values and viewpoints of practitioners should be respected—but that good theory hinges on deep understanding of experience, on what Lee Shulman calls "the wisdom of practice."[18] So, again, "objectivity" does not rule out these inputs, although I do hope that careful and nonpartisan advice is not stifled by ideology, experience, and personal preferences of those providing the advice.

I use the word in this book in its more intuitive meaning, as it appears in essays, official documents, and books related to scientific evidence and the policy process. A good example is from the home page of the NAS, which presents itself as "the nation's pre-eminent source of high-quality, *objective* advice on science, engineering, and health matters." [italics added][19] Similarly, in his very useful book on the history of the OTA, another organization devoted to the synthesis of independent and credible information as input to science and technology policy, Peter Blair notes that "[i]n OTA's early days TAB [the Technology Assessment Board] . . . recognized . . . that in order for the agency to carry out *objective* analysis, it would be necessary to separate the planning and day-to-day operations, including, especially, appointment of project staff and advisory panelists, from the members' individual offices." [italics added][20] In his comprehensive study of think tanks in America, Thomas Medvetz also reveals a belief about "objectivity" held by leaders of these organizations: for example, the head of the Committee for Economic Development is quoted as saying, "[W]e really come at these issues as *objectively* as we can, without any sort of upfront ideological or partisan bias." [italics added][21]

With these caveats and considerations about language, then, I will continue to use the words "objective" and "objectivity" as shorthand for an *aspiration*: to anticipate and contain the effects of preferences or ideology in the framing of studies, to try to separate fact from opinion in the delivery of advice to policy makers, and to prevent the virtues of partisan argumentation so important in a vibrant democracy like ours from choking off the production of independent findings. With gratitude to that anonymous reviewer, for me objectivity means "evidence gathered by researchers who are insulated from the pressure of funders to reach a given set of conclusions and recommendations."

CHAPTER ONE

Whither Altruism?

Philanthropy and Its Discontents

If you haven't got any charity in your heart, you have the worst kind of heart trouble.

—*Bob Hope*

A T ITS INCEPTION IN 1911, the Carnegie Corporation of New York endowment was approximately $130 million, to which was added another $10 million after Andrew Carnegie's death in 1919.[1] That may not sound like much, even when converted to current dollars: $2 billion is a pittance compared to the Bill & Melinda Gates Foundation's current asset base estimated at somewhere between $41 billion and $45 billion. But it is roughly equivalent to the current endowment of the Walton Family Foundation and larger than the asset base of the Broad Foundation ($1.75 billion in 2014 dollars). Contrary to popular complaints that today's big foundations have unprecedented wealth and power, the Carnegie Corporation of a hundred years ago would certainly have been big enough to qualify for membership in that ignominious "billionaire boys club," which Diane Ravitch and others blame for wielding too much influence and causing many of the problems in education today.[2]

But even that comparison is flawed and overstates the relative degree of concentration of wealth and power among the biggest foundations today. First, it doesn't account for change in the *number* of foundations that have become active in the past century. When Carnegie was getting started, there were some other philanthropies on the scene, but they were few in number and small in size. The Russell Sage Foundation, for example, was founded in 1907 with a generous gift of $10 million, hardly enough to dilute the concentrated potential influence of Carnegie. Sage has retained a prestigious place in the philanthropic community and, since its founding, has been a significant supporter of programs and research aimed at "the improvement of social and living conditions in the United States." But with an asset base of about $325 million, it does not make it onto today's list of the top one hundred. In fact, none of the foundations that are currently on that list existed when Carnegie was established; the closest is the Rockefeller Foundation, launched in 1913 and ranked fifteenth (as of the end of 2013) with an asset base of $3.7 billion (in 2012 dollars). Clearly, then, Carnegie's relative clout, or what might be thought of as an indicator of "market penetration," was greater a century ago than that of most foundations in today's much more crowded field.

Second, the argument that today's biggest foundations are too big and too influential ignores other aspects of the philanthropic environment. The most recent data show that in 2012, there were more than forty-one thousand family foundations in the United States that together contributed over $22 billion. Total giving by all foundations in the United States is estimated at close to $55 billion (as of the end of 2013), in the range of 15 percent of the total $360 billion in charitable giving by Americans. The diversity of these organizations, with respect to their missions, management, and impacts, reinforces the argument that there is more competition today than a century or even a half century ago.[3]

Indeed, much of the growth in the foundation sector is relatively recent, which may explain the heightened public attention to magnitudes and targets of philanthropic giving. We are clearly in a new era of private philanthropy, as Joel Fleishman has documented:

> During the first eight decades of the twentieth century, the number of large foundations, those with assets above $1 million or which made grants of $100,000 or above, grew each decade at only single digits—2 percent in the period before 1940, 3 percent in the 1940s, 8 percent in the 1950s and 1960s and 5 percent in the 1970s. Beginning in the 1980s, however, the momentum in foundation creation increased significantly, with 18 percent growth in the 1980s and 37 percent, or 8,139 new large foundations, created in the 1990s.[4]

RECENT TRENDS

In the popular press and professional literature, there is a recurring debate over whether the American culture of publicly supported private giving has made us better off, and there are various claims and counterclaims of excessive foundation influence.[5] I believe that, on balance, private giving has done more good than harm. My principal concern here, though, is whether recent trends in the foundation world compromise the viability of high-quality scientific research generally and education research specifically. My review of selected data is oriented to a few key questions: Is there a discernible pattern in foundation spending, in particular, funding that targets education programs and research, in the past decade? Focusing mostly on the substantial changes in the number and types of philanthropic organizations that have entered the field even in the past twenty years, how have they targeted their investments? Is there evidence of greater market concentration and convergence of strategies among the biggest foundations? Is the problem more acute in the realm of education policy, practice, and research? It is a complicated picture. I will argue that although the rhetoric of excessive and uncontrolled concentration—one that seems to unify extreme left and extreme right on our current political spectrum—is extravagant, there is evidence of changes in the size and orientation of the philanthropic sector to cause concern.

While much is being made of new foundations and their charitable contributions, among the top twenty foundations included in the 2012 compilation by the Foundation Center, which together accounted for more than 70 percent of the total spending by the fifty largest foundations, ten have been in existence longer than thirty years: W.K. Kellogg Foundation (established in 1930), Ford Foundation (1936), Lilly Endowment (1937), David and Lucile Packard Foundation (1964), The Susan Thompson Buffett Foundation (1964), William and Flora Hewlett Foundation (1966), Andrew W. Mellon Foundation (1969), John D. and Catherine T. MacArthur Foundation (1970), Robert Wood Johnson Foundation (1972), and the Open Society Foundations (1979). In 2012, these ten gave close to 6,500 grants totaling roughly $2.9 billion, or 28 percent of the total dollars donated by the fifty largest. Clearly, the redistribution of significant wealth to charitable causes is not a new phenomenon.

On the other hand, new players are making a difference: the Walton, Broad, and Gates foundations, established in 1987, 1999, and 2000, respectively, and often lumped together because of their active education portfolios, gave another $3 billion. As shown in figure 1.1, the Gates Foundation has had a profound impact on the general landscape of charitable giving since its founding a little more than a decade ago. Given its size relative to the other largest foundations, it is important to consider also the breadth of its portfolio. While it has become a major force in education, most of its grants go to other causes. In 2013, almost 80 percent of total Gates giving was in its global development and global health programs, supporting initiatives in agriculture, vaccine delivery, HIV/AIDS treatment, and efforts to eradicate malaria, tuberculosis, and polio in the developing world. As the *New York Times* recently reported, the citizens of Nigeria are close to ending an epidemiological scourge that used to threaten thousands of children, a success story that "is a testament to the persistence, deep pockets and adaptability of the eradication initiative, which is led by the WHO, the Centers for Disease Control and Prevention, the United Nations Fund for Children, Rotary International, *the Bill and Melinda Gates Foundation*, and the United Nations Foundation." [italics added][6]

Domestically, roughly 14 percent of Gates funding in 2013 was for its "United States Program," of which just over 80 percent targeted education. In other words, about 11 percent of total Gates spending went for education-related projects and programs. And a significant proportion of that amount went to postsecondary programs focused on community college success and completion of four-year degrees. Of the foundation's fifty-six largest grants, one was for charter school initiatives ($1.75 million to the NewSchools Venture Fund). Significant support went to enhance teacher effectiveness, including programs that emphasize the use of test scores—for which Gates is often criticized by opponents of testing and test-based accountability—but including also programs to develop searchable video libraries of teaching practices ($1.5 million), to provide an effective teacher in each classroom ($1.8 million), to help school systems train classroom observers ($1.3 million), and to other programs for teacher professional development ($2.9 million). Gates also gave $1.6 million to the National Council of La Raza to address the quality of education for Latinos.

FIGURE 1.1   Top twenty foundations by spending on education, 2012 (in millions)

Bill & Melinda Gates Foundation	$326.6
Walton Family Foundation, Inc.	$172.7
Silicon Valley Community Foundation	$106.5
The Andrew W. Mellon Foundation	$99.5
W. K. Kellogg Foundation	$75.2
Robert W. Woodruff Foundation, Inc.	$67.1
The Duke Endowment	$65.2
John Templeton Foundation	$59.2
The Wallace Foundation	$53.8
GE Foundation	$52.2
Lilly Endowment Inc.	$51.0
Open Society Foundations	$48.2
The Michael and Susan Dell Foundation	$48.2
Carnegie Corporation of New York	$46.7
The William and Flora Hewlett Foundation	$45.4
Robertson Foundation	$43.9
Lumina Foundation	$43.3
The Susan Thompson Buffett Foundation	$42.5
The Walmart Foundation, Inc.	$40.9
Omaha Community Foundation	$39.6

$0 $50 $100 $150 $200 $250 $300 $350

Source: Author's computations based on data from the Foundation Center, 2015.

Grants supporting the Common Core State Standards, another flashpoint in today's reform debates, went to a variety of projects including the development of online games to enhance algebra learning and efforts to help promote the Next Generation Science Standards proposed by the National Academy of Sciences.[7]

This activity was happening during a period of considerable turbulence in the general landscape of American philanthropy. Six of the foundations that spent the most on education in 2002 were no longer on the list of the top ten by 2012: Lilly, the Annenberg Foundation, Carnegie, Ford, the Mississippi Common Fund Trust, and the F. W. Olin Foundation were replaced by the Silicon Valley Community Foundation, Kellogg, the Duke Endowment, the John Templeton Foundation, the Wallace Foundation, and the GE Foundation.[8] Note, in particular, the changes in relative spending by Carnegie and Ford, two of the oldest foundations. The volatility is especially pronounced for Carnegie: in 2012, it ranked fourteenth among foundations investing in education; in 2011, it did not even make it into

FIGURE 1.2 Annual grants for education activities, selected foundations, 2002–2012 (in millions, 2015 inflation-adjusted dollars)

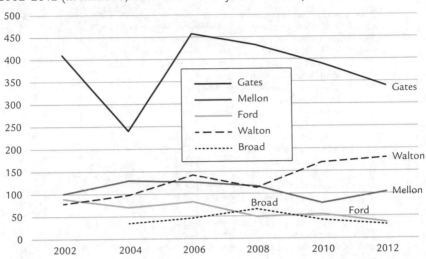

Source: Author's computations based on data from the Foundation Center, http://data.foundationcenter.org/#/fc1000/subject:education/all/top:foundations/list/2012.

the top fifty; and in 2002, it ranked fourth. Lilly and Annenberg, which together had donated roughly $750 million in 2002, had drastically reduced their activity in education.

Even among the four foundations that continued a robust education presence during the decade, there were noticeable shifts: Walton significantly increased its spending, Mellon remained fairly flat, and, perhaps most surprising, both Gates and the Robert W. Woodruff Foundation significantly decreased their spending (as measured using inflation-adjusted 2015 dollars). A snapshot of the volatility in activity among selected foundations is shown in figure 1.2, where we see the changes that occurred among five of the most prominent players in the education realm.

THEORY AND PRACTICE

To gain further insight into the importance of avoiding broad brushstrokes in either praising or condemning the large foundations, information from annual reports and websites can be informative, if not determinative. For example, this passage from the 2011 annual report made public by Carnegie is indicative of the kind of ideological flavor that imbues its philanthropy:

> The National Program's central goal has been to create pathways to educational and economic opportunity by generating change throughout the kindergarten to college (K–16) continuum, particularly secondary and higher education. Our aim has been to enable many more students, including historically underserved populations and immigrants, to achieve academic success and perform at the highest levels of creative, scientific and technical knowledge and skill.[9]

Still, this philosophical orientation, if that's the right way to characterize it, didn't prevent Carnegie from funding charter school organizations, Common Core initiatives, and school turnaround programs, the kinds of initiatives that don't sit well with critics of today's high-stakes standards and accountability reform strategy.

It is perhaps obvious but worth stating that foundations may share basic goals but choose significantly different implementation strategies. Convergence in theory doesn't always translate to convergence in practice, as a few examples will illustrate. The William and Flora Hewlett Foundation, with assets of over $7 billion, donated roughly $350 million in 2011, of which about 10 percent went for education with four basic goals: to increase economic opportunity and civic engagement through "deeper learning," a phrase that may sound like jargon but actually is based on high-quality research about how people learn; to improve the conditions for education reform in California; to enable and improve free access to knowledge relevant to the improvement of teaching and learning, through an exciting and avant-garde program called Open Educational Resources; and to raise educational achievement in disadvantaged communities in the San Francisco Bay Area.[10]

To take another example, the Ford Foundation, still one of the largest, has a remarkable history in education, including experiments such as the decentralization of New York City public schools in the late 1960s and support for major civil rights initiatives through the 1960s and 1970s. Its 2011 annual report was entitled "Justice/Reimagined," a theme that in some ways echoes the rhetoric of opportunity and advancement in the mission statements of Carnegie, Gates, and others. But Ford's strategy was its own, dividing its roughly $450 million of total giving (about what Gates gives for education alone) into three broad categories—"Democracy, Rights & Justice," "Economic Opportunity and Assets," and "Education, Creativity, and Free Expression"—and allocating the funds to specific kinds of projects and programs. The education category accounted then for just under a third of Ford's giving and includes a substantial recent initiative to increase learning time in public schools. Now that the foundation has articulated a singular focus on "inequality" in its current strategy of grant making, it will be interesting to watch how that translates to specific programs of school reform.[11]

The Walton Family Foundation, too, claims to want greater opportunity for all children. Its strategy clearly privileges market-oriented solutions, as telegraphed in this excerpt from its 2014 annual report:

> We envision a future where every child has access to high-quality educational *choices* that prepare him or her for a lifetime of opportunity. We know that empowering parents and students with *options* works, but now we want to do more. We have learned that while choice is vital, it is not enough. Over the next five years, the Foundation will make investments in K–12 education to increase access to *real-time information about school quality for parents*, be more inclusive of teachers and school leaders and ensure that our investments are reaching more of the most disadvantaged kids, especially those living in poverty and those with special needs. [italics added][12]

It is not the rhetoric, then, or the grand goals that provoke hostility from some of the most fervent critics of educational philanthropy, but rather how a foundation chooses to advance the causes it espouses. For yet another example, it might be hard to discern why the Broad Foundation has become the target of so much harsh criticism, given these snippets from its mission statement:

> Our urgency stems from the belief that we cannot afford—as a country, as a society, as individuals—to allow the next generation of children to pass through schools that leave them unprepared for challenging careers, productive citizenship and fulfilling lives . . . Our education

investments are focused on cultivating a personalized approach to learning for all children and on ensuring that the federal and state policies are in place to fully support teachers, students and parents.[13]

Digging a bit deeper, though, we see what might irk the critics. In praising the anticipated education program of the newly elected president of the United States, Broad noted in its 2009–2010 annual report that "with an agenda that echoes our decade of investments—*charter* schools, *performance pay* for teachers, *accountability*, expanded learning time, and *national standards*—the Obama administration is poised to cultivate and bring to fruition the seeds we and other reformers have planted." [italics added][14]

Indeed, the familiar italicized words are exactly the ones that most annoy opponents of reforms that rely on punitive uses of tests and the preference for marketlike alternatives to the bureaucracy of public schools. Hearing Eli Broad enunciate his disdain for schools of education, teacher unions, and other institutions that he associates with the end of the golden age of American education does not inspire confidence.[15] Nor did his enthusiastic support of organizations like Teach For America, Leadership for Educational Equity, Stand for Children, and StudentsFirst, all groups with well-known leanings toward privatization and market-based reforms. On the other hand, there has been some apparent softening, even according to some of the most truculent commentators: referring to Broad's decision to suspend its annual prize for urban schools (aimed at celebrating large schools that show great academic improvement and reduction of the achievement gap), Diane Ravitch cheerfully noted that "Eli Broad was wrong about what was needed to improve public education. He thought that management and charters could overcome poverty, and his cancellation of the prize is his admission that he was wrong. The problems are deeper than he imagined."[16]

From this overview, it is clear that in its size, reach, and complexity, the ecology of educational philanthropy has been changing in subtle ways. But my sense is that, on the whole, the sector is less plagued by a concentration of wealth or, worse, a singular ideological predisposition than one might surmise from reading only its most vocal and vociferous critics. Often overlooked in the anxious criticism of the sector is the possibility that the existence of so many philanthropies of such diverse size and mission creates an atmosphere of countervailing and competitive pressures. For example, it is at least theoretically plausible that the largest and most aggressive foundations' efforts to change education, for example, by doing X, are balanced by other perhaps smaller foundations' cumulative efforts to do Y. Are the reform initiatives of, say, the Walton Family Foundation (total asset base $2.5 billion), which has articulated a strong preference for vouchers, charter schools, and testing, tempered by gifts from organizations with different priorities and more diversified portfolios, such as the Open Society Foundations (total asset base $1.6 billion), the Wallace Foundation (total asset base $1.5 billion), and the Ford Foundation (total asset base $12 billion)? How does the investment of almost $16 million by the David and Lucile Packard Foundation to support science and engineering research fellowships fit into the assessment of concentration?[17]

Along with these considerations, another dimension to the picture warrants attention, especially as it affects education research. Although there is considerable diversity within the biggest foundations' portfolios, which may yield desirable countervailing influences, and in many cases their funding of education-related programs is small proportional to their total giving, a noticeable shift has occurred in the character of the organizations that *receive* the money. Here, in particular, the work of Sarah Reckhow and Jeffrey Snyder has been invaluable. Based on a careful analysis of foundation data and a model that distinguishes among different types of recipient organizations, they offer compelling evidence of a funding tilt in the direction of "national advocacy" organizations that favor particular strategies of education reform and away from traditional institutions like public schools and university-based research centers. For example, they show that "funding for traditional public schools dropped from 16 percent of grant dollars in 2000 to 8 percent in 2010, while funding for charter schools rose from around 3 percent in 2000 to 16 percent in 2010."[18]

Several of the most prominent and influential advocacy organizations with substantial research portfolios, for example, Achieve, the Alliance for Excellent Education, and The Education Trust, receive funding from major foundations and use the resources to promote causes such as the national alignment of academic standards and stronger school accountability systems. Moreover, Reckhow and colleagues present evidence of convergence among at least some of the major foundations, which "increasingly support jurisdictional challengers—organizations that compete with or offer alternatives to public sector institutions . . . top donors are increasingly supporting a shared set of organizations . . . and the combination of these trends has played a role in strengthening the voice and influence of philanthropists in education policy."[19]

And their analysis suggests further that this observed shift toward funding for certain kinds of advocacy and reform organizations has been intensified, rather than attenuated, by the entry of new players: "Rather than undertaking new policy initiatives or supporting a distinct set of organizations, many of the new entrants among the class of top donors distribute funds that overlap with other major funders."[20] The authors end with a compelling question: "Has the rise of interests associated with jurisdictional challengers come at the expense of other sectors of the education policy community, including unions, professional associations, civil rights organizations, or university-based researchers?"[21] This is fine political science applied to a very important policy problem; their modesty of tone should not mask the underlying sense of foreboding that the analysis provokes.

One problem is that, although some of the recent entrants into the educational philanthropy sector came in energized to do good, they relied on entrepreneurial strategies that had served them well in the private sector—and missed opportunities to examine more closely the specific complexities of schools and schooling. For example, the Annenberg Foundation's efforts to create model school districts as well as model schools and the Gates Foundation investment in "small schools" involved huge sums of money and large-scale adoption, but they were launched without the benefit of pilot-level programs that might have yielded more thorough evidence to guide the implementation at scale. Ironically, some of these philanthropists observed correctly that the typical schools they saw bore little resemblance to the traditional or high-tech workplaces where they had made their fortunes, but they underestimated how hard it would be to choreograph the kind of transformation that seemed to them, on the surface at least, most appealing. (I will say more about the alleged failure of large programs like the Gates small-schools initiative later in this chapter.) The painful (and perhaps painfully obvious) truth is that some innovations in management and pedagogy, when imported from the business world, do not result in better teaching and learning. This is a lesson from over two centuries of experimentation in American education policy, but it was not learned or easily digested by at least some of today's big philanthropists.[22]

The real issue here is not so much whether foundations should have the right to invest according to their philosophical or ideological preferences. Indeed, as I will argue, that is precisely one of the virtues of an independent sector that pushes back on public programs and channels resources (often more nimbly than the government can) toward the solution of social and economic problems and the enhancement of civic life. The problem is figuring out if those investments are well thought out and achieving their stated goals. Some of the most prominent foundations with investments in education have devised evaluation strategies that should be emulated more widely. The Hewlett Foundation, for example, adopted in 2012 a set of seven core principles and practices that signify a commitment to learning about the effects of its programs and to transparency with evaluation results. Its statement is remarkably candid, with up-front acknowledgment that not all of its programs can be evaluated and that it will share results "with appropriate audiences." The Wallace Foundation has long been committed to a comprehensive, rigorous, and highly regarded approach to evaluation. Foundations with more focused agendas, such as the Jim Joseph Foundation, which is among the most prominent and active supporters of Jewish education, have admirably expressed their awareness of the need for independent and objective evaluation and are investing in innovative methods and frameworks.[23]

Although there is overlap, it is important to note that *evaluation* of funded programs is different from investments in *research* oriented to production of new or basic knowledge about teaching, learning, or governance of schools and schooling. With a few notable exceptions, many of the most generous funders have been reluctant to support independent research of a more basic or fundamental nature (a distinction that I discuss in greater detail in chapter 2). The best counterexamples are the Spencer Foundation, which continues as one of the most respected sponsors of education research, even as it has become more "strategic" in its programs; the Hewlett Foundation, which invested heavily in research-related activities especially during the period 2002–2010 and which has maintained a part of its large portfolio for support of research and research-related or policy organizations; and the Alfred P. Sloan and William T. Grant foundations, which have programmatic foci but maintain a robust portfolio of grants to researchers working on key issues in education and human development.

There is a subtle tension here. On the one hand, foundations can and should invest in research and evaluation to inform their long-term strategic goals while providing evidence of the extent to which their grantees are succeeding in carrying out the work for which they have been funded. In fact, as I suggested earlier, some of the large foundations with education portfolios have increasingly elaborate evaluation requirements. Many of them engage with external evaluators who have expertise in measurement and provide independent assessments of program implementation and impacts.

On the other hand, the incentives faced by funders to look for proof, or at least strong evidence, that their strategies are sound and their programs are working can introduce tacit or explicit biases that distort the validity of evaluation findings. Here is an extreme example, based on a conversation I had with a high-level officer of a large foundation. (The exchange took place in a meeting where the participants agreed to keep the discussion private and anonymous, so I will not disclose the name of the individual or the foundation he or she represents.) I paraphrase from memory: "Of course we will support objective evaluation studies, *as long as they show that school choice and charter schools work.*" The outgoing head of another large foundation's education program, speaking to a group of early-career researchers, made a similar point, albeit with more nuance, which I again paraphrase: "We have a commitment to wide-ranging and rigorous research . . . *which provides empirical support for our priority programs.*"

In the public sector, where similar opportunistic inclinations surely exist, there has evolved an elaborate system of independent evaluation—for example, the Government Accountability Office, formerly the General Accounting Office, is a federal agency tasked with providing independent and nonpartisan information to Congress on how the government spends taxpayer dollars. Whether an analogous institutional arrangement could provide watchdog functions on the effects of foundation spending is a complicated matter, but one worth considering. (I return to this issue in chapter 4.)

THE ECONOMICS AND POLITICS OF CHARITY

Taken together, the statistics and stories in the preceding section reflect a complex and, in many ways, unique history of charitable giving that clearly has its pluses and minuses. The broader context matters significantly: our history of federalism and separation of powers as well as our tax code shape the distinctive nature of our charitable giving in important ways. These structures and processes are important to understand as a backdrop to our somewhat exceptional record of charitable giving and the complex intertwining of the public and private sectors.

How do we compare to other countries? It is heartening to know that the United States ranks first (tied with Myanmar) in the World Giving Index (WGI), a composite derived from survey data covering three behaviors suggestive of charitable instincts and activity: "helping a stranger," "donating money to a charity," and "volunteering time."[24] Where the United States also stands out is with respect to the organized philanthropic sector, especially through the system of family foundations, a concept hard to find elsewhere. Again, facile comparisons may miss underlying subtleties, but Joel Fleishman's observation about the uniqueness of our civic sector and the role of private foundations is compelling. He argues that foundations in the United States typically perform as the driver, partner, or catalyst for moving forward an agenda.[25]

The contrast with Europe is illuminating. Government there is principally and, in some cases, solely responsible for goods and services that we typically think of in the United States as being a natural part of our civic sector, the private nonprofit world that keeps a safe distance from—but has a complicated and mutually reinforcing relationship with—the workings and prerogatives of electoral politics. Americans have clearly revealed a preference for an arrangement aimed at reaping social and economic benefits from private wealth as supplement—or antidote—to whatever the government provides. History, culture, religion—and *taxes*—all surely play a part in the observed differences with our foreign friends, and no single factor can explain all the differences. France, for example, offers a hefty tax break for charitable giving: according to the *Wall Street Journal*, "French donors can offset between 66% and 75% of the value of their donations against their tax bill." But France ranks ninetieth in the WGI. Sweden, which does not offer a tax incentive, ranks fortieth.[26]

The role of the charitable deduction in our tax code is worthy of special attention (and I will return to it again in chapter 4, in the context of proposed policy options). It is a pillar in the basic architecture of the public-private partnership and guarantees a substantial degree of autonomy to donors in choosing where and how to spend their fortunes. The basic logic is compelling, especially to economists who are always on the lookout for monetary incentives as motivators of human behavior. Simply put, foundations do not pay the full amount of tax due on their fortunes if they agree to disburse a certain portion (the current minimum is roughly 5 percent, including most of the administrative and other overhead costs of running the organization) in gifts or grants to approved types of nonprofit causes or organizations. As the congressional Joint Committee on Taxation puts it, "[M]any charitable organizations rely on charitable donations to finance their operations, and the charitable contribution deduction plays an important role in providing such support. The deduction for charitable contributions reduces the economic cost of making a donation and thus encourages charitable giving."[27]

What this amounts to is an implicit social compact: the opportunity cost associated with lost tax revenues is assumed to be justified by the social benefits that accrue from the transfer of wealth from private hands to the public good. This is surely not the only way to get great libraries and symphony halls and research laboratories. Europe, Russia, Israel, Asia, and Latin America have some of each. On balance, though, we have done well despite (or maybe because of) our unique insistence on rewarding—and, in many cases, amplifying—the charitable impulses of the wealthy with extrinsic economic benefits. The origins, purposes, and underlying significance of the charitable deduction periodically provoke a useful debate. For example, writing in the *New York Times* in May 2015, the founder and editor of *Inside Philanthropy*, David Callahan, warned that "philanthropy . . . is a world with too much secrecy and too little oversight," and blamed the leniency of our tax code: "foundations don't have to prove that they're making good use of billions of dollars of tax-subsidized funds, and nonprofits don't have to identify their donors."[28]

There is an important political and historical dimension that complements these economic arguments. The main issue is power and influence: as Fleishman notes, "Foundations have been criticized for wielding their unaccountable power in the public sphere irresponsibly and thereby influencing democratic processes unfairly," and reminds us that, as early as 1914, such charges were leveled against the Carnegie and Rockefeller organizations (then in their early infancy).[29]

I would submit that the American approach to philanthropy is a central and increasingly powerful cog in the complex machinery of federalism, divided government, and separation of powers. It stems from the general principle articulated in the founding documents of the republic, mostly under the influence of James Madison, which delineated roles for various levels of government, assured a nearly constant state of argumentation and (mostly) healthy partisanship, and influenced just about every aspect of American politics and culture. Why would doctrines of diffused and decentralized governance, at the core of what has sometimes been called "American exceptionalism," not reach into the mechanics of philanthropy? For Alexis de Tocqueville, the nineteenth-century visitor and chronicler of the new American experiment, the uniqueness of our penchant for locally inspired and managed provision of public goods carried over to our emerging approach to charity. As he put it, "[T]he wealth of a democratic society may well be measured by the [quantity and] quality of functions performed by private citizens."[30]

In other words, thinking again about the charitable deduction, there is a notion of limited trust in government, of checks and balances—a phrase with special poignancy given the exchange of money involved. Policy wonks and political scientists have weighed in on these issues and, in particular, on relationships between the public and private sectors. For example, Frederick Hess has argued that "philanthropy provides a vehicle for identifying and supporting promising individuals and ideas outside the public education bureaucracy. Some donors can light the way forward even as others provide a balancing wheel to counter the fads and groupthink of the moment. In the end, as long as philanthropy is independent of government, even muscular efforts that promote certain policies or reshape the system are healthy and even invaluable."[31] Stanford University political scientist Rob Reich highlights the pluralism argument: "Powered by donor preferences and free from the accountability logic of the market and democratic state, foundations can help to provide a welcome pluralism of public goods. The diversity of goods supplied by foundation grantees helps to create an ever evolving, contestatory, and diverse arena of civil society. Such decentralization tempers government orthodoxy."[32]

ACCOUNTABILITY: PROCESS AND SUBSTANCE

Complaints about the role and influence of foundations are often couched in angst about process—who is holding them accountable? It is true that foundations operate with almost no constraints on the purposes or targets of their giving, so long as they abide by the rules for the amount of their holdings they need to disburse if they want to enjoy the tax advantage. But the law does not explicitly prohibit foundations from proactively furthering objectives that may coincide with governmental policies or programs, as long as they respect rules governing advocacy. Nor is the government prohibited from turning to foundations for financial and political support.[33]

Legality aside, there is still the question of whether and to what extent it is a good idea—good policy—to allow or encourage the private philanthropic sector to become aligned with the public governmental sector. Since there will always be some overlap, it is a matter of boundaries, or limits, which are necessarily murky: one person's constructive collaboration is another's conspiratorial collusion. To the extent that some of the biggest foundations working in education today seem, at least for now, rather cozily synchronized with the market-oriented reform preferences of many members of Congress (from both parties) and the executive branch, they may feel they are immune from efforts to curb their influence. But one hopes they are smarter than that and realize that, as times change and political moods swing, their own privilege might become threatened.[34]

This is where the Nixon story can be revealing. Among the people and organizations on the paranoid president's most feared list, the Ford Foundation ranked high. He labeled it "a front for dangerous communism," and his aide Patrick Buchanan accused it of having "become the Exchequer and Command Post for the entire American left." Nixon was one of many elected officials to grouse about philanthropy, especially when it pushed for causes they found distasteful or politically challenging. Involvement of a number of foundations in the civil rights movement, for example, including small ones like the Field Foundation of Illinois and the Berkshire Taconic Community Foundation and giants like Carnegie and Ford, sparked a powerful backlash, leading to congressional efforts in the late 1960s to "drastically restrict their influence on public policy."[35]

Untangling process and substance in arguments about philanthropy is hard. And the murkiness that prevents clear definitions of good versus bad charity ex ante is surely an obstacle to rational policy making: after all, absent clear and enforceable criteria, how can foundations be held accountable fairly? There is less fuss over the quest to eradicate malaria than over the push for civil rights or the plan to evaluate elementary school teachers using standardized tests of their students. Let me be frank: when I asked my friends gathered for that retirement party (see the introduction to this book) what they made of the critiques of the alleged outsized power of foundations, was I really only worried about process? Or was I projecting my own anxiety about the excesses of education reform initiatives supported by foundations pushing choice and charters and privatization? Would I have asked the same question if I were more comfortable with the magnitude and direction of philanthropic involvement in school reform?

But this is in some ways a familiar problem. Tolerance for ambiguity and capacity to muddle through murkiness are requirements for democratic governance, and in American political culture, perhaps even more than elsewhere, the recipe for decision making blends enforceable legal codification and what I would call "mutually acceptable vagueness." The legal analyst Jeffrey Toobin has made a related point in an essay about interpretation of wording in the Affordable Care Act. As he puts it, "The great Supreme Court cases turn on the *majestic ambiguities* embedded in the Constitution. It is not a simple thing to define and apply terms like 'the freedom of speech,' or 'equal protection of the laws,' much less explain how much process is 'due.'" [italics added][36] A perhaps more familiar example was the high court's contemplation of defining obscenity as the basis for setting limits to the constitutional protection of free speech. In a famous 1964 ruling, Justice Potter Stewart finessed the definitional problem: "I shall not today attempt further to define the kinds of material I understand to be embraced within that shorthand description [of pornography]; and perhaps I could never succeed in intelligibly doing so. *But I know it when I see it.*" [italics added][37]

The analogy may be crude, but my point is that it is not surprising to hear criticisms of investments by Gates and other large foundations voiced in terms of how they violate principles of accountability, when in fact the argument is more likely over the substantive goals and ideological underpinnings of their philanthropy. I have a hunch there would be less hand-wringing over unfettered Broad or Gates or Walton foundation involvement in education reform if it was strategically directed to strengthen the role of teacher unions, except, of course, that critics of the unions would then undoubtedly arise in dramatic indignation against the nasty left-wing conspiracy not held to public accountability.

In any case, a perhaps obvious problem with mutually acceptable vagueness, which I believe is a predictable feature of governance when the complexity of problems exceeds the capacity of policy makers to articulate enforceable rules, is that the banner of acceptability tends to flap about in changing political winds. And because there is no obvious way to draw a bright line between good and bad philanthropy ex ante, the risk mounts that politicians and ideologues will be prone to overreact and undo a system that has, on balance, done more good than harm. Mutually acceptable vagueness should not be a precursor to mutually assured destruction.[38]

THE RISKS OF COORDINATION

If the extreme version of contestation is excessive political hostility and intrusion—Nixon going after his foundation nemeses—the potential harm from too much *alignment* between government and private philanthropy is also a legitimate cause for concern. A key question is whether the idealized influence of philanthropy, which is arguably especially important in an era of perceived expansion in traditional federal roles in education, has been compromised by the appearance of increasingly close alignment between some of the biggest foundations and the federal government—and if so, what can be done.[39]

The data on this issue are increasingly clear: as Sarah Reckhow and others have shown, at least some of the biggest foundations are pouring money into projects that are directly and unabashedly intended to bolster favored government initiatives. In education, the preference during the past four presidencies for variants on the theme of competition and choice in American public schooling is echoed in the strategic concentration of resources among at least some of the major foundations. In response, the education blogosphere is bulging with opinion: a good example is the debate over whether private support of the Common Core is too closely aligned with the government's decision to make participation in the state-initiated program a condition for so-called Race to the Top money.[40]

Again, though, we are in a murky zone. It is easier to sense after the fact if the relationship between the private and public funding sectors has become too close for comfort than it is to define a priori the operational limits on closeness. Moreover, with the argument about alignment comes the question about which side in the relationship is actually the driving force. As I noted earlier (see the quotations from Ravitch and Barkan, in the introduction to this book), some of the more strident critics of today's big foundations accuse them of *directing* government policy and politics. In our system of electoral finance, where following big money is (sadly) a necessity for political advancement and survival, there is surely reason to be nervous.

But could the influence not go in the other direction, too? Is it not possible that our elected and appointed officials exert pressure on the private sector and influence the scope and magnitude of charitable giving? We may be tempted to blame the Gates and Broad foundations, for example, for the ills of government-sanctioned test-based accountability. But how then do we explain the 150-year history of testing in the United States that began long before Bill Gates and Eli Broad were born and were driven largely by government? Similarly, if we have a beef with the No Child Left Behind Act (NCLB), a more rational and historically grounded criticism would aim first at its bipartisan framers and supporters in Congress and the White House: senators Ted Kennedy (D-MA) and Judd Gregg (R-NH), representatives George Miller (D-CA) and John Boehner (R-OH), Secretary of Education Lamar Alexander, and, of course, President George W. Bush. NCLB passed the House of Representatives by a vote of 381 to 41, with 182 Republicans and 198 Democrats in favor and 12 abstentions.[41]

Solving the "which comes first" puzzle in the relationship between government policy and foundation strategy has always been challenging. As Ellen Condliffe Lagemann has explained, Andrew Carnegie's interactions with the government were part of his broader interest in understanding—and shaping—public governance. But politicians were not then empty vessels waiting passively to be filled by proactive private citizens and organizations. From their side, politicians eagerly turned to Carnegie (and, later, other philanthropists) for help in promoting their causes.

In any case, regardless of which side appears to be winning at any given moment in the tug of influence between government and the private sector, with so many foundations in the field and so much private money being spent, philanthropy still represents only a small supplement: government investment in scientific, educational, and medical research, and in public goods and services generally, dwarfs private contributions. Consider, for example, total annual giving by the fifty largest foundations, about $10.7 billion in 2012, which covers the full range of their supported activities, everything from day-care centers to opera houses to libraries to charter schools to public radio and television stations to infectious disease treatment and sewage improvements in sub-Saharan Africa, along with the relatively tiny proportions going toward scientific research and program evaluation.

To get a sense of the difference, note that total public expenditures on elementary and secondary education are in the range of $600 billion per year, about 4 percent of gross domestic product (GDP) and more than two hundred times the amount spent by the Gates Foundation on *all* its programs. (I elaborate on the scope and magnitude of federal funding of scientific research, with emphasis on education, in chapter 2.) Of this amount, the federal contribution is in the range of $80 billion—about twenty-five times what Gates gives. All the rhetoric about the virtues of markets and choice notwithstanding, the US education system remains overwhelmingly public: enrollment in K–12 private schools in the United States has until recently hovered in the range of 12 percent for about as long as these data have been collected, charter schools enroll about 5 percent of all public elementary and secondary students, and enrollment in public postsecondary institutions is approximately triple the level of private institutions.[42]

Education is, of course, only one of the public goods funded or supported so dominantly with taxpayer dollars. Public finance is a cherished
tradition of American capitalism, a fact that today may be lost in the din of
quasi-religious worshiping of the market emanating from so many politicians and ideologues. For example, federal, state, and local governments
spent about $160 billion in 2010 to build, operate, and maintain our system
of roads and highways; "almost all of those infrastructure projects were
undertaken using a *traditional* approach in which a state or local government assumes most of the responsibility for carrying out a project and
bears most of its risks, such as the possibility of cost overruns, delays in
the construction schedule, and, in the case of toll roads, shortfalls in the
road's revenues." [italics added][43] Again, in keeping with our tradition of
mixed arrangements, there is a small private sector even for obviously public goods like highways: Adopt-a-Highway programs, for example, which
presumably help with things like litter removal, have become popular, and
in scattered places around the country, there are even privately managed
toll roads. But these are exceptions that prove the rule: provision of public
goods in the United States is still, mercifully, an overwhelmingly public
enterprise.[44]

CHARITY AND ALTRUISM AS PUBLIC GOODS

My argument, then, is that the balancing act between public governance
and private philanthropy is part of the bigger picture of America's political economy. The public side (to be discussed in chapter 2 with reference
to science and education research) is fairly well understood: government's
role is authorized by the people through self-imposed political coercion,
legislatively approved taxation, and regulation enforced through complicated spending formulas and monitored by large public bureaucracies. That
is as it should be and, obviously, other democracies rely even more heavily
on centralized government to distribute or redistribute the national wealth
and attend to the provision of public goods.

The private *voluntary* side, though small in comparison, still plays
a unique and pivotal role. Cultivating and organizing voluntary charity
is actually a public good: while many donors act on their truly altruistic
instincts, the presence of a governmental "hand" ensures continuation and

some accountability. It is important to understand what motivates the decisions and behavior of donors. When Andrew Carnegie first set up his gift, there was no tax incentive—the charitable deduction was first introduced by the War Revenue Act of 1917—which suggests a certain kind of purity in Carnegie's altruistic urges and keeps alive the possibility that similar urges influence today's donors.[45]

Bringing this to the current scene, we might be tempted to be cynical about the motivations of today's ultra-rich, but the claim that they are all driven solely or principally by greed and clever exploitation of the charitable deduction, rather than by a desire to improve the public good, is too facile and not based on hard evidence. Before we sniff at the generosity of Bill and Melinda Gates, who are spending upward of $200 million per year to eradicate malaria in Africa and another $500 million per year to stop the spread of other deadly infectious diseases, we should at least acknowledge that with their money—even after taxes—they (and the next hundred generations of Gates offspring) could spend all their time on a yacht the size of the *Queen Elizabeth 2*, sipping champagne while safely and comfortably using their binoculars to see vistas of poverty, disease, educational failure, and environmental degradation as they sail around the world. Instead, they devote substantial time and energy trying to figure out how—not whether—to share their fortune.

Related, the decision by Warren Buffett to pass some $31 billion to the Gates Foundation is not a symptom of greed: "He [is] giving away, for the public good, the bulk of his lifetime accumulation of wealth—more than two times, in 2006 dollars, what John D. Rockefeller Sr. and Andrew Carnegie . . . gave away *combined!*"[46] The Howard Hughes Medical Institute (HHMI), among the largest private supporters of academic biomedical research, provided over $1 billion for research and science education in 2013 and since 2004 has given more than $7 billion for basic science and programs to enhance science education. Shall we be dismissive of these efforts just because the donors enjoy a tax break?

Some social scientists have argued that altruism can be defined as a special case of self-interest seeking, the basic proposition being that we derive personal satisfaction by doing good for others.[47] If so, the question becomes, Why are impulses of generosity and charity not sufficient? Our elected leaders were apparently not confident that a steady stream of wealth transfer could be motivated solely by altruism: they sought to reinforce even the noblest of those instincts with public policy. It pays to ask why we need laws and complicated tax incentives, the formulation and implementation of which are costly political and procedural undertakings, to hammer down what are correctly viewed as natural (and perhaps, in some cases, religiously derived) behaviors.

One part of the answer is that *the process of organizing and cultivating charity is, itself, a public good*. Its provision cannot be assured without some form of collective and self-imposed coercive intervention. Good intentions of civic-minded citizens are simply not sufficient, a point made more generally by Mancur Olson in his classic work of political economy:

> Patriotism is probably the strongest noneconomic motive for organizational allegiance in modern times . . . but despite [its] force, the appeal of the national ideology, the bond of a common culture, and the indispensability of the system of law and order, no major state in modern history has been able to support itself through voluntary dues or contributions. *Philanthropic contributions are not even a significant source of revenue for most countries.* Taxes, *compulsory* payments by definition, are needed. Indeed, as the old saying indicates, their necessity is as certain as death itself. [italics added][48]

This is an especially eloquent statement about public goods, perhaps most familiar to neoclassical economists but a topic central also to the work of other social scientists, with added emphasis on the *compulsory* nature of collective interventions that are required if certain kinds of desired goods or services are to be provided. The basic logic holds for nearly every situation in which the cumulative effects of individual self-interest seeking do not yield socially desirable outcomes. An example from environmental protection is illustrative: in California, where there is a high concentration of environmentally conscious citizens, *legislation* was required—coercive legislation at that—to ensure that consumers purchased cars with emission control technologies. Many states adopted similar strategies; and the establishment of the Environmental Protection Agency and the passage of abundant regulatory legislation aimed at curbing if not eliminating pollution in its various forms are clearly the result of our willingness to accept—and impose—coercion in pursuit of the common good defined on a national scale.[49]

By analogy, then, let me make two points. First, even the most motivated individuals seeking to enhance the public welfare need reassurance that they are not alone and that their gifts are not expected to solve the big problems. If I contribute annually to a favorite health research organization, for example, the size of my gift is clearly a drop in the bucket, and as a rational investor I would like to think there are other drops in that bucket. So I look for evidence that the organization is receiving funds from others, along with data about what share of the contributions go to overhead. Following this logic, though, I might also be led in the opposite direction: since there are so many other donors, maybe I don't have to add my small amount! Excluding some type of legislated *requirement* to be charitable (the analogy being to the legislated requirement for cars to be equipped with emission control devices), which would clearly be seen as an untenable intrusion of governmental authority, one of the only mechanisms to prevent the total collapse of voluntarism is the provision of information about the size of the donor pool and, importantly, the ways in which even small gifts add value. It is the diffusion of that information that requires some form of coordinated action, the cost of which is necessarily borne, at least in part, by the receiving agency in hopes of encouraging donors to continue giving. The upshot is that to ensure the sustainability of altruism, some type of managed intervention is needed, which I would argue is a variation on the theme of collective action required in pursuit of the provision of public goods.

Second, there is another public goods quality to the *process* of charity—independent of the public goods quality of the projects and goals that it supports—that explains why, even at the local level, some form of coercion, whether through strict rules of membership or more gentle suasion, is a typical feature. Here I am thinking of religious organizations, for example, that rely on individual charity to provide services that benefit the community, and that usually impose membership dues along with regular appeals for support. It's not exactly coercion comparable to taxation, because people don't have to pay their dues and don't have to be members, but there is the sense that "membership has its privileges"—including the opportunity to pay dues—and exclusion is at least theoretically enforceable.

At the federal level, there is actually more latitude in the definition or style of coercion: as we have seen, taxes are compulsory and enforceable by law, as are other mandates, including outright bans on products with known risks. In the case of philanthropy, though, the strategy is more passive: we don't believe charity is or should be compulsory, but we do believe there is a federal role in stimulating it via manipulations of the tax system, most notably the charitable deduction. Acknowledging a useful governmental (collective action) role and the power of incentives in promoting certain behaviors, though, does *not* mean that philanthropy would otherwise not happen. In other words, I'm cautioning that we should not jump to the other extreme and assume that there would be no charity without the existing economic incentives. It is a matter of balance. The possibility of market failure in the strictly voluntary provision of private resources for public goods does not obviate the existence of—or the need to acknowledge with gratitude—genuine altruism.

To reinforce this point, let's review some of the basic facts about philanthropy and charity in the United States. Recall that the list of the top one hundred charitable foundations includes organizations as big as Gates and Ford (roughly $44 billion and $12 billion in assets, respectively) and a slew of smaller ones with endowments ranging from $700 million to $10 billion, each of which donates between $55 million and $750 million per year in support of a wide array of social, medical, educational, artistic, and other causes. Smaller foundations, like Spencer, William T. Grant, and Alfred P. Sloan, which are not in the top one hundred, are important and influential despite their relatively more modest endowments. And then there are literally hundreds of family foundations, too small to make it to the top-one-hundred list, which are the creation of public-minded citizens eager to share their wealth; their combined gifts are truly jaw dropping. Finally, there is the outpouring of charity from individuals, most who are not organized in formal foundation-type organizations. According to the National Philanthropic Trust, "Americans gave $358.38 billion in 2014. This reflects a 7.1% increase from 2013 . . . [I]n 2014, the largest source of charitable giving came from individuals at \$258.51 billion, or 72% of total giving; followed by foundations (\$53.97 billion/15%), bequests (\$28.13 billion/8%), and corporations (\$17.77 billion)."[50]

Yes, there is a tax advantage, but surely *some* of this charity reflects genuine generosity.

ECONOMICS 101: THE TAX CODE AND BEYOND

Moving past whatever suspicions we may harbor about the behavior of the now famous (or infamous) "1 percent," the question remains whether American society would be better off risking a decline in private giving for the sake of reducing the tax revenue loss. I return to this issue in chapter 4, but here will make a related argument. Foundation heads and program officers sometimes forget that "their" money is, in fact, already partly the government's: because of the tax code, philanthropists are essentially stewards of a part of the public trust.[51] Transparency about this aspect of the public-private partnership, and more humility on the part of philanthropists who may overlook this part of the grand bargain, would ease some of the strain in the debate over the charitable deduction.

But the possibility of shifting the responsibility entirely back to the government, along the lines of how things work in other countries, is not an obviously more attractive option. For one thing, returning the financial discretion embedded in philanthropic autonomy back to the government would collide with our preference for diffused authority and checks and balances. The United States does not appear ready for a more Continental style of centralized—and monopolized—governmental authority and responsibility for provision of all public goods. I wish our contemporary political culture was less ignorant of the need for government to ensure the provision of goods and services not well handled by the market (e.g., scientific research, physical infrastructure, public education, disease control, health, defense, criminal justice, to name a few), but at the same time, I am not convinced that obliterating our tradition of private philanthropy as antidote or stimulus to governmental activity would make us better off. The bottom line, if there is one, is squiggly. From our own history, we have learned lessons that relate to the charitable deduction, but the conclusion remains murky: neither reducing nor sustaining the tax advantage guarantees the desired social outcome.

Let me extend the argument about economics. A glaring flaw in the "billionaire boys club" rhetoric is omission of any reference to the demand side. As noted earlier with abundant citations, it has become fashionable to demonize particular foundations for their support of certain initiatives or policies, such as charter schools or test-based accountability or other education reforms. The rhetoric in these criticisms is frequently strident and creates the impression that the foundations are acting unilaterally and in a complete vacuum of public opinion or preference.

But where is the demand side in this equation, the obviously hearty public appetite for strategies that some critics attribute to the outsized power of foundations? After all, school systems (public, private, charter) could say, "no, thank you," and turn away the funds offered. Public schools that accept donations from their well-heeled parents in support of after-school or preschool or athletics or arts programs could also say, "thanks, but no thanks," if they sense that private influence compromises egalitarian traditions and other public education values. Similarly, universities routinely weigh the benefits of philanthropic help against perceived or real threats to academic freedom or other norms, and there are memorable examples of named edifices being suddenly stripped of their donors' identities and the funds returned for various reasons. The demand side does play a role, after all.[52]

These examples reinforce my discomfort with critics of foundation or donor largesse who are raising potentially important questions but who need to reopen their introductory economics texts, reread the sections on "revealed preference" (i.e., that the best way to determine consumer preferences is to examine what they consume, given the choices they face), and avoid treating the recipients of money from Gates, Broad, Walton, and hundreds of other foundations as innocent, powerless, and hapless victims. On the other hand (yes, there is always another hand), although consumers of philanthropic largesse have an obligation to be cautious and selective, especially when they are acting as agents for kids or other groups of citizens likely to be affected, invoking the hackneyed principle of caveat emptor is, at best, inadequate and, at worse, disingenuous. We ignore at our peril the dangers of externalities and the importance of curbing the excesses of market concentration on the supply side. The foundations and other private donors who supply money for various education reforms or other initiatives, and often do so with crusaders' zeal, cannot be absolved from their social responsibility. They need to be held accountable, like all organizations whose actions may produce unwanted side effects.[53]

To cite a recent example, a common allegation is that the Gates Foundation "small schools initiative" proved after the fact to be a waste of money and, worse, a reform that exposed kids, families, teachers, and schools, to what was essentially a risky undertaking. Even some of the principal architects of the program now concede that it was implemented without sufficient prior research or small-scale pilot testing and that the results were disappointing and potentially harmful. And this was not the only example of a large initiative later criticized: the Annenberg Challenge of the mid-1990s, which started with a gift of $500 million from Ambassador Walter Annenberg and attracted matching grants of another $600 million from public and private organizations in thirty-five states, is generally considered a colossal waste; its hodgepodge programs involving 2,400 schools, 1.5 million kids, and 80,000 teachers had little to show for the investment. In econo-speak, the costs of these programs were not justified by observed benefits, and by some accounts, the externalities were mostly negative.

But as if often the case, the harsh rhetoric went beyond the evidence, and the criticisms may have actually been indicators of the high standards of commentators—including the funders themselves. Some analysts have pushed back against the critiques, and have suggested the need for caution in labeling the Gates and Annenberg programs as total failures without accounting for at least some of the potential long-term benefits. Still, the basic issues emerging in this argument are central to understanding and shaping policy options for the future of the American public-private partnership in philanthropy: how to anticipate potentially negative externalities, how to estimate the magnitude and distribution of those externalities, and what to do about them ex ante and/or ex post.[54]

Maybe foundations should be expected or required to conduct or fund objective research before making major grants and/or evaluations of the effectiveness of those grants. And maybe they should be required or expected to provide more evidence in support of their plans and to build their projects gradually. This sounds good, but "start off slow" is not likely to be well received by donors whose motivation derives from a different sense of the meaning of "SOS." If the condition of education in the urban inner city is understood to be an emergency (is there any doubt?), the ethical response cannot be the equivalent of "we'll get back to you in five or ten years after we've collected enough data and are sure we know exactly how to solve all the problems."

Which raises familiar and vexing questions about evidentiary standards in policy formation. How much do we need to know before we act? How certain do we have to be? Setting the bar too low is an invitation to rampant and potentially hazardous experimentation with populations that typically are relatively powerless economically and politically. But setting the bar too high is a recipe for preventing any investment, even in programs that could yield desirable outcomes and benefits that might outweigh downside risks and negative effects. This is, of course, true for government-funded experiments and interventions, too. And the awareness that government can be as culpable as the private sector of indulging in social experimentation sans evidence means that, whatever complaints we may have about the rise of philanthropic influence, we need to recognize that the threat is more general. As I have written elsewhere, "finding the sweet spot between inaction and irresponsible action is part of the art of governing."[55]

I applaud the willingness of at least some of the major foundations to fund independent research and evaluations. In this regard, it is worth recalling that "the [Annenberg] Challenge funded a research evaluation of the program in every one of its participating cities, each led by a local research organization," and that the results were the basis for the overwhelming conclusion that the program was a flop.[56] I am not optimistic that exhortations and appeals to morally upright behavior will suffice. Nor am I convinced that it is fair (let alone realistic) to require organizations that are voluntarily investing in programs or experiments aligned with their vision of the public good to earmark funds from their asset base to support evaluation studies that may yield contrary or confusing findings. Yes, there is that small issue of their tax advantage and the fact that they are, in a sense, stewards of part of the public trust. Nudging them to commit a portion of their funds to research might be legally and morally defensible (and is the basis for one of my policy proposals offered in chapter 4), but devising rules to implement and enforce this sort of requirement will take hard work.

There is a more practical constraint, too, because it is not obvious that such evaluations would be credible. Whether or not appeals to their public consciousness will be sufficient to compel foundations to invest in independent research and evaluations, the results of such endeavors would not necessarily be perceived as independent and provide the needed assurances. I applaud foundations that acknowledge the importance of learning from what they are doing and understand their role in spreading that knowledge widely. But given the likely fragility of such evaluations in the theater of public opinion, especially in an era of growing cynicism about the "truthiness" (*pace* Stephen Colbert) of just about everything we read and hear, the broader question is under what arrangements might external evaluations be feasible and, critically, who would fund and conduct them.

Some of the major foundations in the education world, even those with strong ideological predispositions and with the biggest footprints, *do* fund external studies of their own work and promote investigations aimed at understanding basic phenomena. Again, to their credit, investments by Gates, Hewlett, and others include varying amounts for evaluation. Still, and especially because of the observed shifts in foundation funding away from universities and public schools and toward advocacy-laden "jurisdictional challengers," a legitimate concern is about conditions under which there is a strong likelihood of generating credible and objective analyses of the intended and unintended impacts of philanthropic support.

In this chapter I have made three overlapping arguments. First, much of the grousing about excessive and unregulated philanthropy is out of line with the historical realities. Second, there is nonetheless reason to be wary of patterns of increased wealth concentration and the need for greater accountability and monitoring of charitable gifts that have potentially significant effects on social institutions generally and schools in particular. And third, the politics and economics of our approach to philanthropy and charitable giving are made more complex by the special public-private partnership implicit in our legal and management systems. To better understand those relationships, I turn now to a discussion of the public funding of science and research.

CHAPTER TWO

Good Government Pays

The (Social) Science of Education Research

> Science propose, la politique dispose...
> —*Variation on a theme of fifteenth-century French philosophy*[1]

T HE STORY OF FEDERAL FUNDING of scientific research in America usually starts with homage to the remarkable Vannevar Bush, an MIT engineer who, among other notable accomplishments, had been president of the Carnegie Institution of Washington, directed the Office of Scientific Research and Development during World War II, worked on the Manhattan Project, was an early scientist of analog computing whose work led to the design for the now ubiquitous computer mouse, founded the Raytheon Corporation, and, perhaps most significantly, submitted a report to President Truman in 1945—*Science: The Endless Frontier*—that is credited with fundamentally changing the course of science policy in the United States.[2]

Bush had been President Roosevelt's science adviser, described by one historian of science as one of the "most widely known 'scientific icons' in the U.S., surpassed only by Einstein . . . whom *Time* hailed . . . as the 'general of physics.'"[3] Roosevelt and, then, President Truman were eager to capitalize on the remarkable role of science and technology in the American victory in World War II. As Patricia Pelfrey and Richard Atkinson have noted, the recommendation in Bush's landmark report was to "organize scientists and engineers to work toward a common goal on a scale never attempted before . . . to provide industry and the military with a permanent pool of scientific knowledge to ensure economic growth and defense . . . to define the different roles of government, industry, and universities in the scientific enterprise."[4]

That basic research would be the province of the federal government, because private industry did not have the incentives or resources to invest sufficiently in the production of generalizable (and marketable) knowledge, was among the more radical ideas American politics and policy had yet encountered. To set up a new agency that would fund basic research for medical, military, and other applications was an audacious proposal, comparable in its reach and long-term implications, albeit on a smaller scale, to the New Deal and Social Security Act that were crafted in the previous decade.

Like many attempts to bring the financial and political authority of the federal government to bear on what might otherwise have been left to the private or local government sectors, it faced partisan pushback from the beginning. Two years after the White House received Bush's report, President Truman vetoed the National Science Foundation (NSF) Act (of 1947), a move that reflected the president's reticence about the organizational structure and accountability of the agency more than his antipathy to science. Politicians who were not yet ready to cede financial authority of public funds shared the feeling. William Blanpied highlights the principal argument of the opposition—which at least temporarily prevailed—as voiced by Harold Smith, director of the federal Bureau of the Budget:

> The President would be wrong to delegate his Constitutional authority to oversee the disbursement of public funds to a part time board of private citizens and to a director appointed by that board . . . [O]nly the President and officials directly responsible to him could be accountable for spending such money. The scheme proposed by Bush smacked of arrogance and elitism . . . [and] an agency which is to control the spending of public funds in a great national program must be part of the machinery of government.[5]

If the tension between government and science seems familiar, in the light of contemporary partisan battles over funding, there are some important differences. First, opposition to the creation of the NSF rested mostly on the argument that the government should have a greater—not a lesser—role in the scientific enterprise. The dispute was not so much over the principle of public funding as over public *control* of the funds to be disbursed under conditions of limited governmental oversight and accountability. Nowadays, in contrast, the right wing in Congress is motivated primarily by the desire to shrink government, if not to eliminate it altogether, and the last thing conservatives want is a larger public bureaucracy.

Second, today's political stalemates over science funding are shrouded in ideology and religion: conservative factions in Congress, cheered on by the most extreme of the Tea Party yahoos, brazenly propose cuts in science funding for anything that they claim lacks a clear national security rationale; but alert observers see through the veneer to what is clearly a disdain for any research, *whether funded publicly or privately*, on issues such as climate change, women's reproductive biology, educational standards, and the general social good. Opposition to the creation of NSF seventy years ago was not propelled by the same kinds of religious fervor, but still prevailed for a time even against the clear evidence that science and technology had been so crucial to American military victory and potential economic and industrial expansion.

Remarkably, though, and as a reminder of the tenacity, resilience, and delayed gratification in the American policy culture, the NSF was established in 1950, in no small measure due to yet another report, *Science and Public Policy*, submitted by John Steelman, the chair of the Scientific Research Board that Truman had established in 1946. Though not as well known as the Bush report, Steelman's document played a pivotal role in shaping the federal role and, specifically, in preparing the political terrain for what would soon thereafter become the NSF. As Daryl Chubin wrote in a major report of the congressional Office of Technology Assessment, Steelman "championed a crosscutting policy role for managing federally funded research."[6]

In a time of rapidly evolving understanding of the special role of science in times of war, peace, and then cold war, the combined effects of the Bush and Steelman reports were monumental, especially when viewed in the context of America's historical and cultural allergy to centralized authority. "Before World War II, the federal government provided virtually no support for research in universities . . . [I]n the postwar world, the government committed itself to becoming the major sponsor of scientific research in universities. It was an extraordinary reversal of direction."[7] In the preceding chapter, I discussed aspects of the implicit (and, increasingly, explicit) partnership between the private, nonprofit philanthropic sector and government. In this chapter, I begin with a brief discussion about how and why the workings of science evolved into a complex set of relations between universities, the for-profit corporate sector, and government, which provides a backdrop to understanding recent trends in social science and education research.

SCIENCE AS PUBLIC GOOD: THE ENDLESS DEBATE?

Distinctions between basic and applied research, central to *Endless Frontier* and *Science and Public Policy* and persistent still in today's popular and professional discussions of science policy, understate the more complex trajectories through which foundational scientific inquiry influences—and is influenced by—practical use. But the distinction is still relevant to understanding the role of government, and to appreciating the American strategy of partnership between private and public funding of science. Thinking of extremes can shed light on the more complicated realities.

Suppose, for example, one defined "basic" research strictly as the pursuit of foundational new knowledge with no specific application or intended use, and "applied" research as work leading strictly to technological products and innovations but not contributing to new theoretical understanding or discovery. Although this conventional and intuitively appealing distinction has endured as a tool for understanding certain aspects of science policy, in reality much applied research has basic qualities—and vice versa. This insight was at the core of Donald Stokes's important book, *Pasteur's Quadrant*, which recast the dichotomy in terms of the relative emphasis on *uses* of research and on the notion that even foundational inquiry can be "use-oriented."[8]

Stokes illustrated his model with reference to well-known scientists. Nils Bohr was primarily focused on the *basics* of quantum theory and particle physics, while Thomas Edison's work was targeted at solving specific *applied* problems of electrification. Louis Pasteur occupied the intermediate "quadrant" for which Stokes's book is named. The famous French scientist cared mostly about solving problems in crystallography and microbiology because of their implications for human health, but his work relied on theory and yielded new foundational knowledge that went beyond its original use-inspired goals.

But even this illuminating model may overstate the boundaries between theoretical/basic and use-oriented/applied research. It is worth emphasizing, for example, more than Stokes did, the difference between *intent* and *outcome*. Even if Bohr had been motivated by purely theoretical questions, his work eventually played an important part in the development of atomic bombs, a practical application if there ever was one; and Edison's focus on practical inventions relied on and eventually contributed to theoretical aspects of electric power and electrification. In other words, Pasteur was not alone in his quadrant.

Related to the basic-applied dichotomy is an issue central to understanding the economics of science: the distinction between research-based knowledge as a *general* asset with wide market value and as a *specific* asset with value only to the researcher or to the research organization that produced it. Again thinking in extremes, the idea is that basic science yields discoveries with broad potential use value, for which the standard mechanisms of excludability essential to competitive markets either do not exist or are difficult to enforce. The fruits of purely applied research, on the other hand, are harvested solely and specifically by the individual or group responsible for their invention and development. The simple analytics of this model leads to the now familiar prediction that profit-seeking enterprises will invest primarily (if not only) in hoped-for discoveries that promise a requisite financial return, leaving government as the only viable source of financing for research oriented to broad and generalizable knowledge.

That dichotomy, though, like other stylistically attractive economic models, is wanting. With the advantage of hindsight and decades of analysis of the scientific process, we now know that the imagined fence line between basic and applied research obstructs our view of the murkier contested territory. Indeed, the difficulty—or impossibility—of drawing and sustaining a bright boundary between basic and applied research helps explain, in retrospect, the evolution of the architecture of law and regulations governing intellectual property (patent law in particular), the privileges and obligations of researchers, the protection of human subjects, and the allocation of returns to public and private scientific investment—all components of what is commonly referred to as "science policy." One need only try to imagine the counterfactual—an arrangement in which *all* generalizable knowledge is produced *solely* by the public sector—to see why so much legislative and regulatory attention has been paid to assuring a healthy scientific enterprise that exploits both public and private interests.

Roosevelt, Truman, Bush, Steelman, and other leaders of the postwar period were unlikely to have been motivated by these somewhat arcane propositions, given that most of the relevant literature on the social returns to science and on the economics of information, human capital, and research and development (R&D) appeared well after the blueprint for NSF had been drawn and the legislation passed.[9] Indeed, it is ironic that the fundamental insights, which led to the establishment of a federal role and a vast restructuring of arrangements through which the benefits of science and technology would be harnessed for the greater social good, were rather more intuitive and experience based than being derived from rigorous theoretical or empirical research (use inspired or not).[10]

In any event, and fortunately for us all, these enlightened statesmen had correctly anticipated the vast and long-term bounty that would accrue from public support for science, and they were willing to devote considerable time, political capital, and intellectual energy to laying the building blocks of what eventually became a more complex public infrastructure. Once the principle of a real federal role in science was established and codified in law, the enterprise began to grow. As shown in figure 2.1, by 1955, total federal spending on R&D (as measured by NSF) had already reached roughly $2.5 billion ($22.1 billion in 2014 dollars), almost entirely for national defense; by 1965, both the magnitude and scope had grown, and the total federal investment was $14.6 billion in nominal dollars, or $109 billion in 2014 dollars, a fivefold increase in ten years. The new system was responding well to emerging needs—Sputnik, demand for oil, new health emergencies—and the federal money was dropped into corresponding buckets. By 2014, federal R&D funds had spread to fourteen categories, totaling $133 billion (not including $32 billion in a separate "basic research" category).

This means that, in constant dollars, the federal role in scientific R&D grew by roughly 600 percent between 1955 and the present day. However, the amount of spending recorded in two categories—space flight, research, and supporting activities and education, training, employment, and social services—*dropped* during this period. The latter, of special interest to us here, fell from $1.09 billion in 1967 (in 2014 inflation-adjusted dollars), the first time a number was entered in that category, to $543 million in 2014, approximately a 50 percent decrease over forty-seven years.[11]

I shall return to the specifics of education-related, federal research funding shortly. But first, a few more remarks about the significance of the public investment in science. Recall that one of the most innovative, if not revolutionary, features of the new approach to organizing the nation's science and technology system, stimulated if not fully detailed by the Bush report, was the place of universities: we had embarked on "a national scientific enterprise in which basic research, supported with federal funds *and conducted by universities*, would be *implemented by private industry*." [italics added][12]

I wish to emphasize two points here. First, there was an implicit understanding that the output from basic scientific research, to be conducted primarily in publicly supported university centers and laboratories, was to a significant extent intended as the raw material for productive *implementation*, for the development of tools needed to address and solve practical

FIGURE 2.1   Federal funding for R&D, selected categories, 1955–2014 (in millions, inflation-adjusted 2014 dollars)

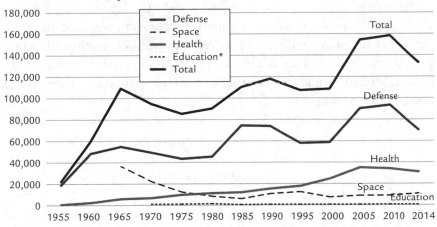

*Education includes "education, training, employment, and social services."

Source: National Science Foundation, http://www.nsf.gov/statistics/2015/nsf15306/pdf/nsf15306.pdf.

problems. From the beginning, the assumption underlying policy was that even basic research was oriented ultimately to *use*, an idea that today plays a central role in concepts like "translational science" and in an aspiration of special relevance to education, namely, that research and practice are (or should be) mutually reinforcing.[13]

Second, the understanding was that the public role (government) would be focused on the "R" in R&D, as a stimulant and partner to the private industrial sector that would assume much of the responsibility for the "D." In other words, translations from laboratory science to technological application would take place largely in organizations that would respond to economic incentives by investing in discovery and bearing much if not all of the risk of failure and, in exchange, would enjoy the chance to capture most of the economic returns. Granted, the private sector has, over the past century, developed a quite robust basic-research capacity, especially in health, pharmaceuticals, and related fields, clear evidence that the boundaries between basic and applied science are fuzzy, but the size and significance of the federal role are key to explaining continued American global prowess (if not hegemony) in science.

American science grew into a complex enterprise with many moving parts. Yet it proved to be agile as conditions changed (perhaps most memorably in response to perceived threats, first from the Russian space program and later from the Japanese auto and video industries and the market penetration of Chinese and Korean technology). For example, concern in the 1970s that research conducted in universities was not moving efficiently enough into industrial application led to policy corrections, including tax credits for research and the relaxation of antitrust regulations to encourage research partnerships.[14]

In retrospect, the evolution of science policy can be seen as another manifestation of the American faith in markets and competition—a faith conditional on the imposition of rules, the agreed-upon delineation of rights and responsibilities of scientists, and the "visible hand" of government. The most ardent believers in free-market capitalism generally fear *too much* government, but the risks of rampant laissez-faire were clearly on the minds of the political elites responsible for America's postwar economy. In somewhat typical fashion, we chose a middle ground: whatever Harold Smith may have felt about keeping big scientific decisions close to the "machinery of government," the way the system evolved was in the direction of a more decentralized arrangement involving government, universities, and the private industrial sector—each operating within its own basic norms and institutional rules. Competition, surely a source of creative and innovative energy in the university and corporate research world, exists within the government, too, where there is vigorous interagency jockeying for budgetary appropriations. Developing so-called strategic plans or national goals is not, in the American culture of pluralist federalism and diffused authority, a task for the faint of heart.[15]

The status of American science and technology is frequently debated, often in terms of our current and future global competitiveness, but the most comprehensive studies show that overall the system has been remarkably productive and remains among the strongest in the world. The government's role in all this, especially through its commitment to funding of research that began with Vannevar Bush et al., has been substantial—the recurrent calls for a reduced federal presence notwithstanding. The government's role in *social science and education*, on the other hand, began differently and followed a different path, and though today there is at least a visible investment, it has always been meager compared to the physical and biological sciences and even more vulnerable to partisan political intrusion. I turn now to a more focused look at trends in education research funding at the federal level.[16]

THE UNSTEADY STATE OF THE EDUCATION SCIENCES

Auditors of current arguments over the quality and funding of education research may be surprised to learn that the debate has actually been underway for more than a century. Even the phrase "science of education," which still rankles physical and natural scientists for whom the work of teaching and learning is perhaps many things but certainly not scientific, appeared as early as 1891. Since then, it has changed meanings, gaining new respect in some quarters and losing ground in others, hailed by some for its contributions to rigorous inquiry leading to new understanding of how people learn and dismissed by others as the interjection of "scientism" into the cultural and social determinants of human development. As Ellen Condliffe Lagemann has so eloquently chronicled, the history of education research is a "troubled" one, and the quest for a real "science of education," an "elusive" one.[17]

A turning point in this history came with the landmark study, *Equality of Educational Opportunity* (*EEO*), commonly known as the "Coleman report" after its lead author, James Coleman. Congress ordered the study as part of the 1964 Civil Rights Act, to survey the "lack of availability of equal educational opportunities for individuals by reason of race, color, religion, or national origin in public educational institutions at all levels in the United States, its territories and possessions, and the District of Columbia."[18]

The Coleman report, more than seven hundred pages, was arguably the most influential contribution by social scientists to the study of education in the twentieth century. As Adam Gamoran and Daniel Long have shown, by 1973 *EEO* was cited more than 2,700 times in more than 130 academic journal articles; it spawned a generation of research on the most urgent problems of access, equity, teaching, and schooling; and it opened a new era of big science applied to education. Key lessons from Coleman have endured, some to our deep collective chagrin: achievement gaps between white majority and African American students, though narrower today than in the 1960s, have persisted; progress in school desegregation has been slowed and in many places reversed, with predictable consequences for the academic achievement of minority children; and the effects of students' and their families' economic conditions continue to limit the gains possible from even the most promising school and systemwide investments in educational resources.[19]

On the other hand, the utility of scientific research to understand the origins and status of educational inequality and related problems, and as a basis for rigorous consideration of policy options, was firmly established, even if the results are at times distressing and the translation of findings into practical solutions is controversial and frustratingly slow. It may seem self-serving to applaud the rise of research—even while mourning the much slower pace of progress in addressing the problems that research is supposed to help us solve—but my point here is different: *even the best scientific research has trouble keeping pace with the growing complexity of the problems to be studied.* This is true in the physical realm (climate change, Alzheimer's disease) and in the social realm (racial disparities, income inequality), but is by no means an indictment of research as much as a testament to the challenges faced by the research community. We may be frustrated by the slow pace of adoption of findings from good research, but we would be in much worse shape if we just dropped the idea of research oriented to practical problems altogether. A more rational response than the one some politicians propose nowadays—to curb research that doesn't succinctly and clearly promise specific solutions to a politically circumscribed set of technological problems—would be to set reasonable expectations for how thoroughly and how quickly science can solve the big problems.

Causal connections should never be assumed casually. But there can be little doubt that the Coleman report led to a substantially increased and energetic federal role in the funding of education research. An abridged timeline since 1964 would include such milestones as the development of a nationally representative and continuing assessment of American students through the National Assessment of Educational Progress, the design for which began in 1963; the formation of the National Academy of Education (NAEd), in 1965, as a private organization made up of US and foreign scholars elected on the basis of outstanding education-related scholarship to advance research and its uses in policy and practice; the creation of the National Institute of Education in 1972 and its subsequent evolution first into the Office of Educational Research and Improvement (OERI) in 1980 and then, with passage of the Education Sciences Reform Act (ESRA), into the Institute of Education Sciences (IES) in 2002; and the development of research as a bona fide and increasingly attractive area of concentration in doctoral-granting graduate schools of education. As noted by the Congressional Research Service, "Collecting statistics and facts on the condition and progress of education was the core function of the earliest version of the Office of Education [established in 1867]. However, a coordinated national undertaking resembling today's research and statistics effort did not begin to take shape until the mid-1970s."[20]

Alongside such a timeline would be markers of the advances in the methods of education research, which now borrow even more consciously than in the past from psychology, economics, sociology, anthropology, statistics, political science, and brain science. Emergence of controlled experimental designs for evaluation of education policies and programs, development and refinement of so-called "education production functions," meta-analytic strategies to summarize and interpret results from multiple studies, longitudinal data collections and their role in understanding education over the life course, and, more recently, the advent of cognitive neuroscience linking the physiology of the brain to progress in learning may not be the darlings of the entire education research community, but they are certainly proof of a vigorous, multidisciplinary, and sophisticated education research enterprise.

Still, complaints about the quality and utility of education research are commonplace, although I would attribute a large amount of the disaffection less to methodological flaws than to discomfort with policy initiatives that the research seems to support and, from another angle, to a misplaced disdain for "scientism" that allegedly ignores sociocultural and affective components of teaching, learning, and schooling. As an analogue to my argument in the preceding chapter—where I suggested that criticisms of our system of philanthropy often confound process and substance—it is also the case that attacks on the quality of education research often mask underlying ideological disagreements with its findings and implications. Education research may still have something of an "awful reputation," but the conclusion reached by careful review of its methods, output, and similarities to other scientific fields—conducted by a committee of the National Research Council—was more charitable.[21] The impact of this conclusion, though, in some ways mirrors the impact of much social science research: it has not translated into significant changes in attitude or policy toward the value of social and education science spending. Political uptake of research is still slow and fitful.[22]

FICKLE FEDERAL FUNDING

The current debate over education research continues on many fronts and in many ways echoes the twentieth-century fights over the meaning of education, the role of values and culture, the persistent discrepancies in resources between minority and majority and rich and poor students, the promise and peril of "mental measurement," the relative relevance of psychology and philosophy to the improvement of educational opportunity, and the uses of data on teachers and learners in systems of public accountability. That word, too, *accountability*, has been in vogue in education policy circles for at least three decades and is today among the hottest flash points in the reform movement. But its underlying meaning—the imperative to provide evidence to taxpayers that their money is being spent smartly and efficiently on their children's schooling—has roots in the founding values of the republic and has been around at least since the "common school" reforms of the early nineteenth century.[23]

One of the more astonishing aspects of education *research*, though, is how little the government actually spends for it, at least relative to the size of the national investment in *education* and relative to the amounts spent on other areas of research. For one perspective on the relative share of total R&D allocated to education, see figure 2.2, which brings into sharper relief the message in figure 2.1.

A reasonable current estimate of the national (as opposed to *federal*) annual outlay on elementary and secondary education, public and private, is $600 billion; add another $500 billion in expenditures by nonprofit colleges and universities, and the total exceeds a trillion, roughly 7 percent of our total gross domestic product.[24] The current budget for the IES is about $570 million, in the range of one-twentieth of 1 percent of the total that Americans spend on education, K–college. IES is by no means the only or largest source, although it is the only federal agency exclusively charged with funding education research and evaluations. The institute's funds are

FIGURE 2.2   Federal R&D spending for health and education, 1970–2014 (in millions, 2014 dollars)

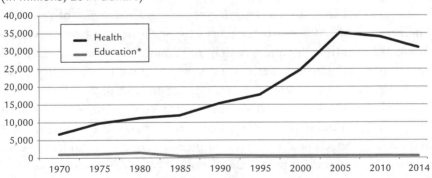

*Education includes "education, training, employment, and social services."

Source: National Science Foundation, http://www.nsf.gov/statistics/2015/nsf15306/pdf/nsf15306.pdf.

organized in four national centers, based on ESRA (the National Center for Special Education Research was added as part of the reauthorization of the Individuals with Disabilities Education Act). In its 2014 review of ESRA, the nonpartisan Congressional Research Service underscored procedural and substantive aspects of IES that are worth reiterating. With respect to the ongoing tension over governmental authority and the diffusion of responsibility, "under the provisions of ESRA, IES operates as an independent institute and is afforded more freedom from ED [the Department of Education] than OERI had as an office (headed by an Assistant Secretary) . . . At the same time, ESRA provides for greater oversight of the work and work processes of IES by a technical panel [the National Board for Education Sciences] in comparison to what was required under provisions in OERI's authorizing legislation."

In terms of its substantive goals and organizational ethos, "The aim of IES is to provide parents, educators, students, researchers, policy makers, and the general public with information on the condition and progress of education, on practices that improve academic achievement, and on the effectiveness of federal education and other education programs. IES is authorized to carry out these aims by compiling statistics, conducting research and evaluations, and disseminating information."[25]

The IES agenda is broad and deep, covering much of the range of plausible topics relevant to the improvement of our understanding of education and, hopefully, leading to continuous improvement. As revealing as the IES range of priority topics, though, is the way in which the authorizing language articulated a preference for certain *methodologies* of research. The wording of ESRA, with references to "scientifically based research standards, scientifically valid research, and scientifically valid educational evaluations," reflected the desire on the part of at least some policy makers and research professionals to import norms and protocols from the so-called "hard" sciences. Randomized controlled experiments, a staple of epidemiological and some social science research that seeks causal evidence of the relative effects of alternative treatments, were now deemed the "gold standard" against which proposals for evaluation of educational interventions would be judged.[26]

Predictably, this shift in attitude—not only away from so-called qualitative studies but also from cross-sectional and even longitudinal studies that relied on correlational data—was met with considerable opposition. On one side was a large and vocal contingent within the established education research community that saw the emphasis on randomized experiments as a politically motivated intrusion; on the other side were advocates of an even more extreme rejection of research that did not meet evidentiary standards of empirical scientific fields like medicine and experimental psychology.

There was political and ideological drama behind the impetus for improvement in the quality and credibility of educational research. Passage of ESRA took place during a period of intensification of principles of high-stakes accountability—for educational performance as well as for the performance of educational researchers. In Washington's acronym-rich environment (which Bill Wulf, the former president of the National Academy of Engineering, once charmingly referred to as our *A.R.E.*), SBR simultaneously stood for *standards-based reform* and *scientifically based research*, a coincidence that was more than semantic. Growing dissatisfaction with education research mirrored frustration with the progress of educational improvement—the latter a feeling widely shared across the political spectrum—and SBR in its twin meanings was the dominant theme not only in ESRA but also in the No Child Left Behind Act, the 2001 reauthorization of the Elementary and Secondary Education Act that reinforced the federal role in public education, even with its limited financial involvement. The connection was powerful, and at the risk of abridging the more subtle arguments that were raging before and during the passage of ESRA, one of the factors that explained the alleged underperformance of the American school system was our disregard for empirical data and an unwillingness to treat the problems with rigorous scientific methodologies.[27]

Against the backdrop of a century's worth of disagreement over what education research is and could be, those arguments of the early 2000s were the latest chapter in what Lagemann had called "the troubled" history of education research. Viewed somewhat more optimistically, though, the debate reflected a positive change in the public discourse and a more favorable attitude toward the investment of money and organizational capital for the gathering of credible scientific evidence relevant to the complex problems of schools and schooling. It is comforting to note that the phrase "education research" has become steadily more common in books published in English, and if we include citations in both the popular and professional media, that trend would surely be even more pronounced.[28]

In terms of the public investment, too, the data suggest a steady commitment, even if at levels that most education researchers deem inadequate. Aside from the postrecession bump in funding in 2010, through the American Recovery and Reinvestment Act (ARRA), the IES budget has remained relatively stable, partisan political fights notwithstanding. There is today considerable respect for both the quality and scope of the IES mission, which strives to anticipate long-term issues, respond to more immediate evaluative concerns, and produce a stream of credible analyses and findings.[29] (The current funding level, which has risen, is part of the discussion in chapter 4.)

The NSF plays a significant role in the federal education research enterprise. NSF's total budget for fiscal 2015 was just under $7.3 billion, including roughly $560 million for awards management, infrastructure, and operating costs. The budget for the education and human resources (EHR) directorate, which invests heavily in research on the improvement of science, technology, engineering, and mathematics (STEM) education, was $846 million, or roughly 12 percent of the total. Other NSF directorates, which focus primarily on what is still considered basic research in all the fields of physical and natural science, allocate resources to universities and other research centers where early-career scholars receive substantial education and training; in a sense, then, much of NSF's budget can be said to contribute to the ongoing education agenda, albeit almost exclusively at the postsecondary (and postdoctoral) levels.

The fiscal year 2015 NSF budget included $5.8 billion for "research and related activities" as compared to $866 million for EHR. Still, in terms of total dollars, EHR ranked fourth out of the nine directorates. We shouldn't read too much into the sometimes strange locutions of bureaucracy, but the fact that the word "education" is separated from the word "research" in NSF's accounts is revealing. Semantics aside, NSF's role in education research has become increasingly important, reflecting on the recurrent anxieties about the general condition of American science and the specific issues related to the current and future STEM workforce.

In fiscal year 2014, the EHR directorate awarded approximately seven hundred new grants, of which about a hundred were for over $1 million.

Although much of this work focuses on STEM education, the portfolio covers a wider swath. Among the larger awards, EHR funds local as well as nationally oriented support for a variety of educational and workforce programming. Examples include grants to specific geographic areas to enhance the quality of STEM secondary educators and more broadly targeted grants such as examining the efficacy of intensified algebra instruction for at-risk students. EHR provides funding for programming for science majors at specific colleges, funding to examine climate change issues such as permafrost, and funding to engage youth in STEM career pathways through clean-energy literacy development. It also funds diversity-related programs aimed at different educational levels. While STEM is the overarching theme, EHR touches upon STEM in many dimensions.

NSF is not alone. STEM education is a topic that has generated a more widespread—if somewhat incoherent—federal role. Most of the so-called "mission agencies" (such as the Department of Energy and NASA), as distinct from the big research agencies, dedicate some of their budgets to education-related activities. Among those with STEM education budgets greater than $300,000, which participated in a federally sponsored survey relating to fiscal 2010 and 2011 budgets, about one-third of the STEM education funding was spent on activities that targeted the specific workforce needs of the mission agencies surveyed, and the remaining two-thirds targeted "broader STEM education activities." But this statistic lumps the mission agencies, whose education spending is almost entirely dedicated to mission-specific training and evaluation needs, together with NSF and the Department of Education, which sponsor the bulk of federal investments in education R&D.[30]

We should not underestimate the importance of the National Institutes of Health (NIH), which is counted under the Department of Health and Human Services. NIH investments for education are more broadly targeted than for STEM through major research programs in several of its main divisions, but there is no standard mechanism for identifying grants (or parts of grants) for specific studies of education. For approximation, I consider three of the institutes that have programs of research related broadly to questions that are relevant to the education and human development research agenda—teaching and learning with special emphasis on brain science, the improvement of education for children with special needs, and cognitive aging. The national institutes of Child Health and Human Development (NICHD), Aging (NIA), and Deafness and Other Communicative Disorders (NIDCD) together operate currently with appropriations totaling approximately $2.9 billion.

These investments represent a small share, roughly 10 percent, of the total NIH appropriation in 2014. For comparison, one of the largest institutes, the National Cancer Institute, accounts for more than 16 percent of the total. Notable in the mix of NIH support are grants for cognition-related issues, early childhood development for the poor, and many that have at least some ostensibly education-related components within their broader remits, for example, research on attention deficit hyperactivity disorders, or on technologies of amplification for children with cochlear implants or who rely on speech recognition to overcome the challenges of hearing loss. A major contribution by NIH has been the NICHD Study of Early Child Care and Youth Development.

A metric that is perhaps more useful than the annual congressional appropriation is the number of awards made by the various institutes. For example, in 2014, there were roughly 5,700 grants made by NIA, NICHD, and NIDCD, totaling close to $2.3 billion. By rough count, $1.7 billion of this amount went to research project grants and related activities, a portion of which is relevant to what would typically be counted as education related.

GOOD NEWS AND BAD

The general picture of education research funding, then, in terms of the federal role, is mixed. Surely the activity level has risen from the mid-twentieth century—if not strictly in dollar terms, then in the scope and influence of programs of the major funding agencies—although relative to the significance of education and human capital development generally, the enterprise is still paltry. The most recent economic crisis and recession of 2007–2009 led to a temporary uptick in research spending generally, through ARRA, but we continue to spend relatively little to address questions about what may be the most significant contributor to the American economy and quality of life, namely, the productivity of schools and schooling. Referring again to the example of NSF, the trend in education funding was flat and slightly declining through much of the previous decade, until

2009, when a slight increase was detected as part of the much more massive increase in total spending. ARRA's effects on NSF's education budget, though positive, were difficult to detect compared to the other programs of research.

To some extent, this pattern reflects misconceptions that have seeped into professional and political discourse. The tropes are familiar: education is not all that complicated, so why do we need a lot of fancy science to figure out how to make it better? The quality of education research still doesn't compare to other fields such as medicine where experimental protocols ensure valid and reliable findings. We have spent lots of money to study the big problems in education like achievement gaps and teacher quality and they still aren't solved. Schooling in America is fraught with so much cultural and political baggage that aspiring to its improvement based on scientific evidence is naive and wasteful. And the beat[ing] goes on. These may not be the exact words we find in editorials or congressional deliberations, but their tone and spirit are all too commonplace—and have been in the air for a long time.

What is different today is that the effects of the historically logy federal investment in education research are amplified by their convergence with two other trends. First, as described in the preceding chapter, the attitudes of private philanthropies toward research and evaluation have shifted in subtle but important ways, from independent support of knowledge production and toward the accumulation of data that more specifically advances particular causes and beliefs. Because education research, like so many fields, relies on a combination of private and public support, trends in either can clearly have significant consequences overall.

Second, the pressures that have historically limited federal support of education research have intensified because of the simultaneous effects of budget cuts and political intrusion into science, on the one hand, and the steady increase in the supply of researchers seeking external funding. The latter point suggests that good news is sometimes not good enough: for a field plagued by public and political misunderstanding about its inherent worth, it is heartening to observe a steady and rising interest in education research as a rewarding career. But with this crowding comes heightened competition for increasingly scarce public dollars, reduced likelihood of winning grants (especially for early-career scholars), and the worrisome possibility that both the quantity and quality of education research will suffer.

Consider, for example, trends in enrollments and completion of graduate degrees in education and related fields. According to data compiled by the National Center for Education Statistics, the number of doctoral degrees awarded by postsecondary institutions increased by 44 percent, from 122,000 in 2002 to 175,000 in 2013. Degrees awarded in health professions and related programs and legal professions and studies made up almost two-thirds of the total; education degrees accounted for 6 percent, while engineering, biological, and biomedical sciences each accounted for roughly 5 percent.[31]

The trend in doctoral completions is even more impressive over the past five decades. As shown in figure 2.3, doctoral degrees conferred in education, per se, grew from about six thousand in 1970 to over ten thousand in 2012. Including other fields (philosophy, history, psychology, other social

FIGURE 2.3   Doctoral degrees conferred, selected fields and years, 1970–2013

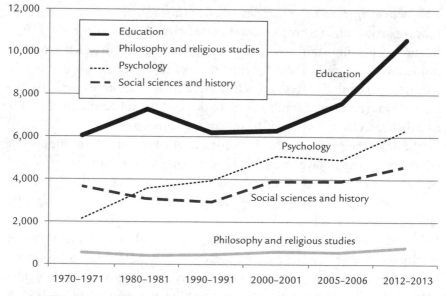

Source: NCES Digest of Education Statistics, http://nces.ed.gov/programs/digest/d14/tables/dt14_324.10.asp.

sciences) that supply researchers whose work often relates to education, the growth during that period was from about twelve thousand to twenty-two thousand, a roughly 80 percent increase.

However, this positive trend is tempered by the obvious competitive strains it produces. Simply put, more scholars are vying for slices of a relatively diminishing pie. Many of these new doctoral degree holders aspire to and obtain tenure track positions in research universities; others go for jobs in the major think tanks not in the university sector and nonprofit research firms; some are hired in private industry. Professional advancement in all these organizations, universities in particular, depends on research productivity, which hinges in part on success at writing successful proposals for external funding.

The situation in research universities warrants special attention. In light of the financial stresses many universities face, an increasingly important criterion for promotion and tenure is not only a record of important research published in peer reviewed journals, but, as importantly, evidence of likely *future* success in winning prestigious federal grants. For many deans and promotion or tenure committees, then, "publish or perish" has been expanded to include "*propose and receive* or perish." But in the major think tanks and contract research organizations that accept government money, whether in the for-profit or nonprofit sectors, similar pressures on early-career scholars are widely acknowledged: friends with long and reputable track records at some of the most distinguished research organizations have shared their sense of despair over how much of their time they have to spend writing grants—and how little time is left for the interesting research itself. The question is whether and how this substantially fiercer competitive environment affects the lives of researchers and the quality of their work.

To its great credit, the NSF has given careful thought to the professional development of researchers and, specifically, to the problems that stem from the competitive pressures of federal grant seeking. Thanks to the foundation's merit review process, data are available that shed light on the changing realities faced by social science scholars. For example, we know that in the late 1990s and early part of the 2000s, overall award rates across all of NSF hovered in the range of 30 percent: of the roughly thirty thousand competitively reviewed proposals received by the agency in 1996, about nine thousand were funded. The EHR award rate was relatively good—34 percent over the period 1996–2000—and in fact, higher than engineering, computer science, and biology. But in the 2000s, the trend took a sharp turn downward. By 2005, the NSF overall award rate had dropped to roughly 23 percent and in EHR to 20 percent. By 2014, the NSF rate was stable at 23 percent, but EHR was down to 17 percent.[32]

Similar trends are discernible from data on NIH and IES competitions. For the three NIH institutes with education-related programs, the odds of winning grants have been falling for the past fourteen years. The NICHD award rate fell from 29 percent in 2000 to 12.5 percent in 2014; for NIA, the drop was from 26 to 15 percent; and for NIDCD, the rate fell from 40 to 26 percent.

IES does not post award data in the same format, but information provided by staff enables an approximation of the trend. Because the data I examined did not separate the number of new proposals received from proposals for continuation of prior grants, I computed an "odds index"

FIGURE 2.4   Odds of success in federal grant-seeking, selected agencies, estimated, 2006–2014

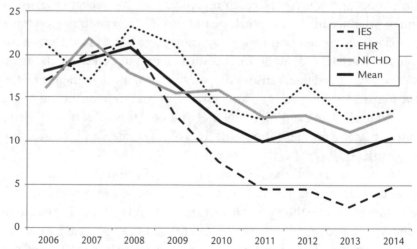

Sources: For NIH: https://report.nih.gov/success_rates/Success_ByIC.cfm; for EHR: http://www.nsf.gov/nsb/publications/2015/nsb201514.pdf; for IES: author's computation of "odds index" = new awards/proposals received, based on data provided by IES staff.

as the simple ratio of total annual obligated funds to number of new proposals received. For example, total obligations in 2006 were roughly $134 million, and there were 409 proposals reviewed, for an odds index of 0.33. Increases in budgetary authority enabled a modest rise in the award rate between 2010 and 2012, but by 2014, the index fell to 0.17. By combing the data from NSF (EHR), NIH, and IES, as in figure 2.4, it is clear that the trend over the past decade was not a happy one for education researchers hoping to obtain federal grants.

CAUSE FOR CONCERN

In the previous chapter, I reviewed data on patterns in philanthropic support for education research, remarked on the possibility that increased competition does not necessarily lead to higher-quality research, and asked if the pressures to please funders may compromise the scientific objectivity of the work. We see now that similar questions arise with respect to the public sector: does the convergence of political and budgetary constraints and the increase in numbers of researchers who need extramural support to advance their professional careers affect the quality and objectivity of federally funded education research?

And the plot thickens. For if these pressures are largely exogenous—brought on by economic and political forces external to the education research community—an additional stress on the system comes from shifts in attitude about evidentiary standards and the quality of research that are, indeed, brought on by the research community itself. Starting in approximately 2002, with passage of ESRA, IES declared and began implementing a sharp preference for certain *kinds* of research, in particular, studies that included randomized designs aimed at establishing firmer causal relations between educational interventions and observable outcomes. This shift, propelled by a simplistic plus/minus rhetoric—medical research is good, education research is lousy—was championed not in the first instance by politicians who don't understand science but by highly credentialed academic researchers working both in and outside the government: the first head of IES, Grover (Russ) Whitehurst, was a former psychology professor determined to upgrade the substance and process of education research, using epidemiological science as his North Star.

Not surprisingly, the subsequent redirection of education research funding took place in a contentious atmosphere; on both sides, the discourse was decorated with claims that jumped far ahead of their own evidentiary base. But the net effect was to shift the burden of proof onto researchers to explain their reticence in applying the gold standard of randomized control trials, even if the range of questions for which such methods were appropriate represented a small subset of the problems worthy of rigorous empirical attention. The fact that "not all questions are causal," as the distinguished statistician Paul Holland once remarked, did not prevent IES from implementing a major reorientation of its (limited) research budget to studies that claimed to offer proof of what works. To paraphrase what I have written elsewhere, "efforts to [impose] a one-method-fits-all mentality, to lock [education] research into a particular evidentiary schema, [were] foolish. Not to pick on one such schema unfairly, but progress in understanding planetary cycles, evolution, or for that matter the effects of smoking on lung cancer, have not relied on randomized trials, so it's not clear why we in education should assume that's the best or only design relevant to our issues."[33]

These pressures to constrain methodological choice—as distinct from the quite legitimate pursuit of higher evidentiary standards regardless of particular research design—create yet more difficulties for an education research community already buckling under fiscal and political siege. And the effects are felt well beyond the confines of the mythic ivory tower: potentially vital work on classroom teaching and the more subtle cultural and pedagogical influences on student learning, so relevant to coping with the changing demographic and socioeconomic realities of schooling in America today, is underfunded and underappreciated just when it is needed most. To the kinds of alarms I sounded about the credibility and objectivity of research under heightened competitive conditions, then, can now be added the scary prospect of researchers forcing themselves to adopt (and adapt) methodologies for which they may be inadequately trained—methodologies that may not be the right ones to address many of the important questions we face anyway.

But let's not overreact—yet. It would be imprudent to rush to definitive judgments based on trend data and frustration with the temporary bursts of enthusiasm for one particular research strategy. But it would be equally irresponsible to ignore the downside risks suggested by current trends and postpone consideration of policy options until it is too late. What kinds of policy mechanisms might safeguard the rigor and credibility of education research? What might be done to stem the erosion of trust in the validity and reliability of research intended to inform, guide, and evaluate policy? What are the implications for the American advice industry generally and for the viability and utility of education research specifically? I turn to these questions in the next chapters.

CHAPTER THREE

Lights unto the Nation

The Rise and Decline of the American Advice Industry

Everyone is entitled to his own opinion, but not his own facts.
—*Attributed to Daniel Patrick Moynihan*

I F FRANKLIN ROOSEVELT and Harry Truman launched an American science policy revolution after World War II, Abraham Lincoln gets the credit for an idea at least as radical almost a century earlier: harnessing the scientific community as a source of advice to the American government. I wrote in the preceding chapter about the fuzzy boundaries separating basic from applied research, and reinforced the argument that government sponsorship of science is a necessary (but insufficient) condition for production of generalizable and "public" knowledge. Now I turn to a different and, I believe, equally important feature of the government's involvement in the R&D enterprise: asking for and using scientific and technological knowledge to inform decision making and problem solving.

Here is the gist of my argument. If government has a public responsibility to sponsor and sustain research with broad, long-term, and often uncertain eventual use, it also has a utilitarian or instrumental need for credible, independent, research-based advice on problems of policy and statecraft. Simply put, the government, perhaps more in the United States than elsewhere, plays three parts in the drama of science: as an enabler, producer, and consumer of scientific knowledge. Like much good drama, the actors often play multiple roles.

What did President Lincoln have to do with this? One of the more poignant examples of the American custom of asking scientists to help the government solve practical problems comes from the Civil War. As high school students are still taught, a remarkable new technology, the famous "iron-clad ship," changed the course of maritime history and gave the Union army a significant military edge. But what few students learn is that in its original design, the iron ship had some fundamental flaws— *which were eventually fixed by scientists working outside of government.* I encourage you to guess, but if you say "rust," you'd be close, and if you say "too heavy," you'd be wrong. No, the most challenging problem was not how to keep the ship afloat but rather how to steer it. The challenge was how to deal with magnetic deviation—*all that iron*—which distorted the accuracy of the ship's compass. Not to strain the poetry here, but in a war defined by the difference between North and South, getting the compass to work and pointing the ship's turrets in the right direction was an applied scientific problem if there ever was one.

Luckily, in the final moments before Congress adjourned in March 1863, it passed a bill that was then signed by the president, establishing the National Academy of Sciences (NAS). And one of the first questions to come before the new body (which had no physical home yet but operated with the nineteenth-century equivalent of virtual connectivity among the members) was about the iron ship. The rest, as they say, is history: a small committee of scientists and engineers studied the compass problem and solved it, thereby engraving permanently into American political culture the principle of science-in-service-to-the-government. When I worked there, we used to kid about how a committee of the NAS won the Civil War. A "stretcher" (as Mark Twain would have pointed out), but the details of this early success story are worth remembering:

> Admiral [Charles H.] Davis requested that the Academy investi-
> gate and report on the subject of magnetic deviation in iron ships
> . . . [which] had hulls of iron construction or decks protected with
> iron plates. The large amounts of iron in these ships caused onboard
> compasses to deviate, thus making navigation an inexact and poten-
> tially dangerous affair. The Compass Committee was thus charged
> with recommending ways to correct this deviation. In January 1864
> the committee issued a substantial, 73-page report in which it recom-
> mended the use of appropriately placed bar magnets to counteract

local attractions acting on ship compasses. Following on its recommendations, the committee itself . . . oversaw the correction of compasses on twenty-seven Union ships.[1]

So it is not surprising that a painting of President Lincoln, which imagines him surrounded by the scientists who had founded the NAS—Alexander Bache, Louis Agassiz, Henry Davis, Joseph Henry, others—hangs handsomely in the boardroom of NAS's headquarters in Washington. Albert Herter allowed himself some artistic license in his rendition of the signing of the NAS charter—there is no actual record of the meeting as depicted—but the symbolism and significance are vivid. As a colleague and I have written elsewhere, "one cannot help but marvel at the coincidence: it was as though, in gratitude for President Lincoln's willingness to establish the Academy, one of its first products was a technological contribution to the eventual northern victory."[2]

It is surely not coincidence that two of the most significant innovations in the organization of American science—founding of the NAS and establishment of the National Science Foundation (NSF) some ninety years later—owed some of their success to the role of science and technology in war. And in both instances, there was a fundamental duality, if not by design, then certainly by effect: government was viewed as a sponsor of generalized knowledge production and simultaneously as consumer of the specific output from that production. The phrase "dual-use technology," which became popular in the twentieth-century literature of innovation diffusion, refers to the ways in which technologies developed for a particular application spawn other and often unanticipated uses. A familiar example is the invention of global positioning systems (GPS), developed originally for satellite and—again—other *military* uses and now ubiquitous in civilian life.[3]

But here I intend a different meaning of duality, to connote the idea of government as a *producer* of scientific knowledge understood as a public good—without always knowing how its results will be translated into practical uses—and as a *consumer* of information derived from science with specific instrumental application. If NSF is largely about the former, the founding of the NAS can be understood mostly in terms of the latter. Note that the NAS doesn't exactly use science to solve its own problems (although arguably some findings from organization research would probably help in the management of the place), but it operates as a credible broker between the research and policy-making communities. There is some murkiness here—surely some NSF funding goes for well-defined problem solving, and some NAS work contributes to the general store of knowledge—which may explain aspects of the debate over what kinds of studies the government should be funding. For example, some advocates of science funding play the national security card in order to camouflage their ideological opposition to inquiries into sensitive topics like climate change or reproductive rights, and seem to have less interest in (and high anxiety about) research with uncertain eventual application; as I argued in chapter 2, these attitudes reflect a narrow and dangerous misinterpretation of the role of government in funding public goods generally and scientific progress specifically.

ADVICE TO THE NATION

How government interacts with science is, of course, a broad topic that goes well beyond the history of the NAS. Most accounts, though, focus on the dramatic technological disruptions of the late nineteenth and early twentieth centuries—a half century after the founding of the NAS—that brought about a reconsideration of the meaning of rationality and the potential for scientific evidence in the otherwise politically dominated workings of government. As Jeff Henig notes, in his excellent study of the role of research in recent policy debates about charter schools, "By the early twentieth century, the institutionalized explosions of science and industry were already requiring specialization of knowledge and role . . . It is against this backdrop that the Progressive movement laid the groundwork for its vision of the relationship between policy makers and policy sciences as one in which social scientists and professional experts would counsel public officials about the best way to maximize democratically defined goals."[4]

It is surprising that this otherwise compelling analysis of the perhaps uniquely American history of relations between scientific reasoning and public policy making omits the founding of the NAS and, for that matter, the American Association for the Advancement of Science (established in 1848), the American Philosophical Society (established by Ben Franklin and others more than a hundred years earlier), and the American Academy of Arts and Sciences (formed in 1780). For these institutions, invented by scientist-statesmen and embraced, albeit haltingly, by the emerging political elites of the new republic, were essential to the shaping of American science policy and the notion of research oriented to the public good. They were the foundations upon which rested subsequent refinements and extensions, such as those now categorized under the Progressive movement of the early twentieth century, and were the first manifestations of what would evolve into today's robust and crowded advice industry.

President Lincoln may have had little involvement in the conception of the NAS, but he was certainly present at its birth. At the risk of overstretching the metaphor, it is safe to say that he gave the new baby a hearty spank that opened its vocal chords and set it on a course of long and productive life. Surely a less inspired leader might have balked at the opportunity to create such an entity, now located about a dozen blocks from the White House, dedicated to the proposition that independent, objective, and critical scientific inquiry had to occupy a respected seat at the table of government. Lest there be any temptation toward over-romanticizing the American passion for science in the service of society, I emphasize that none of these institutional developments came about quickly or easily. The founding of the NAS took place amid political drama similar to what we saw in the case of opposition to the post–World War II efforts to establish a federal research agency. The ideas embodied by the NAS—even as it was understood to be a *nongovernmental* entity in the strict sense—led to head-on collisions between science and politics that today seem at least vaguely familiar.

Although we have no direct evidence of the president's involvement in the intricacies of the NAS charter's wording, two of its most fundamental principles are attributed to Lincoln's peculiar genius—his appetite for seeking consensus from broadly divergent expertise and inclusive debate, and his uncanny ability to apply his knowledge of politics to the politics of knowledge. First, as condition for its establishment (law required congressional approval for the founding of this sort of organization in Washington), the NAS had to provide "advice on demand," to agree to respond to requests from the federal government on all matters of science, technology, and the arts. (The arts then referred to the *mechanical*, rather than the *fine.*) In one small phrase, the relationship of science to government was forever changed: scientists could have their privileges—an academy located in Washington and, eventually, in the only nonfederal building to be erected on the National Mall—but, in exchange, they would serve the nation. Today's various quid pro quos in the relations between the federal government and state or local or private entities, therefore, rest on a sturdy precedent.[5]

There is a distinction here to be underscored: asking the scientific community for advice was never understood as ceding fundamentally political decisions to the academic elite. Science was invited to *advise* on policy, not to do it. This distinction is important, especially in the light of the remarkable growth of the enterprise: by the time Woodrow Wilson was president, the demand for NAS advice vastly exceeded the capacity of its elected membership, which was one reason for the executive order establishing the National Research Council (NRC) as the operating arm of the NAS.[6]

Second, and perhaps even more stunning in terms of its anticipation of what has now become, 153 years after the NAS founding, the all too familiar specter of commercial or political influence that compromises objective professional judgment, scientists providing the requested advice under the auspices of the NAS would receive no compensation. For economists who rightly believe that goods and services that have value must also have a price, the idea that top scientific expertise can be provided pro bono requires acknowledgment of the more subtle impulses of human behavior—altruism, commitment to the public good, willingness to serve—that are not typically featured in the stylized models of neoclassical economic theory. (I have discussed the economics and psychology of generosity in chapter 1 and will return to that topic in chapter 4.) This peculiar institutional arrangement—funding a large organization to enable, encourage, and provide nonmonetary reward for voluntarism among its core members and participants—has persisted as one of the more noteworthy innovations of modern American capitalism.[7]

Noteworthy, indeed, but surprisingly undernoted. One of the more mystifying findings—or nonfindings—from my review of the current literature on the size, concentration, and productivity of organizations (outside the traditional university sector) devoted to providing independent advice to government—which are often labeled as "think tanks"—is the conspicuous absence of reference to the NAS and NRC. I was gratified to see the *New York Times* refer to the NAS as "the nation's most prestigious scientific organization."[8] And I was exhilarated to be in the room for President Obama's salute to its founding as "testament to the restless curiosity, the boundless hope so essential not just to the scientific enterprise, but to this experiment we call America."[9] How is it, then, that using a commonly accepted definition—*public policy research analysis and engagement organizations that generate policy-oriented research, analysis, and advice on domestic and international issues, thereby enabling policymakers and the public to make informed decisions about public policy*—an organization that issues roughly 250 peer-reviewed reports a year on topics ranging across the entire spectrum of policy and takes seriously its mandate to be "Adviser to the Nation," is almost nowhere mentioned in the scholarly and popular literature on think tanks?[10]

Even in the compilations and surveys of the Think Tanks & Civil Societies Program at the Lauder Institute, University of Pennsylvania (the source of the italicized definition above), the NAS and NRC are not included. And the disqualification cannot be attributed to some special meaning embedded in the word "academy": the Chinese Academy of Social Sciences, the Shanghai Academy of Social Sciences, and the Diplomatic Academy of Vietnam somehow all make the list. Similarly, neither in Thomas Medvetz's recent book on the politics and sociology of think tanks nor in earlier works by Andrew Rich, David Ricci, or James A. Smith is there is any mention of or citation to any NAS or NRC work. Louis Menand's engaging intellectual history of the United States includes—in his thinly veiled critique of the elitism of the NAS founders—an acknowledgment of the unique place of the new institution: "a body . . . with limited membership . . . whose pronouncements would carry *incontrovertible authority* [italics added]." The Harvard online guide to think tanks and research centers includes the National Academy of Public Administration, but not the NAS or NRC. Only in Lynn Hellebust's *Think Tank Directory*, published in 2006, is the NRC included.[11]

I leave it to others to speculate on the reasons for this lacuna in the literature. At the same time, though, I want to underscore, and with all respect to readers who detect a bias on my part, that by all reasonable criteria—size, historical significance, and impact—the NAS and NRC occupy a special niche in the complex ecology of think tanks, and moreover, their norms and procedures for funding, review, publication, and dissemination of results provide useful clues to the design of strategies aimed at the sustainability and viability of the independent advice sector more generally. I shall return to some of the specifics of the NAS/NRC—now called National Academies of Sciences, Engineering, and Medicine (NASEM)—its status as a private nongovernmental body with no line item in any federal budget, its multidisciplinary consensus-seeking mode of operation, and its conditional exemption from sunshine laws requiring government advisory groups to work in the open, as I consider prospects for viable and sustained education research that provides credible evidence in support of policy and practice. First, though, some more context.[12]

THE CROWDING OF SOURCES

Surely one compelling lesson from the history of the NASEM is about the robust American appetite for credible, independent, nonpartisan, applied science to inform decision making, enable the effective uses of technology, and improve the workings of government—all of which seems to have started early in the life of the new republic. This is indeed the message embedded in President Obama's paean to our reverence for scientific inquiry. Not to rush into cultural explanations of history and theories of national personality, but one can't help marvel at how the spirit of dissent at the core of the nation's founding was manifest also in the establishment of an organization—the National Academy of Sciences—committed to independent advising, evaluating, and—perhaps most significantly—critiquing of government.

Dissent we've got plenty, as my immigrant great uncle might have said, and it's no surprise that the advice industry has grown into a diffused and competitive hodgepodge. Indeed, our historical allergy to centralized power or authoritarian expertise has spread with epidemiological predictability even to the sector that is supposed to be about disciplined and coherent inquiry to guide policy makers through the thickets of opinion and self-proclaimed expertise. The pursuit of independent information as a credible counterweight to purely political and ideological decisions has resulted in more cacophony—a good thing in democratic society. But whether and how all that information is heard and interpreted by decision makers is not obvious. Politicians are understandably frustrated by the ensuing confusion, and with so much of their time taken up by the important matters of statecraft (fund-raising, campaigning, more fund-raising), they often find that they cannot afford to wade through all the scientific evidence and figure out where they should stand.

The supply side, of course, doesn't operate in a demand vacuum. If today's inchoate advice industry produces a remarkable assortment of research and evaluations, let's not forget that much of that output is *purchased by the government*—and/or funded and cofunded by private philanthropies and donors—to inform policy choices, guide implementation, and assess outcomes on anything and everything that fits under the general rubric of public policy. This advice-giving enterprise has grown more than exponentially: depending on what kinds of organizations are included, estimates of the annual expenditure on social and behavioral science research alone, oriented toward understanding and solving problems of economics, demography, education, and welfare, run into the billions.[13]

The complex advice industry involves universities, corporate R&D departments, evaluation companies, data collection organizations, and individual consultants. Within that somewhat dizzying array of providers, so-called think tanks occupy an increasingly visible and influential place, and a closer look can be informative. However defined, the growth in their number, size, and budgets has been astounding: according to the latest compilation of statistics by the Lauder Institute, there were, as of 2014, 1,989 think tanks in North America, of which 1,830 were in the United States, 90.5 percent of them were created since 1951, the total number has more than doubled since 1980, and close to a third were created between 1981 and 1990.

Perhaps inevitably, with such rapid growth has come the urge to compare, contrast, and even rank these organizations. Leaving aside the apparently insatiable appetite for rankings—another burgeoning subsector of the data-rich advice industry—their contents can provide a useful starting point to consider trends and think about the forces that may affect the quality and utility of the information these organizations supply.[14]

According to the latest reports from the Lauder Institute, expansion of independent research and analysis capacities has been a worldwide phenomenon, with well over six thousand think tanks now operating in the Americas, Europe, Asia, and Africa. Although the rate of increase in establishment of new think tanks has slowed in recent years, to say the field has become saturated with advice givers would be an understatement. In the United States, where 40 percent of our think tanks are doing their thinking in the Washington, DC, area, there is considerable diversity in terms of funding sources, political leanings, publication and dissemination protocols, and topical specializations. Highlights about some of the most prominent think tanks and research organizations suggest a complex mosaic:

- The RAND Corporation, established in 1948 "to connect military planning with research and development decisions," is still one of the largest and most reputable organizations providing evaluations and analyses on the full range of social, economic, educational, and health policy topics. Its total annual expenditures are close to $300 million, with support coming heavily from government grants and contracts as well as private foundations and individual donors.

- The American Institutes for Research (AIR), which also, curiously, is not included in the Lauder reports or in the books by Henig, Medvetz, Ricci, Rich, and Smith, began even earlier, in 1946, with a heavy emphasis on psychological testing related to military personnel. Today, its annual spending of over $325 million is heavily concentrated on education and health, domestically and globally. Like RAND, AIR work is funded by a combination of public and private grants and contracts. Both organizations have developed strict—albeit different—rules governing review of reports and intellectual property; they have maintained a consistently nonpartisan stance, and affiliate with no particular political party or advocacy group.

- FHI-360, created through a merger of Family Health International (FHI) and the Academy for Educational Development in 2011, is the largest of the combined research, evaluation, technical assistance organizations (and is included in the Lauder reports and surveys), with a substantial global footprint and focus on the developing world. According to data from IRS form 990s, FHI-360 has approximate annual expenditures in the range of $660 million.

- SRI International, headquartered in Menlo Park, California, with offices in Arlington, Virginia (outside Washington), and Princeton, New Jersey, is the second largest, according to IRS filing data (roughly $612 million in 2013), and has a sizable education division.
- The Brookings Institution was founded in 1927, with the mission "to promote, conduct and foster research in the broad fields of economics, government administration and the political and social sciences." It is still considered among the most honored and respected American think tanks, with a substantial program in labor economics and education and expenditures of just over $100 million (in 2013). Brookings gets most of its support from donations and sales of its books and other output, and a small amount from government.
- The Urban Institute (UI) was founded in 1968 by President Lyndon Johnson, with a primary focus on alleviating urban poverty and providing a rigorous evidentiary basis for federal antipoverty programs. Total expenditures are about $80 million (in 2013), with the overwhelming majority of funds coming from government sources. According to the Lauder Institute, UI is ranked twentieth among all think tanks in the United States, and first among those with significant education programs.[15]
- WestEd, formed in 1995 from the merger of the Southwest Regional Educational Lab and the Far West Laboratory for Educational Research and Development, has grown into one of the main competitors for federal, state, and foundation grants and contracts relating to education, with emphasis on technical assistance to states for school reform initiatives, and evaluations in many areas including literacy, early childhood, and college-career programs. Total expenditures in 2013 were approximately $148 million, with more than half of revenues coming from federal and state government sources.

Even a quick look at this small sample of the think tanks that now dot the policy landscape in the United States, and in particular those with a strong presence in education, supports the impression that Americans have a hearty appetite for what is perceived to be—hopefully—independent and objective analysis of data to inform decision making. As shown in table 3.1, the annual expenditures of just twelve prominent think tanks—and here I include the NAS—amounted to almost $2.7 billion in 2013; more startling is that this represents a 24 percent increase in just four years (2009–2013).

The source of funding to these and similar organizations, which aspire to be recognized as credible authorities for advice to government, is not the sole or necessarily most significant determinant of their political and ideological independence. For example, the American Enterprise Institute (AEI) takes no federal money, but has long been viewed (and self-identifies) as a conservative institution likely to align with mainstream Republican positions. Brookings, on the other hand, perhaps the most venerable among the establishment think tanks (and rated number one in the world by the Lauder Institute), is almost entirely funded by private gifts and grants, but has been known (at least until more recently) as mostly liberal leaning and generally more sympathetic to Democratic administrations.[16] UI, with a decidedly apolitical ethos, gets most of its revenues from the federal government. SRI, RAND, and AIR have substantial federal grants and contracts and also are known for their aspirations to nonpartisanship. Similarly, one of the very first think tanks, the National Bureau of Economic Research, founded in 1920, is today considered a leading source of high-quality economic research oriented to public policy issues, receives considerable sums in government grants and contracts, and is fiercely independent of political influence. FHI gets substantial funding from the United States Agency for International Development (USAID), along with the World Bank and other international nongovernmental organizations.

The rapid and substantial growth in the number of think tanks has perhaps obvious implications for a concern I am voicing in this book, namely, whether in light of so many competitive pressures, we can still realistically expect the independent advice sector to supply objective and credible evidence to inform or guide policy making in general and with respect to education policy in particular. To the extent that much think-tank funding comes from the private philanthropic sector, which, as I discussed in chapter 1, is undergoing subtle but potentially significant changes in its ethos of knowledge production and its balancing of advocacy and research, the viability of objectivity becomes even more uncertain. It is telling, for example, that Henig's discussion of the role of think tanks in the charter school debates drifts seamlessly into a discussion of the foundations

TABLE 3.1 Annual expenditures, selected think tanks, 2009–2013 (in millions, constant 2015 dollars)

	FHI	SRI	RAND	AIR	WestEd	Brookings	Urban	NBER	AEI	Cato	CAP	NAS	Total
2009	390.9	419.4	286.7	314.7	123.4	100.8	75.0	41.4	29.1	24.6	34.7	321.9	2,162.9
2010	514.5	464.1	289.9	287.8	118.9	95.9	69.8	39.2	31.6	26.6	37.1	342.7	2,317.7
2011	755.4	646.2	298.5	279.3	134.8	100.6	78.1	40.7	34.2	23.5	36.4	369.6	2,797.4
2012	680.2	630.3	286.0	308.9	139.6	100.9	78.0	37.4	33.3	27.0	35.4	342.9	2,699.9
2013	658.9	612.8	288.7	342.7	147.8	102.2	79.6	36.7	35.7	25.5	38.8	313.9	2,683.0

Source: IRS Form 990; for WestEd audited financial statements provided.

that fund the work of researchers and their organizations, suggesting the author's implicit assumptions about the effect of funding on the quality and believability of that research.[17]

The problem can be framed in economic terms, as a hypothesis worthy of further inquiry: crowding of the field leads to greater competition for funding, which introduces implicit or explicit biases in the choice of study topics, an erosion of evidentiary standards, and incentives for opportunistic rather than full disclosure of findings. Granted, it is possible that growth in the number of think tanks is somehow matched by growth in the number of foundations (and the wealth they control), which would level the playing field to some degree, but sufficient anecdotal evidence suggests that we are not exactly at an equilibrium point in this market.

Still, the optimist in me who favors the vibrancy of an argumentative democracy steers toward hoping that more information—more data, more analyses, more interpretations, more recommendations gushing from a diverse and active supply side—is better than less information. After all, why shouldn't government decisions—and the general public—benefit from all this thinking, especially given the variability in findings and conclusions? Yes, there is a cacophony, but overall aren't we better off being compelled to consider the various sides of complex policy debates and the often-conflicting answers provided by outside analysts? And though sifting through myriad and divergent interpretations of data may be frustrating at times, it might be argued that precisely because so many voices are vying for attention (and influence), the overall quality of the work should be increasingly high and those conducting the underlying research increasingly attentive to evidentiary standards and the reliability and validity of their findings. By analogy, competitive instincts among academic researchers seeking to have their work published in the top journals are mostly understood as having a positive influence on the quality of their work. Similarly, the desire for intellectual and financial market share should create incentives for think tanks and other research organizations to prove that their wares are empirically more grounded and methodologically more rigorous.

My optimism is tempered, however. One could argue that the quantity of advice is no more correlated with its quality and credibility than, say, the quantity of hamburgers sold is correlated with their nutritional content. McDonald's still likes to remind passersby of the number of billions of burgers consumed, and cynics might imagine a day when drivers on Massachusetts Avenue or K Street in Washington will see a sign flashing with the number of reports produced by our think tanks and lobbying firms. (To be fair, even McDonald's has begun marketing lower-fat meat, surely as a result of competition with other fast-food vendors.) The analogy is a bit vulgar, but in the light of recurrent episodes of error and fraud in the scientific literature, which, though still a relatively rare phenomenon, are certainly creating increased burdens for editors and publishers of research articles and possibly fueling more antiscientific cynicism in the general population, it is important to examine whether and how competition affects quality.[18]

Thinking about the grim side of oversupply in the information market leads me toward yet another mildly optimistic rebuttal. Think tanks that eschew the seductions of partisanship make extra efforts to diversify their resource base and avoid real or perceived tacking to changing political winds may not get prizes for the loudest and splashiest headlines, but they could attract policy makers' attention precisely for those reasons. If objectivity is becoming a scarce resource, the economist in me says it should become more valued and sought after. But what also seems clear, especially with our growing partisan divides, is that appetite for partisan research to support predetermined positions will remain robust. Whether growth and diversity in the advice industry necessarily compromise the independence and credibility of its products is a question that has started to attract wider attention.[19]

As I've suggested, I would argue that there is an important connection between the data on think tanks (summarized above) and the arguments I advanced in the previous chapters on trends in the philanthropic and government research sectors. Let us recall that one of the virtues of a private philanthropic sector of the size and magnitude we have in the United States is its "contestatory" or argumentative capacity, its willingness and ability to push back against government, its special role in the grand democratic experiment of checks and balances. It stands to reason, then, that policy advice funded *by* the government is sometimes viewed with suspicion, especially if the funding agency is able to wield control over the substance of the research and the process through which it issues results and communicates. Whether such control is real—as in the case of agency review of draft reports from contract research organizations prior to their release—or perceived by a public increasingly pressured to look askance at anything the government does, there is an obvious advantage to reports that are neither funded nor managed by the government, especially when such reports are intended to evaluate or criticize government activity. To their great credit, some think tanks have internalized this philosophy, refuse to take government money, and rely instead on private—and *ostensibly* nonpartisan—sources.

The word "ostensibly" is italicized because it is no longer obvious that think tanks that eschew government funds are as neutral as once imagined and providing hoped-for objective advice to guide public policy; conversely, it is not clear that advice coming from organizations that do receive government funding is less credible than the advice from organizations that the more advocacy-driven private donors or foundations sponsor. (The NASEM receives most of its support from the government, yet its reports get high marks for independence and objectivity.) My sense is that if the conventional opinion on the effects of *private* funding on the objectivity of think tanks now tilts more to the negative, it is for reasons having more to do with the suspicion of wealth as a force in American political and social life than with real evidence of bias.

This issue has created new anxieties, especially as foundations have grown in number, size, and influence. Is policy-relevant research funded by the Gates Foundation, to again pick on the largest and most familiar case, less partisan than research funded by the National Center for Education Statistics or other branches of the Department of Education? It would be foolish to suggest a simple dichotomous answer to this question, along the lines of "any work funded by the [XYZ foundation or the government] is necessarily suspect, while projects supported by [the other] are credible and reliable." A more nuanced approach is called for, especially as we consider the specialized world of research-based education policy advice. Growth in demand for such input during the last half century has led to substantial growth, increased complexity and diversity, and heightened competition for funding among think tanks and policy research/evaluation organizations with education expertise.

THINKING FOR EDUCATION

Diffusion and fragmentation, words that come to mind when thinking about the advice sector and the foundations that support it, are familiar to students of American educational history. But the linguistic coincidence is more than just curious. The ways in which changing norms of philanthropy and public funding of science affect the quality of advice to policy makers take on special characteristics in the realm of education, in part because school leaders operating with considerable autonomy and lack of formal coordination do not have the capacity to conduct their own studies, and are vulnerable to what at times seems like a barrage of recommendations coming from advocates and vendors who frequently claim to have evidence on their side. How states and localities absorb research-based information is a topic that has attracted attention among scholars who care about the links between research and practice, and it pays therefore to rehearse some of the basics about our peculiarly decentralized—and heavily politicized— arrangements for education.[20]

In his final oeuvre before his untimely death, the preeminent education historian Lawrence Cremin reminded us why education (in America, at least) is so political. His argument, that "it is impossible to talk about education apart from some conception of the good life," draws from Aristotle's discussions in chapter 8 of *Politics*. There, Aristotle insisted that education must be public, for the sake of the common good; but he acknowledged, too, that "what should be the character of this public education, and how young persons should be educated, are questions which remain to be considered. As things are, there is disagreement about the subjects. For mankind are by no means agreed about the things to be taught, whether we look to virtue or the best life. Neither is it clear whether education is more concerned with intellectual or with moral virtue."[21]

Disagreements over the substance and purpose of education that Aristotle witnessed and chronicled in the fourth century BCE have not exactly abated. And since education is still central to the multitudinous ways we imagine "the good life," for ourselves and our children, it is inevitable that just about everything related to schools and schooling is sharply politicized. But this is not all bad, especially if one considers the counterfactual case in which education decisions were somehow disconnected from the needs and dreams of citizens. To amend slightly what I have argued else-where, "having devised an intentionally fragmented system of education that privileges argumentation, broad participation, diversity, distributed governance, individual creativity, and locally-inspired innovation over conformist centralism, why should we be surprised—and annoyed—by the intrusion of [politics] in [matters of schooling]?"[22] Or, as one wry observer noted during the 1990s debates over national standards and testing, school-ing in America may be in trouble, but at least the democracy is thriving.

It is worth elaborating on this quip in terms familiar to students of nineteenth- and twentieth-century political and economic theory. The pursuit of the good life, or happiness, or what economists have handily renamed "utility," necessitates a delicate dance between individual desires and preferences, on the one hand, and governance aimed at establishing and maintaining the social order, on the other. The debates over school choice, voucher programs that shift decisions from the collective polity of communities to individual families, and even charter schools that oper-ate with greater managerial flexibility and loosened public control can all be understood as manifestations of the fundamental argument over the best arrangements to ensure that individual preferences yield desirable social outcomes.

Indeed, most debates over politics and policy (in general, and by no means limited to the educational realm) can be simplified in terms of where the debaters stand on the centuries-old core questions of political and eco-nomic philosophy: Does government and centralized authority inhibit or enhance individuals' chances of achieving the good life? How can inevi-table distortions in the translation of individual goals to social outcomes be predicted and preempted? Are there acceptable criteria by which to evaluate the magnitude and distribution of the benefits and burdens of collective (government) decisions? The questions were formulated by Aristotle, to be sure, but, in fact, they were already contemplated by the authors of the Hebrew Bible, and surely some auditors of today's fights over standards-based reform and the Common Core must have new appreciation for the proposition in Ecclesiastes that there is "nothing new under the sun."[23]

Democratic governance, therefore, is both a source and a servant of our somewhat peculiar educational system, which is, in fact, not so much a system as a cacophony. Given that a core principle of American independence and republicanism (note the small "r") was dissent, it is perhaps easier to understand why the first attempt to define in law a set of national education goals didn't happen until 214 years into the life of the new nation and was predictably met with anguished opposition to perceived encroachment into the sanctity of local decision making, and why in general the design, governance, and reform of our education institutions seem to reflect simultaneously a love for learning and a preference for commotion. Put in more negative terms, we suffer from a chronic aversion to centralized authority, which, as former president of Harvard James Conant once suggested, is the reason "we don't have an education system . . . we have an education chaos."

Education is surely not the only chaotic aspect of American democracy, although I am hard pressed to name another activity that provokes as predictable and strident debate about diffusion of authority and the rights of local communities to determine their own destinies. (There are a few places where citizens still say they would prefer their own militias over the national system of defense, but by and large we've gotten past that.) It has always been easier to appreciate intuitively the words on our Great Seal than to make them operational: much of our educational history can be collapsed into the struggle to bring some *unum* to all that *pluribus*. But just because some problems don't lend themselves to straightforward solutions doesn't mean the system is rotten or hopeless. For a more optimistic view consider, again, Conant, whose suggestion that we *prefer* the chaos stems from his contemplation of our Jeffersonian roots:

> To understand the bearing of Jefferson's ideas on the development of American schools and colleges we must realize, of course, that they represented only one aspect of a wider social philosophy. As this philosophy was understood by large numbers of the citizens of the young republic, it included the following points: a belligerent belief in individual freedom; complete confidence in the powers of man's intelligence to overcome all obstacles; the assumption of a society without hereditary classes, without an aristocracy; a differentiation of labors with a corresponding differentiation in the types of education (but no ruling caste, no hereditary educational privileges, everyone to be "as

good as everyone else"); widespread education for all citizens so that political decisions might be "rational." *Dominating all was the doctrine of the maximum independence of the individual, the minimum of social control by organized society.* [italics added][24]

Contemporary scholars have added new empirical evidence to the argument about the advantages of our fragmented system, in terms of its agility and capacity for innovation. How our schools reinvented themselves in response to the twentieth-century challenges of immigration, industrialization, and technology is a story that is often underappreciated by critics who focus on the tumult created in schools that seem always to be "aboil [sic] with change."[25]

Still, the sad truth is that many alleged innovations are foisted on our schools by a seemingly endless parade of hucksters and cheerleaders touting the virtues of the latest fad, leaving little space for consideration and celebration of the changes that might make a real (and positive) difference. Which, perhaps obviously, makes the role of credible evidence all the more important: whether in single-room schools in rural Nevada or the crowded halls of high schools in New York and Boston, whether in district offices or state legislatures or congressional committees or the Department of Education, educators and policy makers striving to improve students' chances of success face a dizzying array of programs and methods—all being sold by marketers carrying thumb drives full of data proving their claims. (I will say more about this in chapter 4 in the context of the latest federal education legislation.)

The good news/bad news metaphor about the inchoate American school system, then, carries forward to the fragmented nature of evidence about what works for children and what doesn't. The logic I'm suggesting goes something like this: our revealed social preference for decentralization in educational decision making leads to a demand for reliable information to inform the choices made by educators and policy makers in their respective schools and jurisdictions, which in turn stimulates a diffused and often conflicted supply of data and advice. At risk of belaboring the obvious, the upside of this is that we know more about how to organize and conduct high-quality research and evaluation, there are more qualified people trained to do this work than in the past, and there is a robust appetite for information about the condition of education—as evidenced by coverage in the mainstream press, professional media outlets, and the blogosphere. The downside, a sad example of unintended consequences, is perhaps as obvious: information overload strains our capacity to know what to believe and ultimately threatens the use of research as a reliable source of evidence to guide policy and practice.

POX AMERICANA?

The problem, again, is illuminated by consideration of some basic economic concepts. Does the increase in supply of education policy advice engender the sort of competition that threatens to compromise evidentiary standards and nurture parasitic impulses that confound advocacy with objective information? Or does the competition lead to better—more valid and credible—products? On the demand side, do potential users of research-based information, the folks who are genuinely trying to improve the quality of education, have the tools (or the patience) to sift through the often-contradictory findings that the research community offers to them? In other words, there is (as always) a simultaneity of supply-and-demand effects: on the supply side, researchers may be induced to tailor their inquiries, and on the demand side, consumers of research may become fed up with all the cacophony and (in the extreme) vote to stop funding it. As Henig had found, public attitudes can become edgy in response to seemingly endless debates among researchers: "Oh my God, these researchers, these social scientists, you know, piddling and piddling and one day it's this and one day it's that: a pox on all your houses."[26]

I am led, therefore, to sound the alarm about the effects of crowding on the quality of education research oriented to public policy. But the story is, again, more complicated. For one thing, expression of anxiety about the increasingly dense ecology of education research (and its allegedly low scientific quality) emanates from researchers who are habitually frustrated by the slow pace of uptake. With all respect to my brothers and sisters in the education research community, let me suggest that those who complain about their limited impact on policy and practice may immodestly be missing the possibility that their influence is inversely proportional to the quantity (not to mention the quality) of their output. Self-promotion doesn't really help in this situation: some of the loudest groaning about lack of receptivity to research findings comes from researchers who think their own work—unlike much of the rest of what is produced—is genuinely excellent and therefore worthy of rather more instantaneous appreciation and application. To put it perhaps too bluntly, along with overproduction of research comes an underproduction of humility.

We are dealing with a variation on the overgrazing phenomenon: it's not too much consumption, per se, but rather too much production that can undermine the possibility for useful application of the research simply because there's just too much of it out there and not enough time or resources for potential users to figure out what it all means. Clearly one of the downsides to the dramatic increase in the energy and productivity of the education advice industry is that it has become harder for its main audiences to decide who is right, what to believe, and whether to take any of the recommendations seriously. (This would not be the first time that policy makers found themselves drowning in floods of data and so-called research. In chapter 4, I will reiterate my earlier reference to the congressional Office of Technology Assessment, or OTA, which was founded in large part to help legislators filter the information coming at them from teems of consultants and other experts armed with "objective" data.)

Nevertheless, on balance, I continue to believe that the burgeoning of the advice industry for education has produced more benefit than harm, the risks and frustrations of oversupply notwithstanding. I base this conclusion on my reading of the popular and professional education policy literature, which has become substantially more relevant and timely and, in many cases, continues to tap into the finest instincts of scientific inquiry. That literature does, of course, include perhaps more than the average amount of self-flagellation found in any professional community: broadsides against superficial, vapid, opaque, and fundamentally irrelevant research, especially of the sort that derives from ideologically driven rebellions against the intrusion of science, are a regular part of our professional discourse.

But we should view them in the broader context and, if I may, with some cheer. Democratic and populist education begets diversity and discord in education research, which is my response to critics of, say, the annual meetings of the American Education Research Association, who love to hate the enormity of the event (easily fifteen to twenty thousand participants occupy the major hotels in whatever city is host to the meetings) and the seemingly silly titles of some papers accepted for presentation. My point is that this sort of internal sniping is symptomatic not of a research enterprise at risk but rather of a community willing and able to invite and sustain important debates over method and meaning.[27]

Partly as a result of the debates within and outside the field, the quality—and utility—of education research has improved significantly, even if Ellen Condliffe Lagemann is basically right and the quest for a full-fledged, respected, and reputable "science of education" remains elusive. And the fact that our community is responsible for important and good work is all the more reason we should focus on the threats to the usefulness of that work as inputs to improved policy making. To summarize what worries me about this situation, I adapt, with gratitude, phrasing from the classic work of Thomas Schelling, a 2005 Nobel laureate in economics: the "micromotives" of education researchers—especially in an increasingly competitive environment—may be threatening the quality and utility of the "macro" education research and advice industry.[28]

RESEARCH, RHETORIC, AND REFORM

It may be helpful to consider some of these abstractions in context. A good example of the basic tension—too much policy advice can be counterproductive—is the debate over the meaning of international comparisons of academic achievement, a topic that stimulates some of the most extravagant rhetoric and policy activity in the United States and elsewhere. On the plus side, again, the quantity of international comparative assessments has expanded significantly since they began in the mid-1960s, and their quality has improved as significantly, thanks to advances in the science of item development, sampling, and score interpretation.[29]

But the ways in which the data from these programs are conveyed to policy makers, in particular by think tanks, at times allows for ideology and advocacy to seep in, usually quite furtively and sometimes rather more blatantly. The rush to partisan judgments can compromise the benefits of a robust supply of interesting and important data: and if think tanks and other organizations wanting to be heard in the cacophony raise their voices while lowering their evidentiary standards, the usefulness of the data becomes severely impaired. The business of international comparisons is not an example of a specific question posed by policy makers for which some body of evidence or data is analyzed; rather, it is a case in which broad policy strategies and the political rhetoric that undergirds them are influenced by—and propelled by—the findings from research. In other words, borrowing and adapting my favorite NAS story (see chapter 3), we're not talking about how to fix the steering problems of the iron ship, but rather about in what direction the ship should be heading in the first place. How does research evidence influence grand strategy?

To place the seemingly incessant debate about American education as it compares to the rest of the civilized world in some historical context, a good place to start is with the famous 1983 report called *A Nation at Risk*.[30] This report, still considered among the most (if not *the* most) rhetorically elegant and politically persuasive documents of its genre, was significantly responsible for setting the nation on a course of school reform that is very much alive and going strong to this day. It was prepared by a presidentially commissioned panel, and convened, ironically, by the very same president, Ronald Reagan, who had hoped to dismantle the youngish federal Department of Education and who found himself, when the report was released, pinned by its rhetoric into acknowledging that our education problems warranted significant federal attention after all.

To have been faithful to the available empirical evidence at the time would have necessitated a modified title—something like "Parts of the Nation Seem to be at Risk in Some Ways Some of the Time." More accurate, surely, but far less compelling to policy makers and politicians, not to mention headline writers.[31] In a class I once taught, I used this example to draw attention to the chasm between rhetoric and evidence, but one of my students grasped a more subtle reality: his humble (and brilliant) response was that if *any* of the nation is at risk, then maybe *we are all at risk*. In other words, we could no longer survive as a nation if we allowed its constituent parts, that vast agglomeration of schools, districts, and states, to perpetuate differences in performance among our radically diverse population and that ignored the increasingly national and global context of trade, technology, and economic interdependence for which our students are ostensibly being prepared. So maybe the title was right after all. (I offered to change places with my student, but he respectfully declined.)

A Nation at Risk paid lip service to the fundamental inequities of educational financing and opportunity that tore at the guts of American public education (and society more generally), but its main argument was less about the ethics of equality and more about the crisis of competitiveness. (There is no reference in the report to the landmark Coleman report, which reshaped American policy about educational opportunity. See my reference in chapter 2.) In economists' lingo, the report claimed its rhetorical edge by emphasizing efficiency and aggregate economic performance rather than equity and opportunity, a technique that, among other things, rekindled powerful new alliances between some educators and businesspeople: the latter had long complained that the workforce was poorly prepared because of the lousy condition of public schools, and here was a report that escalated the argument to new heights of anxiety about the future of the country, now that we had new economic powers to contend with.

The opening lines of *A Nation at Risk* were remarkable proof that government-sponsored writing could transcend the typical jargon that infects much of such work:

> Our once unchallenged preeminence in commerce, industry, science, and technological innovation is being overtaken by competitors throughout the world . . . the educational foundations of our society are presently being eroded by a rising tide of mediocrity that threatens our very future as a Nation and a people. What was unimaginable a generation ago has begun to occur—others are matching and surpassing our educational attainments . . . If an unfriendly foreign power had attempted to impose on America the mediocre educational performance that exists today, we might well have viewed it as an act of war.[32]

Is it any wonder that efforts at gathering international comparative data on student achievement were catapulted from a relatively modestly scaled scholarly activity to one of the most potent tools of policy-oriented research?

PISA ENVY

The original idea of international large-scale assessment emerged during a meeting sponsored by UNESCO in 1958 that focused on problems of educational evaluation and policy analysis. The deliberations there led to the Pilot Twelve-Country Study in 1960, which showed that cross-national surveys of academic achievement were both feasible and desirable, and laid the groundwork for the First International Mathematics Study (FIMS) in 1964. On that one, the United States did not do well: we ranked at the bottom among twelve countries in the test performance of thirteen-year-olds and of students in the last year of secondary school.[33]

The International Association for the Evaluation of Educational Achievement, abridged as IEA, established in 1967, took the lead in organizing a series of studies—the First International Science Study (FISS), the Second International Mathematics Study (SIMS), and eventually the Third International Math and Science Study (TIMSS). This program was the "largest and most ambitious international study of student achievement conducted up to that time. In 1994–95, it was conducted at five grade levels in more than forty countries (the third, fourth, seventh, and eighth grades, and the final year of secondary school)."[34] Since 1995, TIMSS, which now stands for *Trends* in Mathematics and Science Study, collects achievement data worldwide on a regular four-year cycle; today, close to fifty countries participate. IEA is also responsible for the Progress in International Reading Literacy Study (PIRLS), which has been operating on a five-year cycle since 2001.[35]

At the risk of being facetious about the crowding effects of social science and education research, let me suggest that we may now have enough international comparative work underway to warrant an international ranking of the comparisons. Since 2000, the Organization for Economic Cooperation and Development (OECD) has sponsored its own set of international assessments, starting with the, by now, familiar Programme for International Student Assessment (PISA) and extending to the Programme for the International Assessment of Adult Competencies (PIAAC) and, most recently, the Teaching and Learning International Survey (TALIS). Not surprisingly, scholars and policy analysts have strong views about the relative strengths and weaknesses of the OECD and IEA programs. For example, the grade-level data in TIMSS provides different information than the age-specific data in PISA, a distinction that relates to the way in which results from these programs provide relevant information about the specific effects of curriculum variability across schools and countries.[36]

With each large-scale assessment report comes an initial burst of head-line hyperbole and policy punditry, especially in countries that rank poorly. In this, the United States is, perhaps mercifully, not alone: "In Germany, the first PISA report, released in December 2001, caused a sensation. The country that prided itself on its education system, on its contributions to Western science and philosophy—that had produced Einstein, Goethe and Marx—ranked at the lower end of the comparative spectrum. German students did poorly in math, science and reading, with limited literacy effectively lowering performance in all subjects."[37]

Much of the rhetoric in the American media and policy worlds that attends the release of comparative assessments (especially PISA and TIMSS) echoes the themes of *A Nation at Risk* by linking student achievement to long-term economic competitiveness. As Alexandra Killewald and Yu Xie note,

> The news coverage of these test results highlights that, for many Americans, performance in math and science is important both as a measure of ground gained relative to the performance of earlier cohorts of Americans and as an indicator of the United States' ability to remain dominant in an increasingly competitive global landscape . . . policymakers, educators, and journalists have also raised the concern that, in an increasingly globalized world, the United States may not be improving fast enough to keep up. Thus concerns about the competitive position of American science education are related to fears for the economic future of the United States, particularly in comparison with China and other emerging Asian economies.[38]

William Schmidt, a leading expert in science education and international comparative studies, has been among the more vocal advocates for treating the PISA and TIMSS data as warnings of a potentially gloomy future: "Unfortunately there is a large body of evidence indicating that US students are not learning as much about science as their peers in other countries. Any relative advantage that they enjoyed during the 20th century has disappeared."[39] And some of the most strident claims come from the distinguished economist Eric Hanushek: in a recent paper, he and his coauthor argued that cognitive skills as measured by PISA and other

international instruments relate directly to economic growth: "This relationship, which is important and *highly precise*, indicates that relatively
small improvements in the skills of a nation's labor force can have very
large impacts on future well-being." [italics added][40]

There are efforts to dial down some of the heat in these claims, but it's
by no means clear that voices of moderation can be heard in the din of exci-
tation or whether policy makers have criteria by which to weigh rationally
the competing claims. Against the crisis mongering from even the more traditionally staid NASEM, for example, which released a report in 2007 with
the catchy title *Rising Above the Gathering Storm*, how do more cautious
and scholarly analyses of the condition of American science, such as the one
offered by Xie and Killewald, Teitelbaum, or (immodesty alert) my attempt
in 2012 to challenge some of the conventional reasoning about achievement
and economic outcomes, play in the halls of Congress or in a White House
committed to a rather hard-charging standards-based reform agenda?[41]

Theoretically at least, one role for think tanks is to distill key findings
from disparate analyses and offer a balanced judgment of what we know
and what we don't yet know. But in the case of international comparative
assessments, there has been little attempt by any of the major tanks to do
the hard thinking about what the data really mean. Instead, the debate
has intensified with rather more heat than light. Some of the think tanks
mentioned earlier have weighed in with cautions and caveats, which are
necessary but insufficient as the basis for inferring policy-relevant judgments. A 2008 RAND report helped to allay some of the anxiety stemming
from incomplete or wrong interpretations of the data as they relate to the
supply of qualified scientists and engineers, but the report did not attempt
to settle the debate over technical and statistical qualities of the results
and rankings. (That's not meant as a critique of the report as much as an
endorsement, from someone who has long been an ardent admirer of the
organization, of what RAND *could* have contributed to the complex debate
over international comparisons.)[42]

More recently, in the wake of the latest round of PISA results, AEI
posted an opinion piece by AIR scholar Mark Schneider, in which he sauc-
ily suggested that how the United States does compared to Japan, Poland,
and Belgium is of no consequence and we should just take it easy. To which,

Dylan William, a prominent London-based scholar of international education offered an equally crisp rejoinder: "Who cares that Japan, Belgium and Poland beat us in PISA? Anyone who cares about the quality of life that young people attending US schools right now will have when they enter a workplace without the skills that make them better value to employ than a machine."[43] Again, it was a bit surprising and disappointing that AIR, another organization with prodigious capacity for the highest-quality policy research, stopped short of a more comprehensive treatment of these topics.

A later report posted by AEI focused on gender gaps. The author, Mark Perry, who is on the faculty at the Flint campus of the University of Michigan and an AEI scholar, used the occasion to attempt to settle a score with those who had sided with the critics of former Harvard president Lawrence Summers for his statements (mostly misunderstood) about the relative abilities of men and women in mathematics. I imagine that even the most ardent fans of PISA were surprised to hear that the assessment had been validated to confirm a difference in native math abilities or math "intelligence" between boys and girls.[44]

Brookings had little to say about the PISA results, although one of the senior education experts there, Tom Loveless, did raise methodological issues, mainly about sampling in Shanghai, which he alleged had been rigged to inflate average performance. Implicit in this critique was, obviously, a strong warning against overinterpreting the results, especially about Shanghai (which had displaced Finland for top honors in the 2012 PISA score card).[45]

The Heritage Foundation wasted no time looking for ways to use PISA to lambaste the standards movement and the Obama administration's overall education strategy. Politics clearly steered their analysis. Cherry-picking a comment from the addendum in the OECD 2012 report—which suggested that the highest-performing school systems are those that "grant more autonomy over curricula and assessments to individual schools" and that "systems where schools have more autonomy over curricula and assessments tend to perform better overall"—the Heritage author editorialized that "with the U.S. on the brink of establishing national standards and tests through the Common Core State Standards Initiative, which is backed by the Obama Administration, it's worth considering the OECD's suggestion that curricular autonomy might play a part in the high performance of some jurisdictions."[46]

Among the most dogged believers in PISA as a source of evidence of our eminent demise as an international economic force, the National Center for Education and the Economy, headed by Marc Tucker, tops the list. NCEE was established in 1988, with the financial support of the Carnegie Corporation; it defines itself as "both a 'think tank' and a 'do tank.' We like to think that our effort to actually implement the recommendations we make in our major reports keeps us honest by forcing us to confront the real implications of our proposals and that our practical experience in the schools and with district and state policymakers improves the quality and fit of our policy work."[47]

Thinking and doing pays off: according to its 2013 IRS filing, NCEE reported $16 million in expenditures, up from $6 million the previous year. In a 2013 paper, Tucker advanced, again, the refrain made fashionable in *A Nation at Risk* that has since then become ubiquitous in the education policy discourse: "The fundamental changes taking place in the global economy pose an existential threat for high-wage economies like the United States. Countries with high-wage economies will either figure out how to convert their mass education systems into systems that can educate virtually all their students to the standards formerly reserved for their elites or these nations will see their standard of living decline until it meets the now much lower standard of living of countries with much lower wage levels, countries that are producing high-school graduates better educated than ours who charge much less for their labor."[48]

The only other post-PISA report from a think tank that rose to those heights of existential angst came from the Council on Foreign Relations, an organization not typically known for excesses of hyperbole. CFR self-identifies as "an independent, nonpartisan membership organization, think tank, and publisher dedicated to being a resource for its members, government officials, business executives, journalists, educators and students, civic and religious leaders, and other interested citizens in order to help them better understand the world and the foreign policy choices facing the United States and other countries." It established an Independent Task Force on US Education Reform and National Security, which, under the lead authorship of former New York City schools chief Joel Klein and former secretary of state Condoleeza Rice, issued a report in 2012 claiming, in its opening lines, that "[t]he United States' failure to educate its students leaves them unprepared to compete and threatens the country's ability to thrive in a global economy and maintain its leadership role." According to the CFR website, the report "offers guidance to policymakers and others on education reforms that will transform K–12 public school systems to ensure America's economic and political growth and security."[49]

Not as memorable as the "rising tide of mediocrity" and "unfriendly foreign power" wording in *A Nation at Risk*, but potent nonetheless. It is worth noting that Tucker's paper was commissioned by the Center for American Progress (CAP) as part of a project jointly managed with the Thomas Fordham Institute, and funded by the Broad Foundation. But even if these organizations—which are not typically on the same side in debates about politics and ideology—share the anxiety about American economic well-being, and even if they all agree that PISA scores are valid indicators of the pathological ills of American education, their respective policy remedies diverge. Tucker, for example, argues for more *state* control of education, the reduction or elimination of local control, limited federal involvement, increased spending on schools, and reform of our property-tax-based school funding system; he suggests that state legislatures wishing to see examples to "look at the structures, functions, authority, staffing levels, and compensation levels of the ministries of education in the world's top-performing countries."[50]

It is unlikely that the Fordham Institute would be as reticent about local control or as much in favor of pouring more money into school systems, or that the CAP would advocate for a diminished federal role. A roundtable discussion among the leadership of these organizations would be informative—perhaps dizzying—to the policy makers in the room yearning for some guidance about what to do. Whatever "within-group" variance might be apparent in the NCEE-Fordham-CAP-Broad report, the positions articulated by other organizations suggest an even greater degree of "between-group" divergence. In a briefing paper issued late in 2015 by the Economic Policy Institute, another smallish nonprofit think tank with strong labor union backing and well-known Democratic-liberal bona fides, the authors argue that "many policymakers and pundits have wrongly concluded that student achievement in the United States lags woefully behind that in many comparable industrialized nations, that this shortcoming threatens the nation's economic future, and that these test results therefore demand radical school reform that includes importing features of schooling in higher-scoring countries." They recommend that policy makers look to differences across states in the United States (using National Assessment data) for insights about best bets at education reform.[51]

For yet another set of inferences about academic achievement from PISA and other such assessment programs, which also emphasizes the socioeconomic determinants of aggregate test performance, the National Superintendents Roundtable (Horace Mann League) report issued earlier in 2015 analyzed school achievement in nine high-productivity countries. The authors highlight differences in such variables as equity, social stress, and support for families and how those factors influence academic success. Not surprisingly, the report triggered a virulent rebuttal from NCEE, which alleged that the Roundtable report focused on "alarmist rhetoric" rather than on the real problems plaguing American schools.[52]

I have learned a few lessons from these debates that are relevant here. First, all the argumentation notwithstanding, we are better off having good cross-national data on schools and schooling than we would be without those data. Simply put, we learn about ourselves by studying others, and in the process we build new collaborations among scholars and policy makers eager to apply research to the improvement of their respective education systems. It would painful to imagine going back to a time when we knew little about how school systems outside our borders were managed, what children were being taught, and how other societies defined the good life vis-à-vis their citizens' human capital development over the life course. That's the good news, and we should be grateful to the American government for having financed programs that have produced troves of useful information (the US contribution to the OECD annual budget is approximately 20 percent of the total, which was roughly 360 million euros in 2015[53]). The fact that there is more information than we can possibly digest and translate into cogent, unassailable, and definitive policy judgments is certainly not an argument against amassing that information and monitoring its quality.

But as always, there's a downside. With the improvement of comparative survey and assessment methods has come a disproportionate belief in their precision and, worse yet, a willingness to forsake rigorous inquiry and logic for the sake of scoring ideologically motivated points. We might hope, for example, that US economic performance since the debacle of FIMS would provoke at least some skepticism about the precision and reliability of links between achievement scores on a cross-national survey and long-term competitiveness, productivity, and quality of life.[54]

Equally unfortunate, however, is the tendency on the part of some researchers and policy makers to dismiss out of hand international comparative assessments that even hint at the role of teachers as a factor explaining relatively poor performance by American kids. These critics typically bemoan the lack of attention to the socioeconomic context, and some of them seem to argue that until poverty and inequality are addressed, it is unfair and misleading to blame teachers for the achievement results of their students. There is no question that poverty and other socioeconomic conditions need to be included, but even if we don't know how (or don't care) to account for all the complex determinants of academic opportunity, is that a reason to reject the findings about differences in schools, schooling, and student achievement? The most extreme version of this argument is to ascribe tacit or explicit conspiratorial motives—such as the dismantling of public education as we have known it—to the users of various kinds of data, including those from international tests, who make arguments critical of the quality of schools and teachers.[55]

Most unfortunate, for my purposes here anyway, is the possibility that the value of international comparative information will be eroded by the overproduction of advice and the rapid-fire debating that comes with it. *Crossfire* may now be off the air, but we're not exactly short of media outlets that facilitate and thrive on instantaneous punching and counterpunching. In the case of PISA, TIMSS, and the other international tests, the data are complex and therefore will inevitably generate diverse interpretations, which in turn may discourage prospective users of the data who seek more straightforward guidance; and because some of those consumers control the purse strings that fund the collection and analysis of the data, their frustration could very well lead them to advocate for reduction or elimination of public support. That would deal a blow to the scientific study of international educational differences and to the promise of education research generally, and would fan the flames of troglodyte politicians who would have us return to the prescience age of policy making.[56]

WHITHER ADVICE?

I have argued here that the crowding effect, or what I've also called a cacophony problem, raises issues about the viability and credibility of the independent advice sector. To repeat, I am not advocating for a system that drives out disagreement, but rather am raising the concern about unintended consequences of competition when research organizations face financial pressures and incentives to tailor their work toward perceived needs or preferences of their funders. Although not directly germane to problems of education research, lessons might be drawn from recent disclosures of the role and impacts of foreign financing of US-based research.

In September 2014, readers of the Sunday *New York Times* awoke to front-page news about the relationships some of our most distinguished think tanks have with foreign governments. On the face of it, why should this be a problem? With upward of six thousand think tanks worldwide, there is clearly a robust appetite for research-informed advice, and it is not surprising to see leaders across the globe forging ties with the most prominent and reputable US-based policy research organizations. In some ways, it is a natural extension to the long-standing relations that already exist between foreign countries and American colleges and universities. According to the Institute of International Education, there were close to 1 million foreign students in the United States during the academic year 2014–2015, representing almost 5 percent of the total enrolled in American institutions of higher education; roughly 8 percent were funded by their governments, and about 5 percent were doing graduate-level work (including, presumably, some research related to policy issues).[57] From these data, I infer that there is a substantial foreign investment in university-based research, and although it would be difficult to estimate how much of this funding translates to policy-relevant advice of the sort typically associated with think tanks and contract evaluation organizations, my point is more simply to suggest that ties between foreign governments and non-university research organizations in the United States need not be a cause for alarm.

Unless, of course, it turned out that because of these relations, the quality of work taking place in those organizations was skewed by explicit or implicit influences. As with the case of all sources of funding, the possibility that think tanks tailor their messages in response to financial pressure to meet the perceived preferences of their funders is worrisome. On the assumption that foreign governments purchasing advice may face internal political pressure to prove that their policies and programs are working—accountability, after all, is not a uniquely American value—it is at least plausible to expect some amount of meddling in the design of studies and the reporting of results. According to the *Times* story, "[S]ome scholars say the donations [by foreign governments to US-based think tanks] have led to implicit agreements that the research groups would refrain from criticizing the donor governments."[58] Just how pervasive such practices are cannot be inferred from anecdotal evidence, but the underlying logic is compelling enough to warrant at least some further analysis.

A related issue is whether sponsor influence affects the objectivity and validity of advice offered by our think tanks *to US policy makers*. If there is reason to question whether information flowing to foreign sponsors is somehow tainted, it follows that US researchers may also be pressured to avoid telling Congress or the executive branch things that will put sponsors of the research in a bad light. Again, anecdotes are not evidence, but they were obviously troubling enough to appear above the fold in the Sunday *Times*: "'If a member of Congress is using the Brookings reports, they should be aware—they are not getting the full story,' said Saleem Ali, who served as a visiting fellow at the Brookings Doha Center in Qatar and who said he had been told during his job interview that he could not take positions critical of the Qatari government in papers. 'They may not be getting a false story, but they are not getting the full story.'"[59]

I mention these issues surrounding foreign financing and influence to sharpen our focus on the more general problem that has been the subject of this chapter, namely, whether convergent trends in philanthropic and public funding of research compromise the ideal of credible evidence in service to policy. Although the danger signs are real, the evidence so far is not conclusive and I do not (yet) believe there is a fatal fault line running through our think-tank sector, reported cases of poor judgment or opportunistic tampering notwithstanding. By analogy, the fact that a small percentage of scientific studies are withdrawn or retracted after their findings have been published is not a prima facie indictment of the entire research enterprise. On the contrary, one might argue that attention to the bad apples is a healthy response—by the research community as well as the myriad audiences in the public and private sectors who stand to benefit from credible research findings—that will ultimately strengthen the work and protect it from forces that would like to see its destruction.

In the case of the advice industry generally, and with respect to how important credible evidence is to the future of American education specifically, our challenge is to manage the combined threats from overcrowding and opportunistic posturing, a challenge made even more urgent by the convergence of trends in philanthropy and government support. Policy options for addressing these issues are the focus of the next chapter.

CHAPTER FOUR

A Policy Grammar

The Present Is Tense, the Future Imperfect

Q: What's the difference between the optimist and the pessimist?
A: The pessimist has more data.

—Rabbinic wisdom

I N THE FINAL MONTH OF PREPARING the manuscript for this book, three events made me thankful I hadn't finished it sooner. Mark Zuckerberg (the founder of Facebook) and his wife, Dr. Priscilla Chan, announced their plan to eventually transfer roughly $45 *billion* to a new kind of foundation that would provide support for initiatives aimed generally at making the world a better place—for their newborn daughter and, presumably, all humanity. President Obama signed two bills, both passed by Congress with unexpectedly high margins: one reauthorized the Elementary and Secondary Education Act and the second provided increased funding for science, health, and even education research. And representatives from 195 nations, gathered in Paris, the scene of bloody unconscionable evil in the preceding month (a terrorist act claiming 130 lives at the Bataclan theater, the Stade de France, and at cafés and restaurants in Paris and suburbs), demonstrated a rarely seen collective resolve to protect the species—if not from human-inspired terror, then from human-assisted environmental disaster—by signing the Paris Agreement to reduce climate change.

There you have it: an example of philanthropy that does not appear overly driven by preordained ideological goals; the reaffirmation of a federal role in education research; and evidence that even busy heads of state understand voluntary cooperation as a necessary, albeit imperfect, means to mitigate the risks of competition on behalf of the human community. Had I come out sooner with my somewhat nervous contemplation of the combined effects of strategic philanthropy, political reticence to allocate public funds to science, and the apparent erosion of civic responsibility to attenuate the hazards of self-interest, readers might have concluded (with some relief) that I had been unduly pessimistic.

I would have certainly missed some interesting developments, and they do provide at least a glimmer of hope. But I do not believe there is yet sufficient evidence to silence the alarms I have sounded in these pages. The Zuckerberg-Chan announcement may have opened a new chapter in the saga of American charity, with its nontraditional legal architecture—they plan a kind of limited liability corporation, rather than the more typical 501(c)(3) nonprofit foundation—and in that sense, our philanthropic sector seems creatively robust and innovative. Yet the planned gift has also triggered new fears about the risks of "philanthro-capitalism," a term coined by the *Economist* writer Matthew Bishop and coauthor Michael Green about the *virtues* of private giving and that has now been modified, by the more dour critics, into a thinly veiled pejorative. On the one hand, the Zuckerberg gift surely reflects genuinely altruistic, if naively immodest, impulses to repair the world, but it is also causing jitters and stoking renewed fears among those who worry about the camouflaged intentions of wealthy donors intent on preserving their privilege.[1]

Similarly, the reauthorization of the Elementary and Secondary Education Act and the passage of the fiscal 2016 omnibus budget bill create mixed feelings. Passed by a Congress that had demonstrated over several decades (and most acutely during the past seven years) an unprecedented capacity for scorched-earth partisanship, it was mildly reassuring to those of us who wondered if honored traditions of civil argumentation would forever be the focus of a graduate course on political antiquity. But there was also legitimate concern that the new education law, called the Every Student Succeeds Act (ESSA), authorizes a hazardous reversion to the hands-off era during which states and localities were given license to follow their own instincts, ignore or hide the ravages of unequal educational opportunity, and stall—or worse yet, reverse—progress that has been in the making over the past fifty years. As for the budget bill, I was comforted to read that the

US government would remain in business (so to speak), but this law, too, needs to be viewed with caution as it reflects a lingering wariness, a tentative and only grudging acceptance of the need for public participation in the funding of science. The changes to federal research budgets, though positive, were small and came with no guarantee of sustainability.

And finally, national leaders, normally motivated (some would say blinded) by fierce loyalty to their own polities, showed a capacity to resist the temptations of zealous self-interest, reject the antiscientific views of the "climate deniers," and craft an international and necessarily *collective* strategy. That is surely good news, about both the potential for slowing the disastrous effects of climate change and about the possibility for global cooperation that might help solve other problems. But lest we uncork the champagne prematurely, now comes the hard part: the test of reality those signatory nations will have to pass as they get on with implementation and enforcement. It is too early to know if this apparent rejection of the "tragedy of the commons" will turn into something more than a "comedy of errors." Although perhaps not as consequential to human existence as climate change and global environmental degradation, depletion of credible knowledge to inform and advise policy makers working on education and other issues is also a problem that requires sensible political and economic responses.[2]

As readers may guess from my general disposition, reflected in this book and elsewhere, I am inclined to be comforted by the end-of-year examples and to ward off the fretful hand-wringing among those who, shall we say, see every glass of private philanthropy and public policy as half empty. But even I can't get myself much above a 7.4 on my imaginary personal optimism meter, which is why I hope my arguments in this book will arouse increased awareness of the problems and provoke some new thinking about possible solutions. By the end of this chapter, I will reach a more comfortable 8.5.[3]

To get there, I propose a set of four policy options, each with some subsidiary provisions, aimed at curbing the downside risks of changing norms of philanthropy and fitful public funding of science. In presenting these options, I expand on earlier arguments and try to place them in their broader political, economic, and historical context.

Policy option 1: Tweak the tax

- *Impose a modest additional spending requirement (over the current 5 percent rule) on foundations with more than a certain minimum asset base (formula to be determined).*
- *With these funds, establish and maintain a new entity charged with (1) designing—and encouraging—research and evaluation projects that philanthropists with particularly strong "strategic" goals are reluctant to invest in; and (2) producing critical reviews of existing grant programs with respect to their relative reliance on research.*
- *Plan—and possibly organize—the new entity under the auspices of the National Academies of Sciences, Engineering, and Medicine and the National Academy of Education.*

This proposal speaks to two basic issues. It responds to the criticism that foundations should be induced to disburse more of their accumulated wealth in exchange for the broad benefits of the charitable deduction, and it aims to correct the market failure that prevents investments by foundations in generalizable research and knowledge production. Tinkering with the tax code requires a cautious approach: even the most restrained and moderate of commentators on the state of giving in America, generally and with perhaps greater emphasis when it comes to trends in foundation support for education and education research, correctly suggest that if we are not careful, we might compromise the best features of the system. Let me unpack the argument by summarizing and expanding what I've written in earlier chapters.

Uncharitable deductions

One of the greatest risks to complacency in the face of increasingly edgy and advocacy-driven philanthropy would be the erosion of our capacity to generate credible and independently objective knowledge about how education and other social systems are working and how they might be improved. Keeping in mind the idea that philanthropy is a valued source of civic engagement and populist pushback, it would be unfortunate indeed if indifference to concentration of wealth and patterns of giving had the opposite effect. In other words, we need to be attuned to the possibility that under the current system of tax breaks coupled with very loose accountability requirements, the largest and most well-endowed founda-tions might be exacerbating rather than ameliorating the gravitational pull toward excessive ideological and political conformity.

Indeed, commentators lost little time in speculating about the Zuck-erberg-Chan motivations and about the potential risks and benefits of the planned gift. Writing in the *New Yorker*, for example, John Cassidy ruminated about the potential downside to what appeared to be an act of remarkable generosity: "It is . . . worth noting . . . that all of this chari-table giving comes at a cost to the taxpayer and, arguably, to the broader democratic process. If Zuckerberg and Chan were to cash in their Face-book stock, rather than setting it aside for charity, they would have to pay capital-gains tax on the proceeds, money that could be used to fund gov-ernment programs. If they willed their wealth to their descendants, then sizable estate taxes would become due on their deaths. By making chari-table donations in the form of stock, they, and their heirs, could escape both of these levies."[4]

But another *New Yorker* regular offered a more hopeful analysis, one based on a subtler reading of the history of philanthropy and its relation-ship to our system of government and governance. James Surowiecki reminded readers that "hostility toward philanthropy is nothing new," and channeled the anxieties of critics of foundation-supported education reform with this rhetorical query: "Why should unelected billionaires get to exercise their neo-missionary impulses across the globe?" His deft rebuttal, which includes as good a recap of the theory of public goods as one might hope for in a nine-hundred-word opinion column, represents exactly the kind of balance that I believe is necessary as we consider the plus-minus of our unique approach to charity.

Surowiecki concedes that "in an ideal world, big foundations might be superfluous." But, he continues, "in the real world they are vital, because they are adept at targeting problems that both the private sector and the government often neglect . . . Corporations almost invariably underin-vest in public goods, because they can capture only a small fraction of the rewards . . . [and] politicians have to worry about being reelected every few years." Taken together, he argues, neither the private nor governmental sectors can be relied upon to tackle the biggest problems we face. Enter, therefore, the philanthropic community, willing and able "to pour money into controversial causes [and] to make big bets on global public goods."[5]

As for the tax implications, here, too, Surowiecki takes issue with his *New Yorker* colleague and others who argue for reducing or ending the tax advantages to billionaire donors, and bluntly predicts that even with the treasury thereby replenished, big and important social projects will still go underfunded. His evidence for this claim will sound familiar, as it echoes concerns I have raised in this book about the paltry amount the United States invests in education research (see chapter 2): "All public-goods spending is precarious, especially foreign aid, and never more so than with Republicans in charge of Congress. In inflation-adjusted terms, the budget for the National Institutes of Health is lower now than it was a decade ago, and late last year Senator Lindsey Graham warned that budget pressures could put anti-malaria funding 'at risk.'"[6]

Economics of giving

I do not mean to understate or dismiss the anxieties expressed about potential harm from "philanthro-capitalism." The scourge of income inequality, which has risen dramatically in the United States (and many other industrialized nations, especially in the last twenty-five years) is bad enough, but if its impacts on educational opportunity for the disadvantaged are exacerbated by philanthropy—even of the sort that is targeted toward the opposite outcome—that would indeed be a tragic case of unintended consequences.[7]

But let's remember the other side of the argument. Overemphasis on the downside risks associated with the implicit transfer of autonomy to donors, enabled and encouraged by the charitable deduction laws, masks potential financial and political benefits. One factor contributing to the benefits side of the current system, which Surowiecki highlights, is based on a compelling counterfactual, namely, the likelihood that even if more of the wealth controlled by foundations and families such as Gates, Zuckerberg, Broad, Hewlett, and Walton were shifted to the public coffers, government spending on the biggest and most complex public projects—for education and other valued enterprises—would be inadequate.

Another financial or economic consideration, one that is also missed by critics of the charitable deduction, is related to incentive effects. Here I want to strengthen my case (outlined in chapter 1) by borrowing a page from the playbook of the opposing team in this debate, which dismally insists on attributing generosity largely or entirely to tax advantages. Using their logic—and the implicit assumption that monetary incentives are the principal or sole motivator of human behavior—it would follow that lowering the tax break would reduce incentives for exactly the kinds of invention and innovation that enabled the accumulation of all that wealth in the first place.

In other words, if Bill and Melinda Gates, Mark Zuckerberg and Priscilla Chan, and other wealthy philanthropists were motivated in their charity only by their greedy exploitation of the tax deduction, it would necessarily follow that the same implicit risk-return calculus would have deterred them from developing things like Windows or Facebook in the first place, without which they would not have succeeded in amassing the wealth from which they now propose to "give back" to society in the form of charitable gifts and grants. There is no room here for a full-throated discussion of the psychology driving today's high-tech entrepreneurs, though I can't help thinking that many of the young geniuses who brought us things like e-mail, social media, and Internet-based shopping, not to mention a dizzying array of apps—mostly offered pretty much free of charge—were driven by something other than short-term capital accumulation. Whatever propels the development of freeware and shareware is not covered adequately by standard economic "profit-maximization" theory. In any case, I find it inconceivable that people for whom the accumulation of wealth was not their sole or principal motivator should suddenly become philanthropists only because of financial incentives embedded in the tax code. If self-interest is not the dominant driver of invention, it is probably not the main driver of charity either.

Focus on incentives takes us to yet another issue that should give us pause before rushing ahead with a major reform of the tax code. If we again follow the standard economic logic and assume that innovation, like charity, is motivated principally by the anticipation of maintaining wealth or accumulating more of it, then reducing the potential payout (by increasing the tax) would necessarily change the calculation faced by risk-averse technological entrepreneurs. If the result is delay or, worse, cancellation of risky invention projects, the macro effect would be felt not only on the demand side, in terms of consumers' access to technological advances, but also in terms of economic loss on the production side. For example, one would want to estimate the aggregate lifetime earnings of the people employed in the sectors that have blossomed because of inventions that spawned extravagant wealth. Such a computation would enable prediction of the downward effects on the treasury caused by lower taxable income among people who would otherwise have been employed in those industries, an issue that would need to be included in a macro-level analysis of the effects of reduced incentives for investment in risky innovations.

Politics, history, culture

This exercise in economic gymnastics covers only part of the reason for approaching the tax code with caution. As I have argued in previous chapters, political and historical factors need to be considered as well. Privileging individual rights over potential group benefits has been a distinguishing feature of American pluralism, certainly in comparison to other liberal democracies that favor more governmental authority, and on balance we are better off for it. This is a philosophical or moral preference that was important enough to have been enshrined legally in the Fourteenth Amendment to the Constitution and elsewhere; and it is supported too by empirical evidence of the advantages of individualism for creative problem solving and innovation.[8]

Even when it comes to our education "chaos," to borrow again from James Conant's metaphor, some of our most interesting reforms in teaching, learning, and the pursuit of equalization of opportunity came about in large part because of—and not in spite of—our decentralized system. Two examples are illustrative: when the District of Columbia decided in 2008 to provide (and require) universal preK education, for example, it was well ahead of most other jurisdictions in the country; if the citizens of Washington had been told to wait for their national leaders to agree on this kind of program, we would still be waiting. Similarly, initiatives such as TeachingWorks, which aims at fundamental reforms in the preparation of beginning teachers, provide compelling evidence for the innovative capacity of researchers and educators working at times with partial government financial support but without the equivalent of "ministerial" or central government authorization.[9]

No, I haven't forgotten the downside risks of local control, and, in fact, I continue to believe that the pursuit of more rational coherence and, yes, even *standards* on a national level, is the wiser course. Education—a public good with enormous national significance—is too important to be left entirely in the hands of local district officials (or, for that matter, even parents) with neither the resources nor the inclination to apply relevant findings from research, to resist the pressures of clever entrepreneurs hawking various untested interventions, and to conduct the sort of ongoing evaluations needed to ensure proper and effective implementation. Most important, there is just too much historical evidence that ideas like states' rights have been used to justify and perpetuate states' wrongs—the worst forms of segregation and denial of opportunity. For me, those are sufficient arguments for a strong federal role and a commitment to at least some movement in the direction of national goals and standards for teaching and learning.

But it is not a simple either-or proposition: the value of maintaining private authority over some of our national wealth and keeping some investment decisions safe from the national government—which is one implicit purpose of the charitable deduction—should not be underestimated. After all, even the federal government can make wrong choices when it comes to classroom teaching, school finance, the protection of minority rights, or support for long-term research. Political leaders can be unwilling or unable to allocate public resources in ways that accurately reflect the preferences and needs of the people who elected and appointed them, or they can be so preoccupied with implementation of complex decisions in the short term that their view of the future and their willingness to invest in risky or uncertain initiatives become more than partially obstructed. Here I am underscoring a point made in chapter 2 about anticipated benefits that accrue from the diffusion of wealth and power in the provision of public goods, what Rob Reich refers to as "contestatory" effects of the nongovernmental civic sector. I side with him, and with Surowiecki, in favoring an arrangement in which the prerogatives of government are checked and balanced by the actions of individuals and, yes, even corporations.

The complexity of these issues precludes a simple or quick solution to the problem of the charitable deduction, and reasonable people should debate whether the current tax code has it exactly right. My proposal is for a modest adjustment. The substantive effects of a more sweeping change (such as eliminating the deduction altogether) in order to redistribute private wealth back to the government, and the process needed to make such changes (an act of Congress followed by implementation and enforcement by a public bureaucracy known as the IRS and the judiciary), would be perceived as dramatic and intentional shifts in the direction of more governmental control. This is an unlikely scenario in a Congress and White House riven with partisanship and in a political atmosphere poisoned by the fumes of antigovernment ideology. But in any case, the anticipated benefits of such changes, especially if they are viewed as a federal power grab, need to be weighed against the transaction costs associated with effecting them.[10]

Psychology, physiology, and ethics of charity

To this paella of predicaments, we can now add a new spice: research on the psychological and *physiological* benefits that accrue to the generous. Earlier I hinted at my skepticism about stretching the neoclassical economic definition of self-interest to include the benefits accruing to the doers of good deeds. That rendition, in which altruism is essentially flipped into just another form of selfishness, always seemed to me a bit crass, and a methodologically limited, if not fatally tautological, apologia for the removal of government from decisions affecting the public good. The increasingly prevalent rhetoric about self-interest as the motivator of behavior that redounds to the collective benefit generally, based in part on a misreading of Adam Smith's original treatise on the subject, has been the source of much foolishness (and some mischief). For evidence that relying on theories of pure competition, perfect information, zero transactions costs, and the unfettered decisions of private individuals to bring us to the socially optimal allocation of resources can have disastrous consequences, a good place to start is with the victims of the 2007 collapse of the mortgage lending system.[11]

In addition, overemphasis on charity as an act of *self*-interest can dilute the moral basis of acts meant to help *others*. The logic here is that if charity is defined as just another consumption commodity, then there should be no problem relying on monetary incentives—using price as we do to influence demand of most other goods—to stimulate or reward increased giving. Lower the price of giving (by providing the equivalent of monetary reward through a reduced tax burden), and the giving will increase. Or will it? The evidence suggests that the prospect of extrinsic financial gain does not necessarily lead to more generosity. A lesson from the literature about voluntary blood donation showed how converting charitable acts into standard economic quid pro quo transactions alters their "atmospheric" quality and discourages, rather than encourages, the desired altruism. If I donate to charity because the act gives me emotional or moral satisfaction or because it corresponds to a religious or ethical imperative, the offer of financial return might actually sour me.[12]

My reason for elaborating on psychological aspects of charity is to underscore why I believe setting and adjusting the charitable deduction is a complicated and nuanced matter. In my view, these are not tangential issues. Consider, for example, new empirical evidence showing that *satisfaction really does come from giving*. In what may be a new and important application of behavioral economics, the work of a group of scholars from Canada, Africa, and the United States provides compelling arguments not only for the continued bridging of the sciences of psychology and economics but for the idea that altruism does, indeed, provide what I would call "reflective benefits." As reported in one of the top-tier psychology journals, research "provides the first support for a possible psychological universal: human beings around the world derive emotional benefits from using their financial resources *to help others* (prosocial spending)." [italics added][13]

In the age of *selfies*, it is reassuring to see that pleasure derives also from what might be called *otheries*. Apparently, it's not just an emotional benefit, or the type of effect covered handily by the economic umbrella of utility, but also a *physiological* one: these researchers have presented evidence of a causal link between charitable giving and improvement of *the giver's* blood pressure, cardiac condition, and other health outcomes.[14]

The possibility that such benefits reinforce moral imperatives driving charitable impulses is more than scintillating: I am awed by the realization that medical science is now reaffirming ethical traditions that date to the Hebrew Bible (and later Talmudic commentary). At the risk of stating the obvious, neither the biblical lesson from Proverbs that "charity will save from death" nor Maimonides' twelfth-century hierarchy of *tzedakah* (a complicated Hebrew word that covers both justice and charity) were based on epidemiological research. Now we have confirming evidence, worthy of celebration, that not only are the *recipients* of charity likely to enjoy improvements to the quality of their lives but that *donors*, too, are rewarded for their good deeds in the here and now.[15]

As exciting as these new findings are, though, they still do not add up to an argument against extrinsic economic incentives designed to reinforce charitable urges. Again, the possibility that financial reward might suppress, rather than encourage, charity should be taken into account. But it would be imprudent to scrap the tax deduction on the grounds that donors derive enough "psychic reward" from their giving, that they don't need or want the monetary gain, and that the tax break is therefore an unnecessary windfall to donors who would give anyway. For one thing, we don't yet have sufficient empirical evidence to account adequately for the *net* effect: how much of that assumed physiological gain erodes when the economic benefit is eliminated? Moreover, one might argue that just because people (or, more accurately, *some* people: the behavioral economics findings, after all, consist of statistically significant *averages*, which means a lot of donors don't necessarily feel the effects) may profit from altruistic behavior, that's not a rationale to disqualify them from the bonus of a lower tax burden.[16]

The many and the one

Finally, there is the larger issue of our national ethos. Americans love individualism and cringe at too much conformity, but we also have a long history of striving and struggling to define values that bind us as a people. This is in part why the debate about educational standards (see my discussion in chapter 3) is at once so exhilarating and so frustrating; the intuitive appeal of *e pluribus unum* doesn't lead to obvious practical solutions that satisfy complex political and historical preferences.

In this drama of federalism, the tax code plays a leading role. Leaving aside for a moment the predictable financial effects of marginal changes to the charitable deduction, on the whole it conveys, tacitly at least, a message about who we are as a people. Given its centrality to our way of life, the tax system is a particularly good place to embed the equivalent of an endorsement, a kind of seal of approval for the principle of popular participation in the enhancement of the public welfare. Consider the counterfactual: to eliminate the deduction would signal that the voluntary instincts of citizens to give back, whether individually or through large corporate-styled foundations, are no longer as valued and, worse, that big social, economic, and educational decisions will henceforth be managed by the political process only. Not a pleasant outlook, to say the least.

So I come to an argument for moderation (surprise!) as we explore the feasibility of policies that nudge in the direction of increased accountability and transparency in the philanthropic sector without causing fatal structural damage to the whole enterprise. My suggestion for an adjustment to the charitable deduction, which would require the larger foundations to disburse slightly more than 5 percent of their asset base, would hopefully not cause a decline in philanthropy. Rather, it could bolster the credibility of the foundation sector and enhance its overall effectiveness and impact. The additional funds would be used to establish an entity tasked with recommending and supporting independent and objective inquiry of the sort that is otherwise not likely to be undertaken. Its main role would not be to monitor the activities of philanthropies, many of which are responding admirably to the call for more transparency; although a positive by-product would be insights about the extent to which foundations (and other philanthropic organizations) already rely on research to design and implement programs with potentially significant social and economic consequences, whether they are aware of and make use of the relevant theoretical and empirical literatures, whether they have the willingness and capacity to invest in pilot testing of major new initiatives, and whether they support independent evaluations of their programs' impacts (ex post).

My suggestion is to at least begin the process leading to the creation of such an entity through a planning initiative undertaken jointly by the National Academies of Sciences, Engineering, and Medicine (NASEM) and the National Academy of Education (NAEd). Engaging these organizations will signal the importance of scientific and scholarly independence and will facilitate deliberations involving the appropriately wide range of needed expertise and disciplinary specialization. I note, however, that because both NASEM and NAEd rely to some extent on foundation funding, it may be preferable to set up the new entity as wholly separate. Lessons from the establishment of the Corporation for Public Broadcasting, for example, may be instructive, especially as it, too, was established with support from private philanthropy.[17]

POLICY OPTION II: ORGANIZE FOR KNOWLEDGE

- *Establish a new Congressional Education Organization (CEO), a research unit to analyze and synthesize data and the results of research, and advise Congress on education policy options and their potential effects.*
- *Create a similar entity under the auspices of the Council of Chief State School Officers and the National Governors Association to provide credible and objective guidance to states and districts.*

This strategy addresses the problem of information overload, in particular, the challenges decision makers face when confronted with multitudinous and often conflicting recommendations. In the light of shifts in the major federal education legislation in the direction of greater authority for states and districts on key issues of assessment and accountability, the need for a coherent and credible filtering mechanism has become more acute. I discuss this idea now by elaborating on my earlier overview of ESSA and placing it in its broader and more complex historical context.

A perhaps too generous interpretation of ESSA is that its key provisions reflect hard-learned lessons from its predecessor, the No Child Left Behind Act (NCLB). For instance, the new law does seem to reduce the testing burden, which comes as a relief to parents, teachers, and others who had become frustrated by the accountability regime and its effects on teaching and learning. On the other hand, although ESSA continues to require assessment of student progress at various points in elementary and secondary school, it more explicitly affirms the state role in developing the tests and in setting standards of academic performance. Confusion between national requirements and state-level autonomy was one of the major flaws in NCLB, and it may actually get worse under ESSA.

A key question is whether states and districts will have the technical capacity and expertise—and the will—to devise innovative assessments that promote learning and provide valid measures of performance. The flow of recommendations will be robust. Testing companies and other vendors, both nonprofit and for profit, will present their "solutions," surely many of them accompanied by compilations of data and scientific jargon supporting their veracity. Hopefully, this will create heightened demand for filtering, for credible and objective guidance based on good research. Lessons about the origins, goals, and successes of the now defunct Office of Technology Assessment (and its surviving sister agencies—the Congressional Budget Office, Congressional Research Service, and Government Accountability Office)—provide one starting point for the design of financially viable and politically useful agencies to aid Congress and the states.

The federal "roll"

The sigh of relief breathed by the education community upon passage of ESSA was audible inside the famous Washington Beltway, at least to those of us who listen for those kinds of sounds. (It was a noisy month, indeed, with passage of the fiscal year 2016 budget bill a week later.) In a short period, there was enough legislative action to revive hope in the workings of government and, more specifically, in the government's acceptance of its role in the improvement of education for all Americans. The question, though, was whether these actions reaffirmed a real federal role or whether those of us hoping for continuation of a muscular federal presence to boost educational equity and achievement had been rolled.

Because the passage of ESSA bears on aspects of the problems I discuss in this book, I want to revisit its origins and unravel some of its main features. The Elementary and Secondary Education Act (ESEA), originally passed in 1965, was the most significant reform in relations between the federal government and the nation's more than fifteen thousand school districts of the prior two centuries. As the veteran Capitol Hill staff member and leader Jack Jennings noted in his recent book, ESEA was the "ambitious and encyclopedic law [that] reshaped American education and influenced the schooling of millions of American children over a fifty-year period. While the federal government had been peripherally involved in public education prior to 1965, ESEA marked the beginning of broad federal involvement in the daily operation of schools . . . [and] has had a profound effect."[18]

To understand why the new version of the law, ESSA, may trigger the need for even more intensive filtering of policy recommendations and improved technical assistance to states and districts regarding such matters as standards, testing, and accountability, it is worth digressing briefly to explore the historical context of the original 1965 law, ESEA and its 2002 reauthorization, when it was named No Child Left Behind.[19] That version, too, passed with a remarkable bipartisan majority, one that garnered celebratory hugs among strange bedfellows: to see Congressman John Boehner embracing Senator Edward Kennedy prompted many observers to rush to their optometrists for a quick vision check. But NCLB was contested early and often, especially as the realities of implementation began to sink in; critics with opposing views on the philosophy and ideology of education and federal involvement found new grounds for shared disdain.

From one segment of what might be called the progressive or liberal side of the aisle, the fear was that externally imposed accountability requirements—what came to be known as "drop from the sky" assessments—would stifle the imaginations and professional dignity of classroom teachers and their principals and transform the magic of teaching and learning into mindless and formulaic memorization. A key concern for this group was whether the testing mandated in NCLB—states had to show annual progress of students as a condition for obtaining federal aid—would force teachers to abandon the less easily tested parts of the curriculum, drill their students in the material about which they would be tested, discourage creative and open-ended thinking, and perhaps most egregiously, focus their instruction on test prep rather than on the knowledge and skills the tests were ostensibly designed to approximate.[20]

These issues surely caused some cognitive dissonance, at least for some of these critics who were not otherwise known for favoring local control, especially in the light of its sordid historical record. Indeed, for another segment of the left, namely, some of the most vigilant warriors in the battle for equality and the narrowing of achievement gaps between white majority and minority students, NCLB's disaggregation requirement was its most promising feature. Their support was based on the compelling hypothesis that, without transparent accounting for disparities in achievement among children of various ethnic, racial, and socioeconomic backgrounds, there would never be sufficient political will to attend to the inequalities that plague schools and school systems. As one of the more vocal advocacy groups put it, "There is an achievement gap because we have held some students to high standards but not others . . . Low-income students and students of color have consistently been short changed. They've had the least qualified teachers, the least challenging curriculum and the poorest equipped schools . . . [NCLB] holds states responsible for making sure that all students are held to high standards."[21]

Many of these supporters of NCLB acknowledged the downside risks of test-based accountability; after all, they were acutely aware of the long and painful history of the use of tests to perpetuate myths of inherent (and even hereditary) limits to the abilities of children of various racial, ethnic, and national origins. But they concluded, implicitly at least, that the benefits of providing scientific evidence of disparities outweighed the costs of potentially unintended outcomes such as teaching to the test and inflation of scores (resulting from various coaching techniques and, in some extreme cases, outright cheating).

For those in more conservative education policy circles, NCLB caused a different strain of cognitive dissonance. Holding schools and teachers accountable based on valid and reliable indicators of performance (test scores in particular) seemed like a good thing to do. On the other hand, NCLB signified a substantially more energetic involvement by the federal government—in both the setting of educational standards and the measurement of student performance—and was therefore viewed with suspicion and anticipatory derision, especially by the more fervent believers in markets as well as by those who sought to protect the role of states in governance of the schools.[22]

Here was an interesting tension. At least since Milton Friedman's suggestion that the "invisible hand" of markets could cure our educational ills, there had been a persistent agitation and fascination among economists, political scientists, and others for various types of voucher, choice, and charter systems.[23] Leaving aside the question of whether those alternatives actually lead to improvement in valued outcomes of schooling such as improved performance on tests of academic achievement—and the results so far are mixed at best—the implications for *accountability* are worth noting. Market-based systems require reliable information, so it might seem natural for advocates of choice and charters to wish for more measurement. On the other hand, NCLB substantially increased the federal role, which did not sit well with purists who pined for less intrusion by Washington into the decisions of states, districts, and local communities. Tough love—via testing—collided with unconditional love—of markets and choice.[24]

Good information is necESSAry

In the end, disappointment with the bureaucracy of NCLB became a shared sentiment across the aisle. For example, Frederick Hess (of the American Enterprise Institute) wrote harsh critiques of the law, and also of Secretary Duncan's application of the waiver policy under which states were granted relief from some federal requirements. From the left, Diane Ravitch applauded Hess for this position. By the time ESSA passed, just about everyone was ready for a fresh start.[25]

What changes did the new law bring? And, more to the point, how does it relate to the themes in this book? First, it is worth reiterating that ESSA maintains a strong federal presence, with continuing requirements for annual student testing as a condition for receiving federal funds. Years of fighting about the unintended negative effects of NCLB did not culminate in a victory for choice and vouchers and the complete abdication of public authority. Nor did the replacement of NCLB easily satisfy the so-called "anti-testing" crowd—or more accurately, the "anti-test-based accountability" crowd. In that sense, then, the new law represents another grand compromise in American politics of education: the idea of a national ethos is still pursued, with a more than symbolic presence of the national government, while considerable authority and discretion are returned to states and localities.

In the weeks before passage of the new law, President Obama set the stage by acknowledging shortcomings of his own administration's reliance on test-based accountability. He spoke eloquently about the possibility that we had overstepped and that it was time to revisit the purposes and effects of all the testing. The changes embedded in ESSA signaled at least a partial change of course. It

> maintains the same testing schedule and reporting requirements for statewide annual testing, but it gives states the option to give a single summative test, as they do now, or break up the assessment into smaller components that could be given throughout the school year to provide more frequent information on student achievement and

growth. The ESSA also provides local education agencies (LEAs) the ability to use a nationally-recognized high school academic assessment (like the SAT) in lieu of a state-developed assessment, so long as the test can provide comparable data and the state signs off."[26]

At the root of ESSA's underlying strategy, then, lies an implicit and by now familiar faith in the agility and innovative capacity of localities and individual entrepreneurs. But whether the new law represents a real departure from NCLB, under which states were required to test annually all children in grades three through eight and once in high school, in both math and English language arts, is a bit murky. For example, the NCLB requirement to show "adequate yearly progress" enabled states to set their own standards for measuring that progress, which led to confusion (and heated arguments) about comparative performance across the states, clearly an unintended consequence (or necessary political compromise) of a law aimed at establishing some semblance of national standards. As preeminent scholar of educational assessment Robert Linn explained early in the life of NCLB,

> States use different assessments, have adopted their own student performance standards, and have developed different accountability systems. As a consequence of those differences, reports of student achievement and progress are not comparable from one state to another. Although the requirements . . . have led to greater commonality among states in some respects, a great deal of between-state variability remains in many important details in implementing assessments and accountability provisions . . . states still control many aspects in complying with NCLB, such as the specification of content standards, the choice of assessments, and the setting of academic achievement standards."[27]

It is possible, therefore, that ESSA codifies and reaffirms what may have been a de facto but unintended consequence of NCLB, and the risks have quickly become apparent. The extent to which states and districts have the capacity—and will—to make the hard choices they face has always been a limiting factor—under NCLB and again now. As the acting secretary of education cautioned in his first major speech of 2016, "[ESSA] . . . preserves an important role in education for the federal government. But the new and larger role for states should be seen as a clarion call in the civil rights community," a reminder of the risks associated with too much devolution of authority back to the localities where minority opportunities and desegregation were not always the highest priorities.[28]

How this tension will be resolved is on the minds of educators, policy makers, and the general public. One thing should be clear: the history of ESEA and its most recent transformation should warn us that the pipelines carrying research-based evidence to the halls of Congress could stand some cleaning. Although at times I believe the critics are too quick and too severe, there is certainly ample ground for the allegation that knowledge about the uses and misuses of testing for accountability (as an example) was not adequately represented in the deliberations that led either to NCLB or to the new ESSA requirements. Policy makers—at all levels—are becoming increasingly aware of their need for objective and reliable information to guide their choices. This would be a good time to introduce a neutral research arm to inform policy with sound evidence and enable the continuous examination of evidence about the effects of policy decisions.

Vertical integration

How might such an information function be structured? The recurrent turbulence in education policy generally and the latest reminder of the need for independent and objective research to inform practice evoke memories of the origins and purposes of the now defunct OTA. Faced with a barrage of data and advice being proffered by an increasingly diverse group of lobbyists and advocates, Congress chose to establish its own agency aimed at synthesizing available research and providing members trustworthy guidance on the most complex policy problems (mostly involving technology, innovation, and science). I offer here a brief reminder of the origins, goals, and functioning of OTA, in hopes it might stimulate some fresh thinking about ways we might satisfy the need for credible evidence in education.

OTA was established in 1972, and became the fourth congressional think tank, along with the CBO, CRS, and GAO. I had the pleasure of working there for seven years, with a group of dedicated scientists and policy analysts who faithfully aspired to as clean a differentiation—and separation—of opinion from empirical evidence as possible. The mission was to provide "policy options," rather than "recommendations," the subtle difference suggestive of the underlying philosophy that (1) scientists can inform, but ultimately politicians must decide, and (2) arraying alternative courses of action with estimates of their likely effects enabled focused and balanced deliberations.[29]

How OTA was organized and the norms it adhered to are relevant to the problems of educational accountability in the post-NCLB era. Here I will focus on two. Like its sister agencies, OTA represented a type of vertical integration in the market for research-based information. The idea was not to *supplant* the flow of information from universities, think tanks, evaluation shops, and individual researchers and data analysts, or to reject outright the notion that competition was a healthy feature of information markets. Rather the goal was to provide users of all that information (first and foremost, members of Congress and their staffs) with an economical way of summarizing results and their meaning and, most importantly, filtering the myriad and often contradictory findings based on criteria of evidentiary validity and reliability. OTA did not conduct much original data collection, but focused instead on reviewing existing studies, subjecting them to close methodological scrutiny, distilling the core messages, and communicating their implications. The primary audience was Congress, but because all the reports were made available upon release, they became useful source documents for multiple stakeholders and the general public.

The key organizational point here is that Congress derived more credible and consistent information through this vertically integrated arrangement than it could by limiting itself to ad hoc or recurrent "spot contracts" with the hundreds of suppliers of data and advocates promoting research-informed advice. As I have suggested in previous chapters, competition does not necessarily yield higher-quality products; in the case of information to congressional policy makers, the history of OTA supports the notion that a nonmarket alternative—Congress essentially owning its think tanks—was highly valued and that the flow of credible and useful advice was rendered both more efficient and more reliable.[30]

And not only did these congressionally owned research units not diminish the role of the nongovernment providers and purveyors of advice, their place actually became more important and valued. Reports from organizations such as RAND, AIR, and other research shops and think tanks contained data that were crucial to OTA's study panels; to the extent that being included in OTA deliberations and cited in its reports enhanced these organizations' reputations, they faced strong incentives for quality and empirical integrity. Simply put, if OTA and other organizations (including those that are legally independent of government, such as the NASEM and NAEd), rely on synthesis, they must have something good to synthesize.

The second key feature of OTA, without which its principal value to Congress would have been fatally undermined, was the process by which studies were commissioned and designed, how advisers were appointed, and how results were reviewed.[31] The review process, for example, which bears some resemblance to mechanisms that the NASEM and NAEd utilize, is especially significant if we apply the lessons from OTA toward the problems of education research in an era of heightened competition and politicization. Attention to the people involved in review (with respect to their particular areas of expertise and their willingness to separate ideology from analysis of data) and the procedures they used to guarantee (or at least aspire to) the highest standards of balance are among the necessary conditions for ensuring the credibility and utility of the advice (whether in the form of "options" or "recommendations"). On the other hand, these processes are time consuming and, as I noted in chapter 3, an essential ingredient in the recipe for usable evidence is its timeliness: expecting members of Congress, especially those on especially short political leashes, to wait years for a report, is no way to win their favor. Finding the balance between evidentiary and practical standards of inquiry is among the policy analyst's toughest challenges.

The track records of OTA, CBO, CRS, and GAO offer lessons germane to the consideration of what might be done to strengthen the role and credibility of research as input to complex educational decisions. I offer two parallel and possibly overlapping suggestions. The first, focused on the needs of Congress to have an efficient and reliable source of advice on the specifics of ESSA, but even more generally on all its education-related activities, would be to borrow from the acronym of the CBO and establish a new Congressional *Education* Organization (CEO). This entity would be designed with attention to the best (and worst) features of other similar organizations (including the old OTA as well as the NASEM and NAEd). It would be a vertically integrated part of Congress, it would aspire to the highest standards of scientific inquiry, it would enable agile and timely responses to urgent questions while providing room for anticipation of issues not yet on the political agenda, and it would eschew the optics problems by not taking funding from private, philanthropic, or corporate sources. Proposing a new congressional agency in a time of partisan and fiscal stress may seem out of touch with today's reality, but the idea is worth holding onto in hopes of a brighter future, especially as the cost would be relatively low compared to that of other large federal agencies (in its time, OTA operated on roughly a $20 million annual budget).

A concurrent option is for state education leaders (perhaps through the Council of Chief State School Officers and the National Governors Association) to establish their own entity, also borrowing from the methods and mission of the old OTA. With proper funding, such an organization would attract the most qualified education policy researchers, provide a protected environment for careful analysis of data and consideration of options, and produce credible and timely advice for use (or not) by the states. Given the challenges that states and districts now face, for example, with respect to new accountability requirements, pressures associated with the Common Core, and the pursuit of cross-state comparability, being able to rely on advice from such an entity would go a long way toward overcoming the capacity deficits that so many individual states must deal with.

There are many details of governance, funding, and process to be worked through. But my sense is that vertically integrated arrangements aimed at providing federal- and state-level decision makers with a clear set of options, annotated with analysis of their likely benefits and costs, would be broadly appreciated. It would be worth exploring whether to combine these proposals into a single, new organization, though I am not optimistic that it would meet the multiple and diverse needs of decision makers who face different problems and different political environments. In any event, the idea of creating new venues for the flow of credible evidence warrants attention as a potential relief from the pressures outlined in this book, namely, the changes in philanthropy and government funding that affect the objectivity of research-based advice.

POLICY OPTION III: ACCOUNT FOR SCIENCE

- *Amend the charter of the National Academies of Sciences, Engineering, and Medicine to require a regular reporting to the American people on trends in the federal funding of research and development as well as a reporting on the research investments of foundations and other private donors.*

The fiscal year 2016 budget, passed in December 2015, included increases for NSF, NIH, and even the Department of Education's research arm. This is good news, but uncertainties linger about how the omnibus budget bill will be implemented and, in particular, whether the modest increases are a blip on the radar screen or whether the federal role in science is going to be sustained. My rationale for this policy proposal, simply stated, is that providing the public with routine and credible information may discipline Congress (and the executive branch) and prevent wild swings in attitudes and legislation concerning research in general and the education sciences in particular. In addition, given the growing importance of the private sector, in particular, the philanthropic sector as discussed in chapter 1 and again in this chapter, I would make a similar argument for credible and objective information about foundation funding.

The idea of this policy option is to establish a credible monitor of public and private spending on research and development, with the goal of curbing the temptation among elected officials to let short-term political motivations interrupt and undermine long-term stability in the scientific enterprise. To the extent that a robust and sustained "contestatory" role of the private sector is valued as a means for promoting the civic good, objective information to the American people about trends in governmental and philanthropic investment would be a welcomed addition to the mix of reports we already have.[32]

In the preceding section, I focused on implications of the new education act for the development of strategies to ensure that good research continues to be valued and used. Here I will consider together the two other "December surprises," the budget bill and the international climate agreement. They both relate to aspects of the public side of science and provide lessons relevant to consideration of policies to curb the unwanted consequences of changes in philanthropic and government support of research.

Political science

Public funding of scientific research, as discussed in chapter 2, has been both a hallmark of American political ingenuity and a locus of American political insurgence. If one considers some of the most heated political and policy battles of the twentieth and twenty-first centuries—nuclear energy and defense, reproductive rights, tobacco consumption, climate change—what they share is a connection to research and the application of scientific knowledge to public decision making. One of the most controversial studies conducted by OTA, for example, was about President Reagan's so-called "Star Wars" proposal, which called on the scientific and engineering communities to develop a kind of protective shield that would reduce or eliminate the threat of Russian ballistic missile attack. OTA's position on the Strategic Defense Initiative (SDI) was despised by the agency's critics: "Generally speaking, OTA was deeply skeptical of the 'Star Wars' program's technical feasibility, and its critiques struck the Reagan administration in the gut, coming as they did with the official imprimatur of Congress."[33]

In times of heightened partisan stress, it is not surprising that a target favored by opponents of this or that policy is the federal budget under which funding for research is provided. At risk of simplification, it is clear that anger against the alleged liberal-progressive-Democratic policy agenda—on matters such as women's reproductive rights or the role of fossil fuels in causing climate change—has prompted renewed calls in Congress for reining in the spending by the NSF and other federal research agencies. Political intrusion in science is manifest both procedurally and financially, with sudden demands for review of proposals and selection processes and threats to slash budgets.[34]

Against this backdrop, then, I was relieved to see the funding increases for research in the fiscal year 2016 budget. Writing in *Science*, Jeffrey Mervis noted that "NIH is the winner in absolute dollars. It gets a bump of $2 billion, or 6.6%, from its current budget of $30.1 billion. Spending on science programs at NASA would grow by 6.6%, to $5.6 billion, and rise by 5.6% in the Department of Energy's (DOE's) Office of Science, to $5.35 billion. The National Science Foundation would receive an additional $119 million, or 1.6%."[35]

Of special interest here, total funding for the Institute of Education Sciences (IES) grew by 7.7 percent between fiscal years 2015 and 2016, from $574 million to $618 million; the education and human resources (EHR) directorate of NSF received a boost of 1.6 percent, from $866 million to $880 million; and the National Institute of Child Health and Human Development (NICHD) saw an increase of almost 4 percent, from $1.29 billion to $1.34 billion.[36] Table 4.1 shows summary data for funding changes in the three agencies.

These are positive developments, assuming we value the concept of scientific research as a public good to be supported by the federal government. But we should not take that assumption for granted. As noted by the American Educational Research Association, "The increase [in IES funding] is good news for research in the current climate, especially since the House appropriations bill for Labor, Health and Human Services, Education, and Related Agencies that passed in July [six months before the omnibus bill was passed and signed] would have cut funding for Research, Development, and Dissemination by nearly half and cut all funding for the Regional Educational Laboratories."[37]

Embedded in this generally good news are uncertainties about how the budget bill will be implemented—report language accompanying the law

TABLE 4.1   Science funding, FY 2016 (in billions of dollars)

		FY 2016			
	FY 2015 actual	Original White House request	House version, fall 2015	Senate version, fall 2015	Final FY 2016 bill
NSF total	7.3	7.7	7.4	7.3	7.5
EHR	.87	.96	.87	.87	.88
NIH total	30.1	31.3	31.2	32.1	32.1
Department of Education total	67.1	70.7	64.4	65.8	68.3
IES	.57	.68	.4	.56	.62

Sources: National Science Foundation; National Institutes of Health; US Department of Education websites and databases; American Association for the Advancement of Science; American Educational Research Association; Consortium of Social Science Associations.

had not been released by the time this manuscript went into final preparation—and there are traces of politicization in the 2,009-page bill that warrant close attention. For example, mandated revisions to peer-review mechanisms at NSF, which were introduced into earlier legislation on the House side (by Congressman Lamar Smith [R-TX]), seem to have been softened in—but not entirely expunged from—the final version of the bill signed by the president. As noted in the summary prepared by the Consortium of Social Science Associations (COSSA), "The omnibus goes on to direct NSF to 'continue efforts to implement transparency processes, which includes requiring that public award abstracts articulate how the project serves the national interest.' Fortunately, the language falls short of stating what research qualifies as 'serving the national interest,' leaving such a determination to be made by the agency. Other legislation originating in the House this year sought to codify a definition of 'national interest' as it relates to federally-funded research, with an eye on singling out 'wasteful' social science projects."[38]

Modest increases in federally funded research will not, in themselves, bring about a rebalancing of the partnership between private and public support of science, and single-digit improvements in the budget for education research will not lessen the pressure to subject philanthropic investments in reform initiatives to independent and high-quality evaluations. Perhaps most important, the small changes in education research included in the latest federal budget will not enable the kind of scientifically informed advice needed to guide policy makers—at the federal, state, and local levels—through the next phases of standards, assessments, and accountability envisioned in ESSA. (Here I am underscoring a point I made earlier, about the duality of federal investments in science—to support basic knowledge production and to purchase needed scientifically based advice on policy.)

Climate policy and the policy climate

The at least tentatively reaffirmed federal role in research signals, hopefully, acknowledgment that the problems of education are complex enough to warrant more of the best that science can offer, and, as importantly, that these problems are not likely to be addressed adequately by private or corporate investments. Research oriented to improvement of the human condition is a public good. If this development suggests a positive change in the climate of policy, the actions taken by countries gathered in Paris in December 2015, which suggest a positive change in the policy of climate, hold lessons relevant to the future of a sustained public commitment to educational research.

Key elements of the Paris accord are instructive. After years of strenuous and, at times, acrimonious debate within and between countries on the evidence about whether the earth is indeed experiencing real climate change, on its causes (fossil fuels), and on actions that countries of varying size and responsibility for the situation would need to take, they reached agreement at the end of the twenty-first session of the United Nations Framework Convention on Climate Change (UNFCCC). Starting in 1992, this initiative was aimed at negotiating the Kyoto Protocol, which established legally binding obligations for reduction of greenhouse gas emissions.

The details of this agreement, an example of voluntary collective action with some self-induced coercive enforcement provisions, are obviously beyond the scope of this book, but some of the key procedural features are relevant. According to summary documentation prepared by the UNFCCC:

- [A]ll Parties are *required* to undertake national and regional programmes to mitigate climate change . . .
- The Convention provides a forum for *incentivizing* and enhancing action on mitigation by all Parties informed by the latest scientific information and guided by its principles . . .
- The COP and the Conference of the Parties serving as the Meeting of the Parties to the Kyoto Protocol (CMP) have established a variety of arrangements to guide the implementation of these actions and commitments [including] a well established system for *reporting* action undertaken by Parties to implement the Convention; [and] detailed rules for reporting, *accounting*, and *compliance* under the Kyoto Protocol. [italics added][39]

There are several useful lessons here, if one accepts the basic argument that reliable and objective education research is a public good threatened by the convergent forces of private self-interest and reduced involvement of government. The italicized words from the UNFCCC agreement, above, offer kernels of hope. First, there is a sense of *requirement*, which acknowledges explicitly that collective action (of the sort envisioned in the agreement as necessary to confront the challenge of climate change) implies at least some level of coercion. In this case, signatories to the agreement acknowledged their willingness to contain or limit the customary freedoms enjoyed by sovereign nations; they accept the terms of the statement as a type of binding contract, adding the word "requirement" to hint at the importance of self-regulated compliance.

Second, there is a nod to the role of *incentives*, an enlightened appreciation that the pains of implementing the "required" steps enumerated in the contract will be eased by evidence of how the benefits will accrue not only to the collective (Earth) but to the individual countries participating in the plan. Here is a case where the ethics of collective action seem to be aligned with the individualistic instincts of national (self) interest, a convergence that should bolster its chances of success.

Third, there is explicit attention to monitoring and *accountability*, which, given the limits imposed by rules of national sovereignty, are the most important (and maybe the *only*) tools of enforcement. Absent the equivalent of a policing or regulatory function that operates within countries—in the United States, we have developed a considerable infrastructure to monitor environmental externalities and impose civil and criminal penalties accordingly—it is hoped that diffusing information about compliance (or the lack thereof) might create incentives for good behavior.

Taken together, then, the passage of the fiscal year 2016 budget and the international agreement on climate lead me to at least a temporary resurgence of optimism and to consideration of another policy option aimed at protecting the future of education research. With respect to the importance of a sustained (and hopefully) enlarged federal investment in research, the goal is to ensure that the fiscal year 2016 increases are not a fluke but rather the beginning of a sustained trend.

My suggestion to involve the NASEM in an expanded role, reinforced by an amendment to its charter, has several features. On occasion, NASEM has weighed in on the funding issue, in particular as it relates to the condition of research in universities But here I am suggesting a more formal, routine, and sustained activity, which would provide pushback against the changing political winds that interfere with the scientific enterprise.[40]

First, the new R&D monitor would complement the more traditional kinds of "advice on demand" that NASEM offers on specific scientific and technological problems the federal government faces (including the design and evaluation of social, economic, demographic, and educational programs). In addition, NASEM would report on investments of foundations and other nongovernmental providers. Placing such a monitoring function in an independent and respected scientific body, one that thrives on interdisciplinary consensus seeking (as I describe briefly in chapter 3), would protect it at least to some extent from charges that it is just one more outlet for special pleading by whiny scientists.

Second, to further reinforce what might be called the "optical credibility" of the activity, the charter change should reference the importance of including a diverse representation of stakeholders. The amendment could stipulate that the group within NASEM responsible for the new activity be composed of not only so-called "hard scientists" (including those working on the *very hard* behavioral, social, and education sciences), but also an eclectic representation of stakeholders. Scholars from the humanities, local political leaders, parents of children in public schools, and others could be active and important contributors to the effort. Requiring involvement of the NAEd would ensure not only added expertise but the inclusion of multiple and diverse voices of research methods and priorities.[41]

Finally, the new reporting function would provide a vehicle for expansion and enrichment of the kinds of data now provided by organizations such as the Foundation Center, a nonprofit organization that provides information about and resources to the philanthropic sector.[42] Given the existing infrastructure of data and its accessibility (via increasingly agile websites), the added value of involvement by the NASEM and NAEd would be the credibility that derives from the scientific prestige and processes of the institutions and their track record for producing useful syntheses of findings for broad public consumption.

POLICY OPTION IV: ADVISE THE ADVISERS

- *Convene a summit of the major think tanks, research organizations, and foundations to develop and implement performance indicators for the advice industry, which would include measures of the relative strength of peer review and of the advocacy orientation of the organizations.*

The unique history of think tanks and other research and evaluation organizations, as essential contributors to healthy policy discourse, makes it imperative to consider threats to their sustainability and utility. Continued growth in the number of such organizations and in their scope of work, coupled with their pursuit of competitive edge in an increasingly crowded field, creates incentives for behavior that may compromise their credibility as sources of nonpartisan and reliable information derived from objective empirical inquiry.

My proposed policy option is of a more hortatory type. Unlike proposals that have more enforcement capacity, through law or tax requirements, here the idea is to encourage leaders of private organizations to explore together the possibility of joint action aimed at reinforcing their individual and collective purposes. Assuming they can resist the temptation to collude in ways that might violate antitrust laws, the hope is they could reach a consensus on some measures to provide mutual benefit with limited risk.

Collective choices

So far, I have suggested policies or interventions—adjustment to the 5 percent charitable deduction rule, establishment of congressional and state-level research entities—that relate mainly to the philanthropic and government sectors, with emphasis on their respective roles as funders of social science and education research. Here I focus on the advice industry, that increasingly dense ecology of think tanks and evaluation entities supplying billions of dollars worth of options and recommendations for policy makers.

My main anxiety about these organizations, as argued mostly in chapter 3, is that the convergence of institutional, political, and economic changes in the private and government sectors might gradually and somewhat furtively erode research standards and undermine the ideal of objective advice to inform policy. Moreover, prospects for advice-oriented organizations cannot be understood without attention to their financial reliance on private philanthropy and government, which are changing in the ways I have described in chapters 1 and 2.

Given their legitimate interests in maintaining financial and intellectual advantage, private think tanks and research organizations (whether for profit or nonprofit) are not likely—on their own—to be willing or able to overcome the forces of competition and take risks that they may perceive as threatening to their very existence. The challenge is to find ways to encourage some form of collective or collaborative action designed to benefit the sector as a whole without expecting any one organization to take on the responsibility solely. I have in mind a bit of mutually acceptable coercion, enforced voluntarily.

One possibility for this group of think tank leaders to consider would be to take advantage of the work of the Lauder Institute at the University of Pennsylvania (see also the references in chapter 3), which provides survey-based data on think tanks in the United States and abroad. Under the auspices of a reputable and independent group such as this one, regular reporting on peer-review mechanisms—perhaps with a kind of labeling system that categorizes organizations with respect to important indicators of their aspiration toward methodological integrity—would provide useful information to consumers of their reports, while at the same time creating incentives for self-improvement. In addition, occasional case studies of organizations confronting the challenges of maintaining scientific integrity, in an increasingly competitive and difficult funding environment, would provide useful information to the general public and to the current and prospective clients of research organizations. This added set of functions would become a valued resource to the new organizations I recommended earlier, should they be established. The CEO, for example, would use the results of the labeling exercise and related information to guide its choice of studies upon which to base syntheses and develop policy options for Congress and/or the states.

A perhaps obvious challenge is to figure out who would fund this sort of expansion of activity. My recommendation is to convene a leadership summit of the major think tanks and evaluation firms—I would start with those most active in education policy analysis—to present the case for a modest allocation of a portion of the fees they collect toward the costs of these new public accountability activities. They would need to agree on such a plan together (perhaps similar to how members of the Motion Picture Association of America have agreed on the labeling of films with respect to their content). In addition, this strategy might be linked to the proposal I outlined earlier regarding the requirement for foundations to allocate a percentage of their assets toward research and evaluation. Earmarking a portion of those funds to finance the development of a valid and reliable set of indicators of performance in think tanks and related organizations would be a worthwhile endeavor.[43]

A CODA: FREQUENTLY QUESTIONED ANSWERS

My main concern in this book is about the sustainability of independent and credible research as inputs to improved education policy. But I may be guilty of the very sin I have tried to expose. After all, my arguments might be seen as just one more example of special pleading from another self-interested party: as someone trained to believe that policy analysis is about the application of scientific thinking to the design and assessment of public programs and processes, and as someone who continues to make part of his living from that endeavor, my contemplation of how the converging forces of philanthropy and public funding of science threaten policy research is, admittedly, less than pure in its motivations. Still, I will attempt a summary. In keeping with the themes of this book, my concluding recommendations should be viewed as advice intended to stimulate contestation, debate, and dissent.

Here is an abridged version of the basic argument. Changes in the magnitude and direction of philanthropy directed toward social programs generally and education specifically are creating significant pressures on the research community and threatening the viability of objective and independent inquiry as input to policy and practice. What was once a sector devoted primarily to support for general improvements in physical and social infrastructure, including knowledge production and the enhancement of opportunities for cultural and educational advancement, has evolved toward specific programmatic investments aligned with partisan or ideological dispositions.

Acting strategically is not a bad thing. On the contrary, my baseline assumption aligns with views expressed by Paul Brest and Hal Harvey: "A philanthropist's conception of what is good for society determines his or her philanthropic goals, and these values can vary greatly . . . [R]egardless of motive, philanthropists want to use their money to best effect."[44] So the problem is not that donors have strategic goals, which is a good thing; rather it is that their incentives to fund objective research and evaluation—in conjunction with or in addition to their programmatic investments—are not always compatible with their natural proclivities to seek evidence that their projects are succeeding. With only a few exceptions, the major foundations involved in education philanthropy today allocate the bulk of their contributions to programs rather than to the production of general knowledge; researchers seeking private support, therefore, for work that is more basic—especially if it challenges the assumptions implicit in those foundations' activities—face increasingly limited opportunities and are pressured to tailor their studies (ex ante) or communicate findings (ex post) opportunistically in ways that don't risk alienating their funders.

Context and perspective are important. Much of the harsh criticism leveled at philanthropy doesn't address the paucity of research or its quality, per se; it focuses instead on the assumed ideological or political preferences of the funders. Complaints about Gates Foundation support of Race to the Top, for example, have more to do with the general disdain for holding teachers accountable for student performance than with the absence of solid empirical evidence about the effectiveness of such a strategy. In other words, it's not obvious that there would ever be sufficient scientific evidence to change the most fervent philosophical or ideological preconceptions that shape people's attitudes toward various education reforms or the ways in which philanthropists (and others) try to influence those reforms. (It would be nice to believe, though, that evidence can actually help shape or refine people's prior beliefs and attitudes.) As I have argued in previous chapters, dissent from substantive aspects of private or public funding is often camouflaged in complaints about process and methodological impurities.

But none of this should distract us from the possibility that changing patterns and norms of philanthropy are creating significant challenges to a community struggling to acquire resources to support potentially vital research. That would be bad enough—in terms of the effects on research and the public appreciation of the essential role of philanthropy in civic society—but it is exacerbated by the unstable and at times hostile attitudes toward science held by the political elites charged with stewardship of the public good. Here, then, is the second gale force contributing to the storm, which derives its strength from the combination of (1) the rising supply of highly trained social scientists, (2) fiscal constraints that limit federal spending, and (3) political opposition to research on sensitive topics.

The convergence of these forces more than doubles their separable effects, because of the inherent links between the private and public sectors. Scholars facing shrinking odds of getting federal grants increasingly turn to—and are encouraged by—the private foundation sector, but there they confront increasingly circumscribed agendas and, in some cases, explicit resistance to funding anything that might yield results unfriendly to the funders' ideological preferences or political interests. In this context, the brief discussion in chapter 3 about allegations regarding questionable practices that may result from foreign funding of think tanks is germane, even if it doesn't relate specifically to education research. Although I focused in that chapter mostly on the non-university sector, the problem could affect academic scientists, too, especially in an era of financial challenges faced by the institutions of higher education in which they work. At stake here is a more general principle: the possibility that norms of inquiry—including study designs, evaluation methods, and reporting of findings—might be distorted because of competitive pressures.

The upshot of my convergence argument is that the quality and credibility of scientific research oriented (directly or indirectly) toward the improvement of the public welfare, as well as the more focused advice industry that responds to specific questions articulated by government, are at risk; and that the challenges of sustaining and nurturing independent, high-quality, objective education research needed to advance the goals of improved teaching and learning demand the attention of educators, researchers, and policy makers. As a step toward the fuller development of policy strategies to deal with this set of problems, I have offered some preliminary ideas, described earlier in this chapter and summarized in table 4.2.

TABLE 4.2 Policy options: Rationale, benefits, challenges

Policy option	Principal rationale	Additional benefits	Challenges
I. Tweak the tax			
Increase the required amount of philanthropic giving, from the current 5% rule, as condition for continuation of the charitable deduction benefit.	Use the additional resources to establish a new entity for the support of research and evaluations that are not otherwise likely to be funded. (See also "Advise the advisers" below)	Allay concerns that the charitable deduction rules, as currently defined, do not promote sufficient redistribution of private wealth to the public good.	Anticipated resistance by some foundations; difficulty of devising an equitable formula so that large foundations pay a proportionally greater share than small individual and family foundations.
II. Organize for knowledge			
Establish a new Congressional Education Office (CEO) to serve as a vertically integrated research unit to advise Congress on education.	Such an entity, modeled after the Office of Technology Assessment, would filter existing research and data and give lawmakers confidence in the quality of evidence used to guide policy strategies.	Such a unit in Congress would relieve other agencies, including the Congressional Budget Office and Government Accounting Office, from some of their involvement in analyses of education-specific policy.	Congressional resistance to creation of any new entity, and especially one focused on education policy analysis, is likely to be strong during tight budget times and in an era of strident partisanship.

Explore the possibility of a similar entity, attached to the Council of Chief State School Officers or National Governors Association.	Given the pressures on states and localities to devise innovative standards and assessment systems, under ESSA (and other legislation), having a source of credible and objective data would be greatly valued.	Deliberations that would be facilitated by this type of entity would yield opportunities for collaboration and cooperation among states and districts on a wider range of educational issues.	Funding for such an entity would have to come from voluntary donations by the member state education offices and/or state legislatures, which poses challenges of political and collective action.

III. Account for science

Amend the charter of the National Academies of Sciences, Engineering, and Medicine to include a requirement for regular reporting on the condition of federally funded research and development.	This type of report would hold Congress and the executive branch accountable for their willingness and ability to sustain and grow the research enterprise in the United States.	Development of the procedures needed to produce these reports would necessitate regular discussions and cooperative deliberations between the scientific community, the government, and various stakeholders.	Charter amendment requires congressional action, which may encounter resistance from the same factions whose attitudes toward science bring about the need for such an activity.
Consider a special added clause in the amended charter that would mandate collaboration with the National Academy of Education.	The special funding issues regarding education research would be better handled with specific expertise and neutrality of the NAEd.	This collaboration could enhance prospects for other collaborations between the academies, and the possible development of a rationale for a separate NAEd charter.	The same challenges would manifest themselves here and possibly would be more complex, given the particular problems of the reputation of education research in Congress.

(continues)

TABLE 4.2 Policy options: Rationale, benefits, challenges *(continued)*

Policy option	Principal rationale	Additional benefits	Challenges
IV. Advise the advisers			
Convene a summit of leaders of think tanks and other research organizations, along with foundation officers, and explore the possibility of earmarking a portion of the funds from policy option I (above) to support the development and implementation of performance indicators for the advice industry.	Such a system of indicators would provide useful information to consumers of research-based advice regarding its objectivity and credibility.	Developing the indicators, including a possible system of labels that designate relative strength of peer review and other mechanisms aimed at reducing various types of biases, would require facilitated meetings of the leadership of the major organizations, which would have the ancillary benefit of enabling the sharing of information about various research practices and processes.	Deciding which organizations would participate in this indicator system, and reaching agreement on the scope and style of the indicators, would be costly.

In my proposed menu of policy responses are economic and institutional remedies, restated here without a particular sequence or priority ranking in mind but rather to suggest the value of considering them as a package. The four sets of suggestions require the combined efforts of the private philanthropic and government sectors and the cooperation of the leadership of the advice industry. Their direct and indirect benefits need to be weighed against the costs of overcoming obvious (and less obvious) financial and political obstacles, which I have attempted to signal. Nontrivial issues of feasibility warrant continued discussion. Table 4.2 is a starting point, not a presumption of optimality: I am less certain of the positive effects of these proposals than I am of their role in framing the kinds of questions I hope policy makers and researchers will be willing to address.

Indeed, my initial impulse was to lay out the policy options in terms of questions. But this book has already tipped perhaps too far in the direction of asking questions rather than providing definitive answers. Asked why I respond to difficult questions with more questions, I usually rely on the wisdom of the sages and say, "Why not?" But here I will deviate from this policy. To the biggest question that has motivated this book—do we have the political and economic will to preserve, protect, and defend scientific research, generally and as a source of knowledge to ensure the future of education?—I will offer a definitive, objective, unequivocal, and empirically grounded answer. I hope so.

Notes

INTRODUCTION

1. Diane Ravitch, *The Death and Life of the Great American School System: How Testing and Choice Are Undermining Education* (New York: Basic Books, 2010). Full disclosure: Diane and I are friends, and in fact I had read the draft of her book and urged Diane to dial down the strident rhetoric that I felt would obscure the valid points she was trying to make. So much for my influence . . .
2. Diane Ravitch, in interview with Amy Goodman, *Democracy Now!*, http://www.democracynow.org/2010/3/5/protests. Ravitch is one of the most widely read and cited public intellectuals of American education, at least as measured by Rick Hess's annual ranking of the most publicly influential education scholars (see http://blogs.edweek.org/edweek/rick_hess_straight_up/2015/01/2015_rhsu_edu-scholar_public_influence_rankings.html).
3. Joanne Barkan, "Got Dough? How Billionaires Rule Our Schools," *Dissent*, Winter 2011. Barkan is a prolific writer (of, among other things, children's books) and a regular contributor to *Dissent* and other journals and magazines. Her interest in philanthropy continues: see, e.g., her more recent post, "How to Criticize 'Big Philanthropy' Effectively," *Dissent*, April 9, 2014, https://www.dissentmagazine.org/blog/how-to-criticize-big-philanthropy-effectively.
4. Diane Ravitch, "Why I Changed My Mind About School Reform," *Wall Street Journal*, March 9, 2010. There is a courageous side to this turnaround that is often neglected by the punditocracy: knowing Ravitch as I do, I believe her decision was based on an honest rereading of the data and a reconsideration of the benefits and risks of policies she once espoused. Whether it needed quite such an acerbic tone is another matter. In any case, she is not alone in her quest to rethink once strongly held views. For lively and poignant confessionals by education researchers, leading in some cases to substantially revised judgments, see Richard Elmore, ed., *I Used To Think . . . And Now I Think . . . : Twenty Leading Educators Reflect on the Work of School Reform* (Cambridge, MA: Harvard Education Press, 2011).
5. See Foundation Center, Top 100 US Foundations by Asset Size, http://foundationcenter.org/findfunders/topfunders/top100assets.html.

6. Ellen Condliffe Lagemann, "The Politics of Knowledge: The Carnegie Corporation and the Formulation of Public Policy," *History of Education Quarterly* 27, no. 2 (Summer 1987): 209. For more comprehensive analysis, see Lagemann, *The Politics of Knowledge: The Carnegie Corporation, Philanthropy, and Public Policy* (Chicago: University of Chicago Press, 1992). Andrew Carnegie's exceptional stature and role in the early days of American philanthropic life are described eloquently in other literature as well, most notably in Joel Fleishman, *The Foundation: A Great American Secret; How Private Wealth is Changing the World* (New York: Public Affairs, 2009).

7. On the general advantages of taking a longer view in matters of economics especially, see William Baumol, Sue Anne Batey Blackman, and Edward Wolff, *Productivity and American Leadership: The Long View* (Cambridge, MA: MIT Press, 1991). On the evolution of science policy in the United States, which is the focus of chapter 2, see, e.g., Richard Atkinson, "Universities: At the Center of U.S. Research," University of California, https://escholarship.org/uc/item/8cw735xj; and Daniel Sarewitz, *Frontiers of Illusion* (Philadelphia: Temple University Press, 1996). For commentary on misguided efforts to prejudge science, see Michael Feuer and Richard Atkinson, "Absurd Studies of Science's Puzzles Prove Their Worth," *San Jose Mercury News*, July 23, 2006.

8. The debate about the condition of American science is heated. Some of the best research and commentary is in Michael Teitelbaum, *Falling Behind? Boom, Bust, and the Global Race for Scientific Talent* (Princeton, NJ: Princeton University Press, 2014); and Yu Xie and Alexandra Killewald, *Is American Science in Decline?* (Cambridge, MA: Harvard University Press, 2012). For analysis focused on implications of international test score comparisons, see Michael Feuer, "No Country Left Behind: Notes on the Rhetoric of International Comparisons of Education" (William Angoff Invited Lecture, ETS, Princeton, NJ, August 2012); and Michael Feuer, ed., "STEM Education: Progress and Prospects," *The Bridge*, special issue, March 2013, introduction.

9. This is a rough estimate, possibly on the low side, extrapolated from data summarized in Ken Prewitt et al., *Using Science as Evidence in Public Policy* (Washington, DC: National Academy Press, 2012).

10. Selwyn Duke, *The New American*, October 14, 2015, http://www.thenewamerican.com/usnews/crime/item/21760-harvard-gun-control-study-destroys-gun-control-agenda.

11. Thomas Medvetz, *Think Tanks in America* (Chicago: University of Chicago Press, 2014), 237.

12. The phrase "evidence-informed" suggests a subtle appreciation for the role of research in policy making, different from the more conventional rhetoric of "evidence-*based*." The distinction is due to Ken Prewitt, whose contributions

to our understanding of the politics of science have been seminal. See, e.g., Prewitt et al., *Using Science as Evidence in Public Policy.*

13. I am grateful to my former colleague Barbara Torrey for this lovely turn of phrase. A different formulation comes from the comics, which Caroline Chauncey was kind enough to point out: as Marge Simpson discovered while looking for Homer at the Carnival in Rio, "I can dance and worry at the same time!"

14. For this, I use publicly available data on foundations made possible by the work of the nonprofit Foundation Center: http://foundationcenter.org /findfunders/topfunders/top100assets.html. In addition, I rely partly on the fine work of Sarah Reckhow, *Follow the Money: How Foundation Dollars Change Public School Politics* (Oxford: Oxford University Press, 2012); and Sarah Reckhow and Jeffrey W. Snyder, "The Expanding Role of Philanthropy in Education Politics," *Educational Researcher* 43 (May 2014): 186–195. See also Jeff Henig, *Spin Cycle: How Research Is Used in Policy Debates: The Case of Charter Schools* (New York: Russell Sage, 2008); and Frederick Hess and Jeff Henig, ed., *The New Education Philanthropy: Politics, Policy, and Reform* (Cambridge, MA: Harvard Education Press, 2015).

15. Funding of training in the sciences is not without its complexities. Support for early-career scholars provides needed resources to university-based labs and prepares future generations of scientists. But when overall funding for science dips, a result can be the oversupply of highly trained researchers, many of whom are left facing shrinking job opportunities. I am grateful to Peter Blair for bringing this important reminder to my attention.

16. A book like this one, about the importance of credible evidence, should be extra careful with words like "anecdotal." Here I want to emphasize that I'm not necessarily buying the criticism about financial influence impeding the work of think tanks, as implied by articles in the mainstream press. I borrow the notion of "clinching" an argument, as distinct from "vouching" for one, suggesting different levels of evidentiary certainty, from Nancy Cartwright, *Hunting Causes and Using Them: Approaches in Philosophy and Economics* (Cambridge: Cambridge University Press, 2007).

17. See Michael Feuer, L. Towne, and R. Shavelson, "Scientific Culture and Education Research," *Educational Researcher* 31, no. 8 (November 2002): 28–29; Michael Feuer, L. Towne, and R. Shavelson, reply to comments on "Scientific Culture and Educational Research," *Educational Researcher* 31, no. 8 (November 2002): 28–29; and Michael Feuer, response to "Scientifically Based Research in Education: Epistemology and Ethics, " by Elizabeth St. Pierre, *Adult Education Quarterly* 56, no. 4 (August 2006): 267–273.

18. See Lee Shulman, *The Wisdom of Practice: Essays on Teaching, Learning, and*

Learning to Teach, ed. Suzanne Wilson (New York: Jossey-Bass, 2004); and Michael Feuer, "Evidence and Advocacy," in ed. Michael Feuer, Amy Berman, and Richard Atkinson, *Past as Prologue: The National Academy of Education at 50* (Washington, DC: National Academy of Education, 2015).

19. See the home page of the NAS, and the link to "What We Do," http://nas.edu/about/whatwedo/index.html.

20. Peter Blair, *Congress's Own Think Tank: Learning from the Legacy of the Office of Technology Assessment (1972–1995)* (New York: Palgrave, 2013), 32.

21. Medvetz, *Think Tanks in America*, 259.

CHAPTER 1

1. Two authoritative sources provide slightly different numbers for Carnegie's initial endowment. Ellen Lagemann has it at $125 million, while Joel Fleishman says it was $135 million. See Ellen Condliffe Lagemann, *The Politics of Knowledge: The Carnegie Corporation, Philanthropy, and Public Policy* (Chicago: University of Chicago Press, 1989), 12; and Joel Fleishman, *The Foundation: A Great American Secret* (New York: Public Affairs, 2009), 10.

2. See, for example, Diane Ravitch, *The Death and Life of the Great American School System* (New York: Basic Books, 2010); and Matthew Lynch, *Huffington Post* blog, http://www.huffingtonpost.com/matthew-lynch-edd/how-the-billionaire-boys_b_6383298.html.

3. I rely on two sources for these estimates: the Foundation Center, http://data.foundationcenter.org/#/foundations/all/nationwide/total/list/2012; and Giving USA, http://givingusa.org/giving-usa-2015-press-release-giving-usa-americans-donated-an-estimated-358-38-billion-to-charity-in-2014-highest-total-in-reports-60-year-history/.

4. Fleishman, *The Foundation*, 342.

5. See, for example, John Cassidy, "Mark Zuckerberg and the Rise of Philanthrocapitalism," *New Yorker*, December 3, 2015, http://www.newyorker.com/news/john-cassidy/mark-zuckerberg-and-the-rise-of-philanthrocapitalism; and James Surowiecki, "In Defense of Philanthrocapitalism," *New Yorker*, December 21, 2015, http://www.newyorker.com/magazine/2015/12/21/in-defense-of-philanthrocapitalism. I will have more to say about their commentaries in chapter 4.

6. Donald G. McNeil, "A Milestone in Africa: No Polio Cases in a Year," *New York Times*, August 11, 2015, http://www.nytimes.com/2015/08/12/health/a-milestone-in-africa-one-year-without-a-case-of-polio.html?_r=0.

7. On the origins and prospects for the "Common Core," see, e.g., Matthew Frizzell and Tara Dunderdale, *A Compendium of Research on the Common Core State Standards* (Washington, DC: Center on Education Policy, 2015),

http://www.cep-dc.org/index.cfm?DocumentTopicID=1. For the status of the science standards, see http://www.nextgenscience.org/next-generation-science-standards.

8. Silicon Valley is a community foundation and operates differently from the other foundations listed here. See http://www.siliconvalleycf.org/who-we-are.

9. Carnegie Corporation of New York, 2011 Annual Report, https://www.carnegie.org/media/filer_public/a8/16/a8169ca7-cc1c-4e2c-8c46-c471b082bd47/ccny_annualreport_2014.pdf.

10. Hewlett's Global Development and Population Program made $87 million in grants—almost three times the amount allocated in its domestic education programs—focused on governance, education in the developing world, family planning and reproductive health, and reducing teen and unplanned pregnancy in disadvantaged communities in the San Francisco Bay Area. The Performing Arts program made $14 million in grants to support the arts generally and to enhance community engagement among disadvantaged populations in the Bay Area specifically.

11. See "How We're Challenging Inequality," homepage, Ford Foundation, April 2016: https://www.fordfoundation.org/. For commentary, see, Larissa MacFarquhar, "What Money Can Buy: Darren Walker and the Ford Foundation set out to conquer inequality," *New Yorker*, January 4, 2016, http://www.newyorker.com/magazine/2016/01/04/what-money-can-buy-profiles-larissa-macfarquhar.

12. Walton Family Foundation, 2014 Annual Report, http://www.waltonfamily foundation.org/newsroom/foundation-releases-2014-annual-report.

13. "Entrepreneurship for the Public Good In Education, Science and the Arts: The Broad Foundations 2013–2014 Report," http://www.broadfoundation.org/asset/101-2013-14tbfreport.pdf.

14. Ibid.

15. I recall hearing Mr. Broad's carte blanche of education schools during a conference sponsored by the Milken Family Foundation, in 2012 or 2013. Unfortunately, I do not have a citation to offer.

16. Quoted by Motoko Rich, "Billionaire Suspends Prize Given to Schools," *New York Times*, February 9, 2015.

17. See "2015 Packard Fellowships in Science and Engineering Awarded to Eighteen Researchers," https://www.packard.org/2015/10/2015-packard-fellowships-in-science-and-engineering-awarded-to-eighteen-researchers/.

18. Sarah Reckhow and Jeffrey W. Snyder, "The Expanding Role of Philanthropy in Education Politics," *Educational Researcher* 43 (May 2014): 190. This article expands on analysis in Sarah Reckhow, *Follow the Money: How Foundation Dollars Change Public School Politics* (Oxford: Oxford University Press, 2012).

19. Ibid., 186.

20. Ibid., 193.

21. Ibid.

22. Several histories of American education have made this point eloquently and forcefully. See, e.g., David Tyack and Larry Cuban, *Tinkering toward Utopia: A Century of Public School Reform* (Cambridge, MA: Harvard University Press, 1997); the agility of the American public school system and its capacity for innovation is discussed also in Claudia Goldin and Lawrence Katz, *The Race Between Education and Technology* (Cambridge, MA: Belknap Press, 2008).

23. See Fay Twersky and Karen Lindblom, "Evaluation Principles and Practices," William and Flora Hewlett Foundation, 2012, http://www.hewlett.org/uploads/documents/EvaluationPrinciples-FINAL.pdf. For the Wallace Foundation strategy, see: http://www.wallacefoundation.org/learn-about-wallace/approach-and-strategy/Pages/our-approach-to-philanthropy.aspx. The founding executive director of the Jim Joseph Foundation, Chip Edelsberg, and colleagues Sandy Edwards and Stacie Cherner deserve credit for their enlightened approach to the thorny problems of program evaluation. (Full disclosure: I have been involved in a project to help the Jim Joseph Foundation develop a framework of common metrics.)

24. Charities Aid Foundation, November 2014.

25. See Fleishman, *The Foundation*, 329–330. Although he underscores the role of the tax exemption perhaps more strongly than I would, in the light of data from the World Giving Index, Fleishman's salute to the uniquely American traditions of "polyarchy" is critical to understanding the current and future status of philanthropy.

26. See Peter Davy, "The Power of Perks," *Wall Street Journal*, March 1, 2010, http://www.wsj.com/articles/SB10001424052748703787304575075400171203026.

27. US Congress, Joint Committee on Taxation, "Present Law and Background Relating to the Federal Tax Treatment of Charitable Contributions," February 14, 2013, https://www.jct.gov/publications.html?func=startdown&id=4506. For discussion of the rules pertaining to the deduction, see, e.g., http://grantspace.org/tools/knowledge-base/Funding-Resources/Foundations/payout.

28. David Callahan, "Who Will Watch the Charities?" *New York Times*, May 30, 2015, http://www.nytimes.com/2015/05/31/opinion/sunday/who-will-watch-the-charities.html?_r=0.

29. Fleishman, *The Foundation*, 103.

30. Alexis de Tocqueville, *Democracy in America*, English trans., ed. Harvey C. Mansfield and Delba Winthrop (Chicago: University of Chicago Press, 2000),

x. Cited also in Fleishman, *The Foundation*, 72. I have taken the liberty to add the bracketed words.

31. Frederick M. Hess, "Philanthropy gets in the ring," American Enterprise Institute, https://www.aei.org/publication/philanthropy-gets-in-the-ring/.

32. Rob Reich, "What Are Foundations For?," *Boston Review*, Forum, March 1, 2013, http://www.bostonreview.net/forum/foundations-philanthropy-democracy.

33. Where to draw the line between permissible foundation-government inter-action and what would be deemed lobbying for partisan causes is one of the more important judgments that foundation officers need to make. Advocacy has to be backed by evidence derived from studies that have been undertaken and is not merely the expression of political or ideological preference. Murki-ness here is one reason that foundations need legal teams. Influence that goes in the other direction—from government to foundations—may bump into other obstacles, such as public resistance to excessive meddling by political agencies in the workings of the private sector, but government is not subject to the kinds of threats (or incentives) faced by foundations eager to maintain their tax benefit. I am grateful to Mike McPherson for alerting me to the subtleties of the law with respect to partisanship and advocacy.

34. On the current relations between the federal government and private founda-tions, see Stephen Sawchuk, "Foundation Cash Boosts Education Advocacy Groups," *Education Week*, May 16, 2012. Fleishman (*The Foundation*) issues a friendly warning to foundations about the importance of some form of self-monitoring and regulation.

35. Olivier Zunz, *Philanthropy in America: A History* (Princeton, NJ: Princeton University Press, 2011). The Nixon irony, which I also alluded to in the intro-duction, goes even deeper. This was, after all, the president who was what my friend Peter Blair calls "a study in contrasts." As Peter notes, with his keen appreciation of nuance, this was the president who "created EPA [Environ-mental Protection Administration], OSHA [Occupational Safety and Health Administration], NOAA [National Oceanic and Atmospheric Administra-tion]; integrated public schools in the South, established a federal affirmative action program, indexed social security for inflation, imposed wage and price controls, appointed three justices who voted with the majority in Roe v. Wade, and even advocated a single payer comprehensive national health insurance for all Americans! There aren't even many Democrats today who would go along with all those." How times change!

36. Jeffrey Toobin, "Hard Cases," *New Yorker*, March 9, 2015.

37. US Supreme Court, 378 U.S. 184,84 S.Ct. 1676,12 L.Ed.2d 793,Nico JACO-BELLIS, Appellant, v. State of Ohio, No. 11. Reargued April 1, 1964. Decided June 22, 1964.

38. For a discussion of rationality in the face of complexity and ambiguity, see Michael J. Feuer, *Moderating the Debate: Rationality and the Promise of American Education* (Cambridge, MA: Harvard Education Press, 2006). For these issues, the seminal sources are Oliver E. Williamson, *Markets and Hierarchies* (New York: Free Press, 1975); and Herbert Simon, "Theories of Bounded Rationality," in eds. C. B. McGuire and Roy Radner, *Decision and Organization: A Volume in Honor of Jacob Marschak* (Amsterdam: North Holland, 1972).

39. Frederick Hess was one of the first policy analysts to ignite the argument about philanthropic involvement in school reform. See his edited volume, *With the Best of Intentions: How Philanthropy Is Reshaping K–12 Education* (Cambridge, MA: Harvard Education Press, 2005). For a recent rebuttal and discussion among philanthropists, see http://www.philanthropyroundtable. org/topic/excellence_in_philanthropy/rethinking_americas_schools.

40. See, e.g., Valerie Strauss, "Gates Foundation pours millions more into Common Core," *Washington Post*, May 12, 2015, http://www.washingtonpost .com/blogs/answer-sheet/wp/2015/05/12/gates-foundation-pours-millions -more-into-common-core/.

41. Keeping in mind the irony noted in my preface, readers will enjoy reading Diane Ravitch's open letter to Lamar Alexander, former secretary of education (and Ravitch's boss) and now chairman of the Senate Committee on Health, Labor, and Pensions. See http://dianeravitch.net/2015/01/20/from-diane-ravitch-to-senator-lamar-alexander-dont-forget-rule-84-in-the-little-plaid-book/.

42. Data summarized here are from these sources: US Department of Education, National Center for Education Statistics, *Digest of Education Statistics, 2013,* Table 106.10: "Expenditures of educational institutions related to the gross domestic product, by level of institution: Selected years, 1929–30 through 2012–13," http://nces.ed.gov/programs/digest/d13/tables/dt13_106.10.asp; and US Department of Education, National Center for Education Statistics, Digest of Education Statistics, Table 421, https://nces.ed.gov/programs/digest/d12/ tables/dt12_421.asp. Recent data provided by Richard Murnane (in a personal communication, for which I am grateful) suggest a downturn in the enrollment of children in private elementary schools, from roughly 12% in 1970 to 9% in 2010; at the high school level, the enrollment has been fairly stable, at roughly 8% during that time period. Other sources provide different estimates of the federal role, depending on definitions and methodology. See, e.g., National Science and Technology Council, "A Report from the Federal Inventory of STEM Education Fast-Track Action Committee on STEM Education," White House Office of Science and Technology Policy, 2011; and

Jason Delisle, "Putting a Number on Federal Education Spending," *New York Times*, February 27, 2013, http://economix.blogs.nytimes.com/2013/02/27/putting-a-number-on-federal-education-spending/?_r=2. US Department of Education, National Center for Education Statistics, *The Condition of Education*, January 2014, http://nces.ed.gov/programs/coe/indicator_cgc.asp; and *Digest of Education Statistics*, 2013, http://nces.ed.gov/programs/digest/d13/tables/dt13_303.10.asp. No wonder that education researcher Jay Green has likened the effect of philanthropy on education reform to the effect of spitting on changing the course of ocean waves. See Hess, *With the Best of Intentions*.

43. US Congress, Congressional Budget Office, "Using Public-Private Partnerships to Carry Out Highway Projects," January 9, 2012.

44. See http://adoptahighway.net/about-us/. Ironically, the United States is one of the few countries where toll roads are mostly owned and operated by the public sector; see World Bank, http://www.worldbank.org/transport/roads/toll_rds.htm.

45. A fundamental reality of American philanthropy is the extraordinary sums donated by individuals and families. The dedicated philanthropist Carrie Morgridge has noted, "[I]ndividual American households donate five times as much to charities and other nonprofits as all the foundations in the country combined." See Carrie Morgridge, *Every Gift Matters* (Austin, TX: Greenleaf Book Group Press, 2015). For data on charitable giving by individuals, families, and so on, see http://www.nptrust.org/philanthropic-resources/charitable-giving-statistics/.

46. Fleishman, *The Foundation*, 45.

47. For example, Robert E. Schenk, "Altruism as a source of self-interested behavior," *Public Choice* 53, no. 2 (1987): 187–192. For a lovely contemplation of how doers of good deeds, generosity, and "grace" benefit from their own behavior, see Sarah Kaufman, *The Art of Grace: On Moving Well Through Life* (New York: W. W. Norton & Company, 2015). I discuss these issues in greater detail in chapter 4.

48. Mancur Olson, *The Logic of Collective Action: Public Goods and the Theory of Groups* (Cambridge, MA: Harvard Economic Studies, 1971), 13. Whether the coercion implied by taxation has to be "self-imposed" raises the question of the relationship between tax policy and political organization. As Olson notes, the extreme view, held by people like Knut Wicksell, for whom "coercion is always an evil in itself" and that therefore the state should never exact taxes from a citizen without his consent." A more moderate view, which seems to characterize the acceptance of coercion in American democracy at least, is that legislative majorities that are assumed to reflect the general will of the public are the source of tax and other compulsory policies.

49. For the basic arguments, see Edwin Mills, *The Economics of Environmental Quality* (New York: Norton, 1978).

50. National Philanthropic Trust, http://www.nptrust.org/philanthropic-resources/charitable-giving-statistics/. It is worth noting that corporate foundations, which may operate with a different blend of private and public interest strategies, donated roughly $5 billion, from an asset base of about $25.5 billion, in 2013. For data, see http://data.foundationcenter.org/#/foundations/all/nationwide/total/list/2013.

51. See, e.g., Stephen Ohlemacher, "New Limits On Tax Deductions May Reduce Donations, Charities Fear," *Huffington Post*, January 16, 2013, http://www.huffingtonpost.com/2013/01/16/tax-deduction-limits-charity_n_2489696.html. See, also, Rob Reich's *Boston Review* commentary (Reich, "What Are Foundations For?"), in which he relays an anecdote about the philanthropist George Soros, as recounted by Mark Dowie: "During a meeting to resolve a disagreement about grant-making priorities, Soros is alleged to have announced, 'This is my money. We will do it my way.' At which point a junior staff member interjected that roughly half of the money in the foundation was not his money, but the public's money, explaining, 'If you hadn't placed that money in OSI . . . about half of it would be in the Treasury.' Dowie reports that the junior staffer did not last long in the Soros foundation's employ." See Mark Dowie, *American Foundations: An Investigative History* (Cambridge, MA: MIT Press, 2001).

52. When I was an officer in my children's elementary school parent-teacher organization, circa 1988, I learned that we were funding the purchase of standardized tests to be administered in years not mandated by the Washington, DC, public schools. When I asked about this, I was told it was to make sure the kids had as much practice time as possible for college admissions tests they would take ten years later. As I recall, we didn't seek support from foundations, which in retrospect would have become easy scapegoats. The truth is I probably should have and could have advocated against the additional testing for my kids and their peers, regardless of who was paying for it, but I didn't. It seems wrong, or at least incomplete, to single out test developers for our overuse of tests without mentioning that there is a demand side that continues to purchase and use those tests. See, e.g., my article, "Future Directions for Educational Accountability: Notes for a Political Economy of Measurement," in *The Future of Test-based Educational Accountability*, ed. L. Shepard and K. Ryan (New York: Routledge, 2008).

53. "Revealed preference" and "externalities" are linchpins of microeconomic theory. For a quick overview, see, e.g., https://en.wikipedia.org/wiki/Revealed_preference; also Thomas Helbling, "Externalities: Prices Do Not Capture All

Costs," International Monetary Fund, March 28, 2012, http://www.imf.org/
external/pubs/ft/fandd/basics/external.htm.

54. To his credit, Bill Gates offered an honest appraisal of the small-schools initiative. See his 2009 letter, http://www.gatesfoundation.org/Who-We-Are/
Resources-and-Media/Annual-Letters-List/Annual-Letter-2009. Fleishman
is also complimentary of Gates for this public statement, an example of the
kind of self-monitoring that Fleishman believes is necessary for the philanthropic sector to save itself. See also David Marshak, "Why Did the Gates
Small-High-Schools Program Fail?," *Education Week*, commentary, February 19, 2010; and Peter McElroy, "The Annenberg Challenge: Lessons and
Legacy," Duke University, Center for Strategic Philanthropy and Civil Society, 2014, https://cspcs.sanford.duke.edu/sites/default/files/Annenberg%20
Challenge%20-%20Peter%20McElroy.pdf. Indeed, the evidence is mixed,
and as is often the case, the negative reviews tended to crowd out the more
optimistic findings. See Mary Anne Raywid, "Synthesis of Research / Small
Schools: A Reform That Works," *Educational Leadership* 55, no. 4 (December
1997/January 1998, http://www.ascd.org/publications/educational-leadership/
dec97/vol55/num04/-Small-Schools@-A-Reform-That-Works.aspx.

55. See my foreword in Jennings, *Presidents, Congress, and the Public Schools:
The Politics of Education Reform* (Cambridge, MA: Harvard Education Press,
2015), xi. For an extraordinarily interesting and important commentary on
the tendency to dismiss proposed action on grounds of incomplete data or the
likelihood of undesired consequences, see Albert Hirschman, *The Rhetoric of
Reaction: Perversity, Futility, Jeopardy* (Cambridge, MA: Harvard University
Press, 1991).

56. McElroy, "The Annenberg Challenge," 12.

CHAPTER 2

1. With apologies to the French philosophers who summarized their attitude
about man and God in just four words: "*L'homme propose, Dieu dispose.*" See,
e.g., http://www.age-of-the-sage.org/quotations/quotes/man_proposes_but
_god_disposes.html.

2. Vannevar Bush, *Science—The Endless Frontier: A Report to the President
on a Program for Postwar Scientific Research* (1945, repr.; Washington, DC,
National Science Foundation, 1990), https://www.nsf.gov/od/lpa/nsf50
/vbush1945.htm.

3. William Blanpied, "Inventing US Science Policy," *Physics Today* 51, no. 2
(February 1998): 34. Reprinted with permission by the National Science
Foundation, https://www.nsf.gov/about/history/nsf50/science_policy.jsp.

4. Patricia Pelfrey and Richard C. Atkinson, "Science and the Entrepreneurial University," *Issues in Science and Technology* 26, no. 4 (Summer 2010): 40; see also Richard C. Atkinson, "Vannevar Sets the Stage," in *Past as Prologue: The National Academy of Education at 50. Members Reflect*, ed. Michael Feuer, Amy Berman, and Richard C. Atkinson (Washington, DC: National Academy of Education, 2015).

5. Blanpied, "Inventing US Science Policy," 35. Also, J. M. England, *A Patron for Pure Science: The National Science Foundation's Formative Years* (Washington, DC: National Science Foundation, 1982), 30.

6. See Daryl Chubin et al., *Federally Funded Research: Decisions for a Decade* (Washington, DC: United States Congress Office of Technology Assessment, Government Printing Office, May 1991), 4, fn. 8. For the original Steelman report, see J. R. Steelman, *Science and Public Policy* (Washington, DC: Government Printing Office, August 1947; New York: Arno Press, 1980). And for additional discussion and interpretations of the Bush report, see Daniel Sarewitz, *Frontiers of Illusion: Science, Technology, and the Politics of Progress* (Philadelphia: Temple University Press, 1996).

7. Pelfrey and Atkinson, "Science and the Entrepreneurial University," 40.

8. See Donald Stokes, *Pasteur's Quadrant: Basic Science and Technological Innovation* (Washington, DC: Brookings Institution, 1997). For discussion of how Stokes's model relates to education research, see Michael Feuer, "Pure and Applied Science and Pasteur's Quadrant," in *Encyclopedia of Educational Theory*, ed. D. Philips et al. (Los Angeles: Sage Publications, 2014), 674–676. For earlier and influential treatment of these issues, see the classic by Charles Lindblom and David Cohen, *Usable Knowledge: Social Science and Social Problem Solving* (New Haven, CT: Yale University Press, 1979).

9. Note that Stokes's work appeared in 1997 and therefore had the advantage of fifty years of data on the realities of science funding. On the importance of "general" versus "specific" assets in economic theory, the classic statement is in Gary Becker, *Human Capital* (Cambridge, MA: National Bureau of Economic Research, 1964). For amendments to Becker's theory as related to education and training in the private sector, see Henry Glick and Michael Feuer, "Employer-Sponsored Training and the Governance of Specific Human Capital," *Quarterly Review of Economics and Business* 24, no. 2 (Summer 1984): 91–103; and Michael Feuer, Henry Glick, and Anand Desai, "Is Firm-Sponsored Education Viable?" *Journal of Economic Behavior and Organization* 8 (1987): 121–136. Economic perspectives on science, with emphasis on the social returns to research, began earlier—circa the mid-1950s—but still a decade or more after the Bush-Steelman papers. The classic work is by Robert Solow, "A Contribution to the Theory of Economic Growth," *Quarterly Journal of Economics* 70, no. 1 (1956): 65–94. See also E. Mansfield, "Contribution

of R and D to Economic Growth in the United States," *Science* CLXXV (February 4, 1972): 477–486.

10. I am grateful to Daryl Chubin for alerting me to a nuanced amendment to this history. Science policy may have benefited from intuitive insights among some of the key players, but at least according to the OTA report that Chubin edited (*Federally Funded Research*), policy was also influenced heavily by testimony from Nobel laureates in physics. This reminds me of what some wags refer to as "eminence-based" rather than "evidence-based" recommendations, a distinction that may sound familiar to people who have worked in agencies like OTA and the NAS. It is beyond the scope of this book, but my favorite example of the role of intuition in the scientific process concerns Galileo's theory of gravity: see, e.g., Roger N. Shepard, "The Step to Rationality: The Efficacy of Thought Experiments in Science, Ethics, and Free Will," *Cognitive Science* 32 (2008): 3–35.

11. Estimates based on data in National Science Foundation, "Federal Funds for Research and Development," 1955–2015, http://www.nsf.gov/statistics/2015/nsf15306/pdf/tab23.pdf. For conversion to constant dollars, I relied on readily accessible tools such as US Department of Labor, Bureau of Labor Statistics, CPI Inflation Calculator, http://data.bls.gov/cgi-bin/cpicalc.pl. Note that these estimates of federal R&D spending are slightly different from those provided by the American Association for the Advancement of Science; see http://www.aaas.org/page/historical-trends-federal-rd.

12. Pelfrey and Atkinson, "Science and the Entrepreneurial University," 40.

13. One of the best discussions is in Suzanne Wilson, ed., *Lee Shulman: The Wisdom of Practice* (New York: Jossey-Bass, 2004).

14. For discussion of the landmark Bayh-Dole amendments that enabled universities to benefit from the R&D conducted by their faculty, and other policy changes, see Pelfrey and Atkinson, "Science and the Entrepreneurial University."

15. Only recently, for example, did the White House Office of Science and Technology Policy decide it was time for a strategic plan regarding federal investments in STEM education. See "Federal Science, Technology, Engineering, and Mathematics (Stem) Education, 5-Year Strategic Plan," White House, National Science and Technology Council, May 2013, https://www.whitehouse.gov/sites/default/files/microsites/ostp/stem_stratplan_2013.pdf. For an especially lucid account of national education goals in a system designed for diffusion of authority and decentralized governance, see Maris Vinovskis, *From a Nation at Risk to No Child Left Behind: National Education Goals and the Creation of Federal Education Policy* (New York: Teachers College Press, 2009).

16. For empirical analyses of the condition of American science, see Michael

Teitelbaum, *Falling Behind?: Boom, Bust, and the Global Race for Scientific Talent* (Princeton,NJ: Princeton University Press, 2014); Yu Xie and Alexandra Killewald, *Is American Science in Decline?* (Cambridge, MA: Harvard University Press, 2012); and Chubin et al., *Federally Funded Research*. An excellent historical economic treatment of the effects of American investment in science, technology, and education is in Claudia Goldin and Lawrence Katz, *The Race Between Education and Technology* (Cambridge, MA: Belknap, 2008).

17. Ellen Condliffe Lagemann, *An Elusive Science: the Troubling History of Education Research* (Chicago: University of Chicago Press, 2000). The phrase "how people learn" is borrowed with gratitude from the eponymous report of the National Research Council: John D. Bransford et al., ed., *How People Learn: Brain, Mind, Experience, and School*, expanded ed. (Washington, DC: National Academy Press, 2000).

18. James S. Coleman et al., *Equality of Educational Opportunity* (Washington, DC: US Government Printing Office, 1966).

19. See Adam Gamoran and Daniel Long, "Equality of Educational Opportunity: A 40-Year Retrospective" (Madison, WI: Wisconsin Center for Education Research, 2006), http://www.wcer.wisc.edu/publications/workingPapers/index.php. On the Coleman report as "big science," see Ken Prewitt et al., *Using Science as Evidence in Public Policy* (Washington, DC: National Academy Press, 2012). For the most compelling recent evidence of the effects of economic inequality on educational opportunity and academic performance, see Greg Duncan and Richard Murnane, ed., *Whither Opportunity* (New York: Russell Sage Foundation, 2011).

20. Jeffrey J. Kuenzi and Adam Stoll, "The Education Sciences Reform Act" (Washington, DC: Congressional Research Service, 2014), https://www.fas.org/sgp/crs/misc/R43398.pdf.

21. "Awful reputation" is the phrase made somewhat famous by Carl Kaestle's paper, which contrary to some popular misunderstanding showed that the reputation was *undeserved*. See Carl Kaestle, "The Awful Reputation of Education Research," *Educational Researcher* 22, no. 1 (January–February 1993). For a summary judgment on the overall significance, quality, and contributions of education research, see Richard Shavelson et al., ed., *Scientific Research in Education* (Washington, DC: National Academies Press, 2002). For a reasoned postmodernist response, see Elizabeth St. Pierre, "Scientifically Based Research In Education: Epistemology And Ethics," *Adult Education Quarterly* 56, no. 4 (2006): 239–266; and for continuation of the debate, my "Response to Elizabeth St. Pierre, 'Scientifically Based Research in Education: Epistemology and Ethics,'" *Adult Education Quarterly* 56, no. 4 (August 2006): 267–273.

22. There is no room here for a full discussion of peer review, but it is worth noting its significant role not only in quality control of science but as a "symbolic demarcation of where scientific expertise ends and political judgment begins." I am grateful to Daryl Chubin for this insight.

23. See Carl Kaestle, *Pillars of the Republic* (New York: Hill and Wang, 1983); David Tyack, *The One Best System: A History of American Urban Education* (Cambridge, MA: Harvard University Press, 1974); and Lawrence Cremin, *Popular Education and its Discontents* (New York: Harper and Row, 1990).

24. US Department of Education, National Center for Education Statistics: Expenditures of educational institutions related to the gross domestic product, by level of institution: Selected years, 1929–1930 through 2012–2013, http://nces.ed.gov/programs/digest/d13/tables/dt13_106.10.asp.

25. Kuenzi and Stoll, "Education Sciences Reform Act," 1–2.

26. For brief discussion of the different approaches taken by the first two directors of IES, see Feuer, "Pure and Applied Science and Pasteur's Quadrant."

27. For a review of some of the issues salient in this debate, see, e.g., Suzanne Franco, "Reauthorization of NCLB: Time to Reconsider the Scientifically Based Research Requirement," 2007, http://nonpartisaneducation.org /Review/Essays/v3n6.htm#sthash.zDoUv5I9.dpuf. I discuss other aspects of NCLB, and its successor, the Every Student Succeeds Act (ESSA, passed in late 2015), in chapter 4.

28. For a pictorial representation of changes in common usage of the phrase "education research," see https://books.google.com/ngrams/graph?content =education+research&year_start=1950&year_end=2008&corpus=15&smoo thing=3&share=&direct_url=t1%3B%2Ceducation%20research%3B%2Cco. Increased public use of the phrase "education research," however, does not necessarily mean that subtle differences between education and other fields of inquiry are either well understood or easily embraced. The fact that products of educational research are not as easily marketed for financial gain as, say, biological findings that fuel the pharmaceutical industry; that debates over equity are more heated in education than in other branches of science; and that uncertainty and disagreement over exactly what it means to be "educated" poses challenges to the definition of measurable outcomes, are among the principal reasons that education research, while sharing fundamental methodological principles with other sciences, remains special and in many ways more vexing. I am grateful to Richard Murnane for suggesting that I reiterate these points. See also Shavelson et al., ed., *Scientific Research in Education*.

29. Full disclosure: I was appointed by President Obama to serve on the National Board for Education Sciences, which has oversight responsibilities for IES, in November 2014. Anything I say about IES in this book is my opinion and

does not necessarily reflect the positions of the US Department of Education or any of its units.

30. See "Federal Science, Technology, Engineering, and Mathematics (Stem) Education, 5-Year Strategic Plan."

31. US Department of Education, National Center for Education Statistics, Condition of Education, April 2015, http://nces.ed.gov/programs/coe/indicator _ctb.asp.

32. National Science Foundation, "Report to the National Science Board on the National Science Foundation's Merit Review System, Fiscal Year 2000," Appendix Table 1, http://www.nsf.gov/nsb/documents/2001/nsb0136 /nsb0136_6.htm; and Fiscal Year 2014, Appendix Table 1, http://www.nsf.gov /nsb/publications/2015/nsb201514.pdf.

33. See my short essay, "Evidence and Advocacy," in *Past as Prologue*. For the most cogent and balanced rebuttal to the prevailing "gold standard" logic of the early 2000s, see Shavelson et al., *Scientific Research in Education*. For a recent critique of the flaws of randomized trials in education research, see Alan Ginsburg and Marshall S. Smith, "Do Randomized Controlled Trials Meet the 'Gold Standard'? A Study of the Usefulness of RCTs in the What Works Clearinghouse" (Washington, DC: American Enterprise Institute, March 2016).

CHAPTER 3

1. See Rexmond Cochrane, *The National Academy of Sciences: the First Hundred Years, 1863–1963* (Washington, DC: National Academy of Sciences, 1978). Plates with diagrams from the magnetic deviation report are maintained in the academy's archives.

2. Michael Feuer and Christina Maranto, "Science Advice as Procedural Rationality: Reflections on the National Research Council," *Minerva* 48 (2010): 262. But see also Louis Menand, *The Metaphysical Club: A Story of Ideas in America* (New York: Farrar, Straus and Giroux, 2002).

3. For an overview of dual-use technology and innovation diffusion, see Barry Bozeman, "Technology transfer and public policy: a review of research and theory," *Research Policy* 29, no. 4–5 (April 2000): 627–655.

4. Jeff Henig, *Spin Cycle: How Research is Used in Policy Debates—the Case of Charter Schools* (New York: Russell Sage, 2008), 18–19.

5. The idea of the federal government creating inducements to states and districts became a hallmark of the Obama administration's Race to the Top initiative, but it was certainly not the first time. The No Child Left Behind Act in 2001, for example, required states expecting to receive federal funds to show "adequate yearly progress." For details, see http://www.edcentral.

org/edcyclopedia/no-child-left-behind-overview/, and http://www2.ed.gov /programs/racetothetop/rttfinalrpt1115.pdf.

6. Again, a major institutional development connecting science to government took place during wartime. For detail, see Cochrane, *The National Academy of Sciences.*

7. For more information about the NAS charter and early history, see Frederick Seitz, "A Selection of Highlights from the History of the National Academy of Sciences, 1863–2005," http://www.nasonline.org/about-nas/history/high-lights/. On the theory of altruism as expression of self-interest, see, e.g., Susan Rose Ackerman, "Altruism, Nonprofits, and Economic Theory," *Journal of Economic Literature* 34 (June 1996): 701–728).

8. Editorial, *New York Times*, February 21, 2009, A20, http://www.nytimes .com/2009/02/21/opinion/21sat2.html?_r=3.

9. President Barack Obama, remarks at the National Academy of Sciences, April 27, 2009, https://www.whitehouse.gov/the-press-office/remarks -president-national-academy-sciences-annual-meeting.

10. The NAS annual report says that the institution issues 400 reports per year; however, of those, approximately 250 are peer-reviewed (most of them "consensus" reports), with the remainder including documents mostly issued by the Transportation Research Board that do not undergo full-fledged review. I am grateful to Bill Skane for this clarification. See "Report to Congress—The National Academies of Sciences, Engineer-ing, Medicine," http://www.nationalacademies.org/annualreport/. The quoted definition is from James McGann et al., "2014 Global Go To Think Tank Index Report," Think Tanks & Civil Societies Program, Univer-sity of Pennsylvania, 8, Scholarly Commons, http://repository.upenn.edu /think_tanks/8.

11. Works cited in this paragraph are Thomas Medvetz, *Think Tanks in America* (Chicago: University of Chicago Press, 2014); Andrew Rich, *Think Tanks, Public Policy, and the Politics of Expertise* (Cambridge, UK: Cambridge Uni-versity Press, 2004); David M. Ricci, *The Transformation of American Poli-tics* (New Haven, CT: Yale University Press, 1993); James Allen Smith, *The Idea Brokers: Think Tanks and the Rise of the New Policy Elite* (New York: Free Press, 1991); Louis Menand, *The Metaphysical Club* (New York: Far-rar, Straus and Giroux, 2001), 158; Harvard Kennedy School, "Think Tank Search: A Google Custom Search of more than 590 think tanks and research centers," http://guides.library.harvard.edu/hks/think_tank_search/US; and Lynn John Hellebust, ed., *Think Tank Directory: A Guide to Independent Nonprofit Public Policy Research Organizations*, 2nd ed. (Topeka, KS: Gov-ernment Research Service, 2006). I would have been surprised at not finding the NRC included in the literature of think tanks even if I had not worked there for seventeen years.

12. The NAS implemented its most recent organizational changes in 2015, resulting in elimination of the NRC. For details, see http://nas.edu/.

13. If the word "purchased" seems incompatible with the notion of pro bono scientific advice, it is worth noting that the NASEM qua *institution* does receive reimbursement for expenses associated with the organization of the myriad volunteer committees of scientists who are responsible for the actual work. For discussion of the demand for social and behavioral science as input to government policy analysis, see, e.g., Kenneth Prewitt, Thomas Schwandt, and Miron Straf, eds., *Using Science as Evidence in Public Policy* (Washington, DC: National Academies Press, 2012). The numbers cited here are from McGann et al., "2014 Global Go To Think Tank Index Report," 10. But see also Medvetz, *Think Tanks in America*, 31–33, for comment on the vagueness of definitions and why all such counts should be taken with more than a grain of salt.

14. For discussion of behavioral and technical aspects of ranking systems, with emphasis on institutions of higher learning, see Michael Feuer, Henry Braun, Amy Berman, and Nancy Kober, "A Hearty Appetite, But Is It a Healthy One? The Promise and Pitfalls of Rankings of Higher Education Institutions" (monograph, George Washington University, Washington, DC, 2015).

15. These rankings are obviously subject to considerable fluctuation: in just the past few years, the education program of the Urban Institute, especially on the K–12 side, has shrunk considerably.

16. Changes in the politics of education make labels like "liberal" increasingly ambiguous. At least since the Clinton-era reshaping of its ideological agenda, through the efforts of the Democratic Leadership Council, the Democratic Party has become increasingly sympathetic to market-based education reforms and test-based accountability. Meanwhile, the Republican Party's successes at claiming some of the "equity and opportunity" territory that had traditionally been associated with the other side of the aisle, manifest for example in the bipartisan passage of the No Child Left Behind Act in 2001, have further muddied the conventional partisan waters. See, for example, Al From, *The New Democrats and the Return to Power* (New York: St. Martin's Press, 2013). On the other hand, this façade of closeness, at least on some of the core issues in education, is not reflected in today's angry and discordant political rhetoric.

17. Henig, *Spin Cycle.*

18. See Richard Van Noorden, "The Trouble With Retractions," *Nature* 478 (October 6, 2011), http://www.nature.com/news/2011/111005/pdf/478026a.pdf.

19. As noted by McGann et al., "[I]nstitutions have found that they can stand out by adopting a more strident ideological bent—a practice that had led

to think tanks' increasing politicization" ("2014 Global Go To Think Tank Index Report," 24).

20. See W. M. Cohen and D. Levinthal, "Absorptive capacity: A new perspective on learning and innovation," *Administrative Science Quarterly* 35 (1990): 128–152.

21. See Lawrence Cremin, *Popular Education and its Discontents* (New York: Harper and Row, 1990), 85. The quote from Aristotle is in the translation by Benjamin Jowett, http://classics.mit.edu/Aristotle/politics.8.eight.html.

22. Michael Feuer, "Evidence and Advocacy," in *Past as Prologue: The National Academy of Education at 50*, ed. Michael Feuer, Amy Berman, and Richard Atkinson (Washington, DC: National Academy of Education, 2015), http://www.naeducation.org/cs/groups/naedsite/documents/webpage/naed_169315.pdf.

23. On the Hebrew Bible's concern with individualism and the common good, see, e.g., Daniel Elazar, "Obligations and Rights in the Jewish Political Tradition: Some Preliminary Observations," *Jewish Political Studies Review* 3, nos. 3 and 4 (Fall 1991). For the classic treatment of individual rights and the social good, see, e.g., Adam Smith, *The Wealth of Nations* (1776); Kenneth J. Arrow, *Social Choice and Individual Values* (New Haven, CT: Yale University Press, 1963); and John Rawls, *A Theory of Justice* (Cambridge, MA: Belknap Press, 1971). For the debate over the Common Core, see Matthew Frizzell and Tara Dunderdale, *A Compendium of Research on the Common Core State Standards* (Washington, DC: George Washington University, Center on Education Policy, February 2015), http://www.cep-dc.org/index.cfm?DocumentTopicID=1.

24. James B. Conant, "Education For A Classless Society: The Jeffersonian Tradition" (Charter Day Address, University of California, May 1940), https://www.theatlantic.com/past/docs/issues/95sep/ets/edcla.htm.

25. The quotation is from Richard Elmore, *Building a New Structure For School Leadership* (Washington, DC: Albert Shanker Institute, Winter 2000). Elmore has been an advocate for standards as a vehicle driving toward more coherence and, in particular, for reducing the disparities in resource allocation that continue to plague the American educational landscape. But it is important to consider the benefits side of the equation here too: for evidence on the successes of American schooling through much of the twentieth century, attributable to the collective investment in expanded access and increased participation in traditional high school but also to innovations that were made possible by local and school-level decisions. See, for example, Claudia Goldin and Lawrence Katz, *The Race Between Education and Technology* (Cambridge, MA: Belknap Press, 2010). The best history of how local schooling decisions enabled the integration of immigrants during the early part of the twentieth century is in Jeffrey Mirel, *Patriotic Pluralism: Americanization*

Education and European Immigrants (Cambridge, MA: Harvard University Press, 2010).

26. Henig, *Spin Cycle*, 59. A related point is about how education decision makers actually use research. See, e.g., C. E. Coburn and J. E. Talbert, "Conceptions of evidence use in school districts: Mapping the terrain," *American Journal of Education* 112, no. 4 (2006): 469–495.

27. My friend Fredrick (Rick) Hess seems to have perfected the art of schaden-freude in his occasional send-ups of the AERA meeting bulletin. See, for example, his suggestion that attendees at the 2010 conference might have wanted "to get the scoop on the sophisticated-sounding inquiry into paper airplane utilization, [by listening to the paper called] 'Examining Exclusionary Activity Through Mediated Discourse Analysis: Looking Critically at Play, Peer Culture, and Paper Airplanes,'" http://blogs.edweek.org/edweek/rick_hess _straight_up/2010/04/making_the_most_of_the_first_day_at_aera.html). For a more tempered (and surely less entertaining) argument about the hazards of dismissing research when it doesn't obviously lead to productive application, see Richard Atkinson and Michael Feuer, "'Absurd' Studies of Science's Puzzles Prove their Worth," *San Jose Mercury News*, June 23, 2006.

28. References here are to Ellen Condliffe Lagemann, *An Elusive Science: The Troubling History of Education Research* (Chicago: University of Chicago Press, 2002); and Thomas Schelling, *Micromotives and Macrobehavior* (New York: W.W. Norton, 2006).

29. See, for example, Board on International Comparative Studies in Education, *Methodological Advances in Cross-National Surveys of Educational Achievement* (Washington, DC: National Academies Press, 2002).

30. *A Nation at Risk: The Imperative for Educational Reform* (Washington, DC: National Commission on Excellence in Education, April 1983), http://www2. ed.gov/pubs/NatAtRisk/index.html.

31. Questions about the empirical validity of claims made in *A Nation at Risk* were raised fairly soon after its publication. See, e.g., L. Stedman and M. Smith, "Recent reform proposals for American education," *Contemporary Education Review* 2, no. 2 (1983): 85–104.

32. *A Nation at Risk*, 5.

33. I cite this early result in my introductory note, *The Bridge*, Spring 2013, http://www.nae.edu/Publications/Bridge/69735.aspx. For detailed analysis of the results of FIMS and subsequent comparative data, see E. Medrich and J. Griffith, *International Mathematics and Science Assessments: What Have We Learned?* (Washington, DC: US Department of Education, Office of Educational Research and Improvement, National Center for Education Statistics, 1992.) Table B2 in Medrich and Griffith shows the United States at the bottom and Israel at the top. It is interesting to note that both countries'

standing on international comparisons has fluctuated considerably over the last half century. Israel's macroeconomic performance, productivity growth, technology exports, and international competitiveness suggest that maybe the math scores in 1964 were predicting something real; the problem is that the economic story of that "start-up nation" has continued to be stunning— declines in average test scores in recent years notwithstanding (Israel scored below the mean in mathematics, reading, and science on the 2012 PISA). For a popular account of Israel's economic development, see Dan Senor and Saul Singer, *Start-up Nation: The Story of Israel's Economic Miracle* (New York: Twelve, Hachette Group, 2009).

34. http://timssandpirls.bc.edu/timss1995.html.

35. For a synopsis of the history of IEA, see http://www.iea.nl/brief_history.html.

36. See, for example, Mark Schneider, "The International PISA Test: A Risky Investment for States," *Education Next* (Fall 2009), www.educationnext.org; and William Schmidt, "What do PISA and TIMSS Tell Us?," *Education Week*, April 24, 2014, http://blogs.edweek.org/edweek/assessing_the_assessments/2014/04/what_do_PISA_and_TIMSS_tell_us.html.

37. Kerstin Martens and Stephan Leibfried, "The PISA Story," *German Times for Europe*, January 2008, http://www.german-times.com/index.php?option=com_content&task=view&id=3205&Itemid=81. For a more scholarly treatment, see E. Ertl, "Educational standards and the changing discourse on education: The reception and consequences of the PISA study in Germany," *Oxford Review of Education* 32, no. 5 (2006); and Laura Engel, James Williams, and Michael Feuer, "The Global Context of Practice and Preaching: Do High-Scoring Countries Practice What U.S. Discourse Preaches?" (working paper number 2.3, Graduate School of Education and Human Development, George Washington University, April 2012).

38. Alexandra Killewald and Yu Xie, "American Science Education in Its Global and Historical Contexts," *The Bridge*, ed. Michael Feuer (Washington, DC: National Academy of Engineering, Spring 2013).

39. William H. Schmidt, Nathan A. Burroughs, and Leland S. Coganin, "On the Road to Reform: K–12 Science Education in the United States," in *The Bridge*, Feuer, ed.

40. Eric Hanushek and Ludger Woessmann, "The High Cost of Low Educational Performance: The Long-Run Impact of Improving PISA Outcomes" (Paris: OECD, 2010); see also Eric A. Hanushek and Ludger Woessmann, *The Knowledge Capital of Nations* (Cambridge, MA: MIT Press, 2015).

41. See Yu Xie and Alexandra Killewald, *Is American Science in Decline?* (Cambridge, MA: Harvard University Press, 2012); Yu Xie, "Is U.S. Science in Decline?," *Issues in Science and Technology* XXX, no. 3 (Spring 2014); Michael S. Teitelbaum, *Falling Behind?: Boom, Bust, and the Global Race for Scientific*

Talent (Princeton, NJ: Princeton University Press, 2014); and Michael Feuer, "No Country Left Behind: Rhetoric and Reality of International Large Scale Assessment" (William Angoff Memorial Lecture, Educational Testing Service, Princeton, NJ, 2012).

42. See T. Galama and J. R. Hosek, eds., *US Competitiveness in Science and Technology* (Santa Monica, CA: RAND, 2008).

43. See https://www.aei.org/publication/pisa-in-perspective/.

44. See https://www.aei.org/publication/math-test-results-from-500000-students-in-65-countries-reveal-significant-gender-differences-in-favor-of-boys/.

45. See Tom Loveless, *Lessons from the PISA-Shanghai Controversy* (Washington, DC: Brookings Institution, March 18, 2014), http://www.brookings.edu/research/reports/2014/03/18-pisa-shanghai-loveless.

46. Lindsey Burke, "Stuck in the Middle: American Student Performance Stagnates on New PISA Exam," Heritage Foundation, December 10, 2013, http://dailysignal.com/2013/12/10/stuck-middle-american-student-performance-stagnates-new-pisa-exam/.

47. See http://www.ncee.org/about-ncee/history-of-ncee/.

48. See Marc Tucker, "Governing American Education: Why This Dry Subject May Hold the Key to Advances in American Education," National Center for Education and the Economy, May 2013, http://www.ncee.org/wp-content/uploads/2013/10/Governing-American-Education.pdf.

49. Joel I. Klein and Condoleezza Rice, *US Education Reform and National Security* (Washington, DC: Council on Foreign Relations, March 2012), http://www.cfr.org/united-states/us-education-reform-national-security/p27618.

50. Ibid., 32.

51. M. Carnoy, E. García, and T. Khavenson, "Bringing it back home: Why state comparisons are more useful than international comparisons for improving US education policy" (EPI Briefing Paper #410, Economic Policy Institute, Washington, DC, October 30, 2015), http://www.epi.org/files/2015/bringing-it-back-home-final-pdf.pdf.

52. See Jim Harvey et al., "The Iceberg Effect: An International Look at Often-Overlooked Education Indicators," Horace Mann League of the National Superintendents Roundtable, January 2015, http://www.superintendentsforumtest.org/wp-content/uploads/2015/01/Released-Iceberg-Effect.pdf; and for Marc Tucker's rejoinder, http://www.ncee.org/2015/09/the-iceberg-effect-reports-that-set-us-ever-further-behind/. It will perhaps be of interest to readers that Jim Harvey was among the lead authors of *A Nation at Risk*.

53. See http://www.oecd.org/about/budget/member-countries-budget-contributions.htm.

54. For additional explanation of the dubious nature of these links, and in particular with reference to abysmal US performance on FIMS, see my short essay in *The Bridge*.

55. See, for example, David Berliner and Bruce Biddle, *The Manufactured Crisis: Myths, Fraud, And The Attack On America's Public Schools* (New York: Basic Books, 1996). Surely there are some ideologues who persist in their criticism of public education, using whatever data they can muster, because they are so convinced that privatization (vouchers, choice) is "the answer." In that sense, Berliner and Biddle performed an important service by exposing errors in how certain data (from test scores, mostly) were interpreted. But the notion of a "manufactured crisis," which smacks of conspiracy, would be difficult to substantiate using even the most elegant of statistical techniques.

56. See, for example, "Academics call for pause in PISA tests," *Washington Post*, May 13, 2014, https://www.washingtonpost.com/news/answer-sheet/wp/2014/05/13/academics-call-for-pause-in-pisa-tests/. Here I have singled out the uses and interpretations of international large-scale assessment data, but clearly there are other hot-button education policy issues for which the major think tanks either take rather predictably partisan views or avoid the topic altogether. The effectiveness of charter schools, for example, compared to traditional public schools, deserves high-quality analysis and believable interpretation, but the politics of research, as Jeff Henig chronicled, creates formidable obstacles. For a sampling of the ways in which the charter school debate has been handled in the think tank'ocracy, see, P. Baude, M. Casey, E. A. Hanushek, and S. G. Rivkin, "The evolution of charter school quality," no. 16, *Research Briefs in Economic Policy*, CATO Institute, December 2014; J. Butcher and L. Burke, *Expanding education choices: From vouchers and tax credits to savings accounts* (Washington, DC: Heritage Foundation, 2013, http://thf_media.s3.amazonaws.com/2013/pdf/SR136.pdf; and T. Loveless, *Charter school study: Much ado about tiny differences* (Washington, DC: Brookings Institution, July 3, 2013), http://www.brookings.edu/research/papers/2013/07/03-charter-schools-loveless. The most thorough treatment of the overall problem of research-into-policy as related to the charter school debate is in Henig, *Spin Cycle*.

57. See Institute of International Education, "International Students by Primary Source of Funding, 2014/15," Open Doors Report on International Educational Exchange, 2015, http://www.iie.org/opendoors.

58. Eric Lipton, Brooke Williams, and Nicholas Confessore, "Foreign Powers Buy Influence at Think Tanks," *New York Times*, September 6, 2014.

59. Ibid.

CHAPTER 4

1. See Matthew Bishop and Michael Green, *Philanthrocapitalism: How the Rich Can Save the World* (New York: Bloomsbury Press: 2008). For a supportive review, see Joel Fleishman, "The New Noblesse Oblige," *Stanford Social Innovation Review*, Winter 2009, http://ssir.org/book_reviews/entry/philanthrocapitalism_how_rich_can_save_world_mattew_bishop_michael_green. For the negative side to philanthropy by the wealthy see, e.g., the commentary on the Zuckerberg-Chan announcement by George Joseph, "Why Philanthropy Actually Hurts Rather Than Helps Some of the World's Worst Problems," *In These Times*, December 28, 2015, http://inthesetimes.com/article/18691/Philanthropy_Gates-Foundation_Capitalism; and for more on the "plutocracy of philanthropy," see Lindsay McGoey, *No Such Thing as a Free Gift: The Gates Foundation and the Price of Philanthropy* (London: Verso, 2015). For a thoughtful analysis of Zuckerberg's efforts in school reform, see Dale Rusakoff, *The Prize: Who's in Charge of America's Schools?* (New York: Houghton Mifflin Harcourt, 2015).

2. For the classic treatment of free-rider effects when enforcement is not possible, see Garrett Hardin, "The Tragedy of the Commons," *Science*, December 13, 1968. For the more optimistic view, see Elinor Ostrom, *Governing the Commons: The Evolution of Institutions for Collective Action* (Cambridge, UK: Cambridge University Press, 1968). Ostrom shared the 2009 Nobel Memorial Prize in Economic Sciences with Oliver Williamson, whose work is cited later in this chapter.

3. I am reminded of the quip by Woody Allen, who once responded to a query about his chronic pessimism by conceding that "OK, the glass is half full. Of poison." For a more scholarly and serious contemplation of the habits of researchers (especially in the behavioral and social sciences) to find flaws in proposals for social change, see Albert O. Hirschman, *The Rhetoric of Reaction: Perversity, Futility, Jeopardy* (Cambridge, MA: Harvard University Press, 1991). Readers of Hirschman will appreciate the eulogy by political scientist Francis Fukayama, "Albert O. Hirschman, 1915–2012," http://blogs.the-american-interest.com/fukuyama/.

4. John Cassidy, "Mark Zuckerberg and the Rise of Philanthrocapitalism," *New Yorker*, December 3, 2015, http://www.newyorker.com/news/john-cassidy/mark-zuckerberg-and-the-rise-of-philanthrocapitalism.

5. James Surowiecki, "In Defense of Philanthrocapitalism," *New Yorker*, December 21, 2015, http://www.newyorker.com/magazine/2015/12/21/in-defense-of-philanthrocapitalism. A recent example underscores Surowiecki's argument: bureaucratic and other constraints delayed governmental action, worldwide, to the Ebola crisis, while the more nimble Gates Foundation was able to quickly infuse $50 million toward the emergency response. See, e.g., http://

www.gatesfoundation.org/Media-Center/Press-Releases/2014/09/Gates-Foundation-Commits-$50%20Million-to-Support-Emergency-Response-to-Ebola. I am grateful to David Brooks for alerting me to this story. To the best of my knowledge, there has been no criticism of the foundation's power and influence in this dreadfully tragic situation. For a reminder of the tendency to focus on the hazards of philanthropy, in education matters, see Valerie Strauss, "Bill Gates keeps pushing Common Core, with big money (and a bid to get Charles Koch to like it)," *Washington Post*, December 27, 2015, https://www.washingtonpost.com/news/answer-sheet/wp/2015/12/27/bill-gates-keeps-pushing-common-core-with-big-money-and-a-bid-to-get-charles-koch-to-like-it/.

6. Surowiecki, "In Defense of Philanthrocapitalism."

7. For the best treatment of inequality and its effects on education, see Greg J. Duncan and Richard J. Murnane, *Whither Opportunity: Rising Inequality, Schools, and Children's Life Chances* (New York: Russell Sage, 2011). For application of the *Whither* framework to analysis of trends in other countries, see, e.g., work underway by the Israel Academy of Sciences and Humanities Initiative for Applied Education Research, http://education.academy.ac.il/Uploads/BackgroundMaterials/english/Inequality-background-en-101213.pdf. For a printed summary of this work, see "Inequality and Education: The Relationship Between Rising Economic Inequality and Educational Attainment and Achievement," ed., Oded Busharian, Jerusalem, The Initiative for Applied Education Research/The Israel Academy of Sciences and Humanities, 2016.

8. In economics, there is a long and deep literature about the trade-offs between equity and efficiency: "The economist can say whether a particular state of the economy involves an efficient allocation of resources . . . [but] has no more competence than anyone else to say that a particular move [to a different allocation] is desirable if it has unfavorable effects upon some members of society." James Henderson and Richard Quandt, *Microeconomic Theory: A Mathematical Approach* (New York: McGraw Hill, International Student Edition, 1971), 255. It is the rarer cases when ethical principles or political preferences, which are based on value judgments, enhance productivity or efficiency rather than detract from them. The possibility that our historical preference for decentralized and diffused decision making for education (and other things) has contributed to improved economic performance, by enabling and nurturing innovation, has not received much attention by education or economic historians. Two especially noteworthy exceptions are Claudia Goldin and Lawrence F. Katz, *The Race Between Education and Technology* (Cambridge, MA: Harvard University Press, 2008); and Richard Murnane and Richard Nelson, "Production and innovation when techniques are tacit: The case of education," *Journal of Economic Behavior and Organization* 5, no. 3–4 (January 1984): 353–373.

9. For the story of universal preK in Washington, DC, see Simone Zhang, "A portrait of universal pre-kindergarten in DC" (Washington, DC: Urban Institute, May 1, 2014), http://www.urban.org/urban-wire/portrait-universal-pre-kindergarten-dc. For more information about TeachingWorks, at the University of Michigan, see http://www.teachingworks.org/.

10. Attention to transaction costs, a linchpin of the "new institutional economics," provides insights to policy options, as I will show later. The basic reference for this line of reasoning is the work of Oliver Williamson, who has had a powerful influence on my thinking. See, e.g., his *Markets and Hierarchies* (New York: Free Press, 1975).

11. It is always a bit jarring to see advocates for "pure" capitalism citing Adam Smith, who understood more than most of his peers the limits of markets. See, for example, Gavin Kennedy, "Misunderstanding Self-Interest Yet Again," http://adamsmithslostlegacy.blogspot.com/2014/05/bernard-ginns-business-editor-writes-25.html. The original works are: Adam Smith, *Wealth of Nations* (original edition: London, Methuen and Co., 1776); and *The Theory of Moral Sentiments* (original edition: London, A. Millar, 1759), http://www.econlib.org/library/classicsauS.html#smith. For a tempered and sound analysis of the economics of altruism, see Susan Rose-Ackerman, "Altruism, Nonprofits, and Economic Theory," *Journal of Economic Literature* 34 (June 1996): 701–728.

12. I refer here to the interpretation offered in Williamson, *Markets and Hierarchies*, of the study by Richard M. Titmuss, *The Gift Relationship: From Human Blood to Social Policy*, updated ed. (New York: New Press, 1997).

13. Lara B. Aknin et al., "Prosocial Spending and Well-Being: Cross-Cultural Evidence for a Psychological Universal," *Journal of Personality and Social Psychology* 104, no. 4 (April 2013): 635–652.

14. For the research on physiology of charity, see Ashley V. Whillans, Elizabeth W. Dunn, Gillian M. Sandstrom, Sally S. Dickerson, and Ken M. Madden, "Is spending money on others good for your heart?" (working paper, University of British Columbia, Department of Medicine, n.d.), https://ashleyatubc.files.wordpress.com/2011/01/ha_final_approved.pdf. This work and related findings were the subject of an opinion piece in the Sunday *New York Times* on December 25, 2015, coauthored by Elizabeth Dunn and Ashley Whillans, which ended on this cheery note: "Our research points to the conclusion that embracing the spirit of generosity may not only be heartwarming; it may also be good for the heart. Call it the Grinch effect." See http://www.nytimes.com/2015/12/25/opinion/give-if-you-know-whats-good-for-you.html?emc=edit_th_20151226&nl=todaysheadlines&nlid=18789091&_r=0.

15. I am grateful to my friend and teacher, Rabbi Danny Zemel, for pointing me to this biblical and Talmudic wisdom. See Proverbs, 10:2, http://www.chabad.org/library/bible_cdo/aid/16381/jewish/Chapter-10.htm. On Maimonides and antecedent references to *tzedakah*, see Moshe Halbertal, *Maimonides:*

Life and Thought, English trans. from Hebrew (Princeton, NJ: Princeton University Press, 2014).

16. Timing issues are worth exploring. Suppose we could find a population of prospective donors who don't know (or care) about the tax code, and we then tried to figure out whether the health effect has more or less influence on their decision to keep on giving than does the introduction of a monetary incentive. Here's a topic for some new behavioral-economics research.

17. For history of the Corporation for Public Broadcasting, see http://www.cpb .org/aboutcpb/history-timeline. I am grateful to Bill Skane for reminding me that NASEM does, indeed, rely increasingly on philanthropic support. Whether that is sufficient to disqualify it from becoming the permanent home for the new entity I am proposing is, obviously, a matter for continued discussion.

18. Jack Jennings, *Presidents, Congress, and the Public Schools: The Politics of Education Reform* (Cambridge, MA: Harvard Education Press, 2015).

19. The 1994 reauthorization was called "The Improving American Schools Act," and included "Goals 2000," one of the more important milestones in the standards movement. See https://www2.ed.gov/offices/OESE/archives/legislation /ESEA/brochure/iasa-bro.html.

20. Sadly there is evidence of all these outcomes. See, e.g., Daniel Koretz, "Moving past No Child Left Behind," *Science* 326 (November 6, 2009): 803–804; and Sharon Nichols and David Berliner, *Collateral Damage: How High-Stakes Testing Corrupts America's Schools* (Cambridge, MA: Harvard Education Press, 2007). On the general question of whether test-based accountability has brought about desired improvements in teaching and learning, see Michael Hout and Stuart W. Elliott, eds., *Incentives and Test-Based Accountability in Education* (Washington, DC: National Academies Press, 2011).

21. "Improving Your Schools: A Parent and Community Guide To No Child Left Behind" (Washington, DC: The Education Trust, 2003), http://edtrust.org /wp-content/uploads/2013/10/userguidebw1.pdf. For one of the most poignant and informed reflections on the history of school reform relating to minority improvement and civil rights, see William Taylor, *The Passion of My Times: An Advocate's Fifty-Year Journey in the Civil Rights Movement* (New York: Da Capo Press, 2004). The education and civil rights communities lost a hero when Bill died suddenly in 2010; for a poignant summary of his extraordinary life and career, see Emma Brown's obituary in the *Washington Post*, June 29, 2010, http://www.washingtonpost.com/wp-dyn/content /article/2010/06/29/AR2010062905117.html. For a nuanced and balanced scholarly analysis of the effects of NCLB, see Adam Gamoran, ed., *Standards-Based Reform and the Poverty Gap: Lessons for "No Child Left Behind"* (Washington, DC: Brookings, October 2007). For an example of how the misuse of test scores perpetuates obnoxious stereotypes of racial and ethnic inferiority,

see, e.g., Richard Herrnstein and Charles Murray, *The Bell Curve: Intelligence and Class Structure in American Life* (New York: Free Press, 1994).

22. Some years earlier, an idea was proposed that seemed like a logical way to reconcile the need for accountability measures with the protection of state and local control. Reacting to the proposal for a "voluntary national test," in 1998, Republican congressman Bill Goodling requested from the National Academy of Sciences a study on the feasibility of "linking" the existing state and commercial tests and reporting the disparate results on a common scale. Why this plan to solve the *e pluribus unum* problem with psychometrics proved to be methodologically impossible was the topic of Michael J. Feuer, Paul W. Holland, Bert F. Green, Meryl W. Bertenthal, and F. Cadell Hemphill, ed., *Uncommon Measures: Equivalence and Linkage Among Educational Tests* (Washington, DC: National Academies Press, 1999).

23. The original argument for vouchers is laid out in Milton Friedman, *Capitalism and Freedom* (Chicago: University of Chicago Press, 1962). Joseph Stiglitz, awarded the Nobel Memorial Prize in Economic Sciences in 2001, offered a cogent rebuttal of the "invisible hand" metaphor in an interview that appeared in the *International Herald Tribune*, October 11, 2006: "Adam Smith, the father of modern economics, is often cited as arguing for the 'invisible hand' and free markets . . . But unlike his followers, Adam Smith was aware of some of the limitations of free markets, and research since then has further clarified why free markets, by themselves, often do not lead to what is best . . . [T]he reason that the invisible hand often seems invisible is that it is often not there." From interview with Daniel Altman, http://economists-view.typepad.com/economistsview/2006/10/joseph_stiglitz.html. One of the more comprehensive—but ultimately flawed—analyses about the advantages of privatization in education was in John Chubb and Terry Moe, *Politics, Markets and America's Schools* (Washington, DC: Brookings, 1990). On the mixed results from empirical research of choice and charter schools, see the work of the Stanford Center for Research on Education Outcomes (CREDO), http://credo.stanford.edu/pdfs/Online%20Press%20Release.pdf; the analysis by Mathematica Policy Research, http://www.mathematica-mpr.com/our-publications-and-findings/publications/inside-online-charter-schools; and critiques such as the one by the National Education Policy Center at the University of Colorado, http://nepc.colorado.edu/newsletter/2013/07/review-credo-2013.

24. I believe this conflict explains what I observed at meetings during the early years of NCLB, when I detected some relief, if not a whiff of schadenfreude, among conservatives who savored the prospect that the whole law with its cumbersome regulations would collapse of its own bureaucratic weight. For them, school choice solves the accountability problem more efficiently. Rather

than spend lots of time and energy developing and then arguing about imperfect metrics like test scores or performance assessments, and empowering the federal government to hold states accountable, the quality of schools could more easily be measured by watching the behavior of rational educational consumers: schools that attract enrollment must be better than those that lose enrollment. The bottom line, following this remarkably circular logic, is that accountability is better left to the magic of markets than to the bullying of bureaucracies. Those tempted by this theory should apply another lesson from market economics: *caveat emptor.*

25. The intricacies of NCLB waivers, an attempt by the Duncan administration to provide relief to states from certain provisions of the law, are beyond my scope here. For details, see "Federal Education Policy & Programs: NCLB/ESEA Waivers," Center on Education Policy (George Washington University), http://www.cep-dc.org/index.cfm?DocumentSubTopicID=48; Frederick Hess, "Duncan's Trip Down the Waiver Rabbit Hole," *Education Week*, April 28, 2014, http://www.frederickhess.org/2014/04/duncan-trip-down-the-waiver-rabbit-hole; and Diane Ravitch, "Rick Hess Blasts Duncan's Waiver Policy," May 6, 2014, https://dianeravitch.net/2014/05/06/rick-hess-blasts-duncans-waiver-policy/.

26. Tamara Hiler and Lanae Erickson Hatalsky, "How the Every Student Succeeds Act Changes No Child Left Behind," *Third Way*, December 1, 2015, http://www.thirdway.org/memo/how-the-every-student-succeeds-act-changes-no-child-left-behind.

27. Robert Linn, "Test-based Educational Accountability in the Era of No Child Left Behind," University of California, National Center for Research on Evaluation, Standards, and Student Testing (CRESST), Center for the Study of Evaluation (CSE) Center CSE Report 651, April 2005, http://files.eric.ed.gov/fulltext/ED488732.pdf. The education policy, research, and measurement communities mourned the loss of Bob Linn in December, 2015. His career contributions were legendary, as was his generosity as a colleague and mentor. See the tribute by the National Academy of Education, http://www.naeducation.org/cs/groups/naedsite/documents/webpage/naed_169871.pdf.

28. For Secretary King's remarks, see http://www.ed.gov/news/media-advisories/acting-us-education-secretary-give-remarks-national-action-networks-martin-luther-king-jr-day-annual-breakfast. For commentary and analysis see Alyson Klein's blog, http://blogs.edweek.org/edweek/campaign-k-12/2016/01/john_king_to_call_for_emphasis.html; and reporting by Emma Brown in the *Washington Post*, https://www.washingtonpost.com/news/education/wp/2016/01/18/acting-u-s-education-secretary-civil-rights-community-must-be-vigilant/?wpmm=1&wpisrc=nl_lclheads.

29. The distinguished head of OTA, John Gibbons (of blessed memory), had a

keen and witty understanding of the role of science in politics. When testify-
ing before Congress and presenting "options" based on findings from OTA
reports, Gibbons frequently encountered frustrated representatives or senators who would say, "Yes, those are interesting options, *but what should we
do?*" To which Gibbons would wryly reply, "That's why you were elected." For
the best history of OTA, see Peter Blair, *Congress's Own Think Tank: Learning from the Legacy of the Office of Technology Assessment (1972–1995)* (New
York: Palgrave Macmillan, 2013). Inter alia, Blair's nuanced assessment of
the organizational and cultural differences between the OTA and NAS are
worthy of attention and discussion. OTA was closed in 1995, as part of the
reforms initiated by Congressman Newt Gingrich. The details of that intrusion of nasty partisanship serve as reminder of the hazards of political and
ideological interference in the workings of science.

30. For the analysis of vertical integration as an alternative to market-type
transactions, the most important source is Oliver E. Williamson. See *Markets
and Hierarchies* (New York: Free Press, 1975); also his address upon receiving
the Nobel Prize in 2005, http://www.nobelprize.org/nobel_prizes/economic-
sciences/laureates/2009/williamson-lecture.html.

31. It is worth noting that one of the virtues of the OTA process—only requests
from the chair and ranking member of standing committees of Congress
could ask for studies—was also a factor in the agency's undoing. When
control of the House or Senate switched parties, and committee leadership
changed, OTA found itself without steady allies and could not rely on the
rank and file for continuing support. See Blair, *Congress's Own Think Tank.*

32. I do not intend this in a vengeful sense, although I suspect the strategy will
appeal to critics of test-based accountability, which is based in part on the
notion that providing information about school performance will somehow
be sufficient to bring about its improvement.

33. Chris Mooney, "Requiem for an Office," *Bulletin of the Atomic Scientists* 61, no.
5 (September-October 2005): 40, https://www.princeton.edu/step/seminars
/previous/fall-2005/Mooneyreading2005No2Requiemforanoffice.pdf. The
current secretary of defense, Ashton Carter, then a professor of physics at
Rockefeller University and MIT, wrote an early and important background
paper on this topic, which is included in an anthology on the "strategic
defense initiative" that covers technical and policy considerations. See Steven
E. Miller and Stephen Van Evera, ed., *The Star Wars Controversy: An International Security Reader* (Princeton, NJ: Princeton University Press, 1986).

34. The story is, of course, more complicated, and worthy of closer examination than possible in this book. For excellent coverage of the battles between
an increasingly conservative Congress and NSF, see Jeffrey Mervis, "Battle
between NSF and House science committee escalates: How did it get this

bad?," *Science*, October 2, 2014, http://www.sciencemag.org/news/2014/10
/battle-between-nsf-and-house-science-committee-escalates-how-did-it-
get-bad; and "Congressional Republicans split over climate, social science
spending," *Science*, June 15, 2015, http://www.sciencemag.org/news/2015/06
/congressional-republicans-split-over-climate-social-science-spending.

35. See Jeffrey Mervis, "Budget agreement boosts U.S. science," *Science*,
    December 18, 2015, http://www.sciencemag.org/news/2015/12
    /updated-budget-agreement-boosts-us-science.

36. See the compilations of the American Educational Research Association,
    http://www.aera.net/Newsroom/AERAHighlightsE-newsletter/AERA
    HighlightsDecember2015/FY2016OmnibusBillBoostsFundingforEducation
    Research/tabid/16146/Default.aspx.

37. Ibid. For a characteristically lucid and balanced appraisal—and rebuttal—of
    arguments against public funding of research and development, see Rich-
    ard Nelson, "Book Review: A Science Funding Contrarian," *Issues in Science
    and Technology*, XIV, no. 1 (Fall 1997), http://issues.org/14-1/nelson/. In his
    critique of a book by the economist Terence Kealey (*The Economic Laws of
    Scientific Research*), Nelson reminds readers that "the principal arguments
    for public support of science are that knowledge won through fundamental
    research is nonrivalrous in use, and that in many cases it is difficult for a per-
    son or an organization to keep that knowledge out of the hands of others or
    to force all who use it to pay a fee." And his bottom line, with which I agree
    (see my discussion in chapter 2) is that "Kealey's view that government should
    just get out of the business of supporting science is particularly wrongheaded
    and dangerous."

38. Consortium of Social Science Associations, "Analysis of the FY 2016 Omni-
    bus Appropriations Bill and Implications for Social and Behavioral Sci-
    ence Research," December 17, 2015, http://www.cossa.org/wp-content/
    uploads/2015/12/FY-2016-Final-Omnibus-Analysis-Dec-2015.pdf.

39. See Ad Hoc Working Group on the Durban Platform for Enhanced Action,
    http://unfccc.int/resource/docs/2013/adp2/eng/info2.pdf.

40. For example, *Research Universities and the Future of America: Ten Break-
    through Actions Vital to Our Nation's Prosperity and Security* (Washington,
    DC: National Academies Press, 2012).

41. I am aware of my bias in this proposal, given my current leadership role in the
    NAEd. But I hope the idea will last beyond my tenure as president.

42. See http://foundationcenter.org/about/index.html.

43. Organizing such a summit could be a task undertaken by the Education
    Funders Strategy Group, a consortium-styled entity that enables and encour-
    ages cooperation and sharing of ideas among major philanthropies. See http://
    www.npesf.org/education-funder-strategy-group.

44. The quotation is from Paul Brest and Hal Harvey, *Money Well Spent: A Strategic Plan for Smart Philanthropy* (New York: Bloomberg Press, 2008). I have taken the liberty of changing the order of those two sentences. The idea that what some people call "strategy" is actually "tactics" is an insight of Mike McPherson's for which I am grateful.

Acknowledgments

I SUBJECTED THE ASSEMBLED MEMBERS and friends of the National Academy of Education to an early version of the basic arguments in this book, in my presidential address, in November 2014. My colleagues were, as always, graciously attentive. Mike Smith, Susan Fuhrman, Jim Banks, Marilyn Cochran-Smith, and Maris Vinovskis spoke to me after my talk, and I thank them for the extra time and attention. Mike's more detailed comments on drafts of selected chapters were in keeping with his reputation for insight, wit, generosity, and all-around brilliance. I have shared the ideas in this book, if not the actual draft chapters, with my various George Washington University faculty colleagues, and thank them for their kindness as I occasionally strayed from the demands of the day-to-day. Maria Ferguson and Nancy Kober gave me helpful comments, and Touran Waters advised wisely on outreach. Meg Holland magically manages me and our office, and was wonderfully supportive. Outside my university home, many friends and colleagues took time to read, think, and comment. Daryl Chubin, a dear friend who is also a leading authority on US science policy, was generous with constructive and learned comments. Dick Atkinson reads everything I send him and, as always, challenged my assumptions and helped me refine my arguments; his friendship and mentorship mean the world to me. Mike McPherson read an early version of the introduction and encouraged me to keep going; he then read other sections and suggested improvements in tone and substance. Richard Murnane, from whom I have been learning since 1976, provided thoughtful suggestions and some fresh data, for which I am thankful. Avital Darmon, a friend whose contributions to the improvement of education research in Israel are now legendary found time to read selected chapters in depth, and her reactions helped me think about whether and how my arguments would be received outside the United States. Roy and Judy Eidelson have been inspiring and challenging me for thirty years, and their reactions to pieces of the draft were, as always, on point and extremely useful. Ellen Condliffe Lagemann has been a coach and mentor for a long time; her wisdom and generosity are reflected in the foreword to the book, for which I am ever so grateful. Colleagues from my years at OTA and the NAS, Peter Blair and Bill Skane, came through with their predictably astute comments and suggestions, many of which I have happily integrated into the text or notes. Ericka Miller has withstood my rants on the subject for over a year, and pushed me with her own brand of wisdom and literateness. Many thanks also to Judge David Tatel, Diana Hess, and Anna McColl for wise and constructive reactions. Thanks to Marty Orland, Michael Neuenfeldt of WestEd was quick and graciously helpful with needed financial data. Adam Zemel provided tip-top assistance with references. The production and marketing team at Harvard Education Press—Chris Leonesio, Jane Gebhart, and Laura Cutone Godwin—are wonderfully talented and I thank them for efficient and gracious work on the text, graphs, and cover art. My family came through, as always: Sarah read various sections and offered sensitive and deep insights in her typically humble manner. Jonathan's sense of the language of politics—and the politics of language—helped me refine key points. Special thanks to Regine for enjoying a few weeks without me while I took advantage of the serenity of Lake Lariat to dive into the project, and for reacting to my descriptions of what and why I was writing.

My biggest thanks are saved for two very special colleagues: Caroline Chauncey, my editor at Harvard Education Press, a regular source of inspiration, came through again with off-the-charts literary skill, nuanced understanding of the subject, and cheerful guidance about how to make things more readable. And Amy Berman, my graduate assistant at the George Washington University, deserves more credit and gratitude than is possible in this kind of acknowledgment summary. I can't imagine how I would have taken on this project without them.

About the Author

M ICHAEL J. FEUER is a native of New York City. He attended public schools in Jamaica and then went to Queens College, where he majored in English, dabbled in radio, and edited the student newspaper. After living and studying in Israel (during the period that included the 1973 Yom Kippur War) and teaching English in Paris, he returned to Philadelphia for his MA and PhD at the University of Pennsylvania. His career has included five years on the faculty of Drexel University, seven years at the congressional Office of Technology Assessment and seventeen years at the National Academy of Sciences; he is now completing his sixth year as dean of the Graduate School of Education and Human Development at the George Washington University. Feuer was elected to the National Academy of Education in 2003 and to its presidency in 2013. He has published in economics, policy, education, and philosophy journals and books, and has had reviews, essays, and poems in various newspapers and magazines. His first book, *Moderating the Debate*, was published by Harvard Education Press in 2006. Feuer lives in Washington with his wife, Regine, a physician specializing in addiction. Their two grown children live and work in the DC area.

Index

academic achievement
  gaps in, 56, 124–125
  international comparisons of,
    95–106
  of minority students, 56
  socioeconomic factors in, 105
academic freedom, 42
academics
  See also researchers
  affiliations of, 11
Academy for Educational
  Development, 82
accountability, 23
  climate policy and, 137
  education policy and, 58–59
  of foundations, 31–33, 43, 121
  high-stakes, 61
  test-based, 18, 23, 34, 122–123,
    124–126
achievement gaps, 56, 124–125
adequate yearly progress, 127
Adopt-a-Highway programs, 36
advice industry, 6, 10–11, 73–108
  competition in, 106
  credibility of, 88, 108, 139
  crowding effects in, 80–88, 98,
    106
  education policy and, 89–108
  foreign financing in, 106–108, 143
  government and, 77–81, 87–88
  growth and diversity of, 80–88
  objectivity and, 107

performance indicators for,
    138–141, 146
  quality of, 86–87
advocacy-driven philanthropy, 9
advocacy organizations, 24–25
Affordable Care Act, 32
African American students, 56
agility, 92
Alexander, Lamar, 34
Alfred P. Sloan Foundation, 27, 40
Ali, Saleem, 107
altruism, 110, 119, 120
  defined, 37
  as public good, 36–41
ambiguity, 32–33
American Academy of Arts and
  Sciences, 77
American Association for the
  Advancement of Science, 76
American culture, 5, 17, 120
American Education Research
  Association, 94–95, 134
American Enterprise Institute (AEI),
  84, 100–101
American exceptionalism, 30
American Institutes for Research
  (AIR), 7, 82, 84, 101
American Philosophical Society,
  76–77
American Recovery and
  Reinvestment Act (ARRA), 62,
  64, 65

Andrew W. Mellon Foundation, 17, 20
Annenberg Challenge, 43
Annenberg Foundation, 19, 20, 25
applied research, 50–51, 53–54, 73
Aristotle, 89, 90
assessment, 122–123, 126–128

Barkan, Joanne, 2, 34
basic research, 50–51, 53–54, 73
behavioral economics, 119
Berkshire Taconic Community Foundation, 32
Bill & Melinda Gates Foundation, 3, 15, 20, 25, 34, 35, 88
    education spending by, 18–19, 43, 142
    influence of, 18
    programs supported by, 18–19
billionaire boys club, 1, 15, 42
Bishop, Matthew, 110
Blair, Peter, 13
Blanpied, William, 48
Boehner, John, 34, 124
Bohr, Nils, 50, 51
Brest, Paul, 142
Broad, Eli, 23
Broad Foundation, 15, 18, 22–23, 34, 103
Brookings Institution, 7, 83, 84, 101, 107
Buchanan, Patrick, 31
Buffet, Warren, 37
Bush, George W., 34
Bush, Vennevar, 47–48, 55

cacophony problem, 106
    See also crowding effects
Callahan, David, 29
Carnegie, Andrew, 35, 37

Carnegie Corporation, 3, 15, 16, 19–20, 21, 30, 32
Carnegie Endowment for International Peace, 7
Cassidy, John, 113
Center for American Progress (CAP), 103
Center for Education Policy, 7
Chan, Priscilla, 109, 110, 113, 115
charitable deductions, 28–31, 37, 41–42, 112–114, 117–118, 120–121, 144
charity. *See* philanthropy
charter schools, 18, 21, 23
    enrollment in, 35
    funding of, 24
    research and, 76
checks and balances, 41, 87
Chubin, Daryl, 49
civic responsibility, 110
civic society, 28, 117
Civil Rights Act (1964), 56
civil rights movement, 32
Civil War, 74–75
climate change, 109, 111, 135–138
coercion, 38–39, 40
cognitive neuroscience, 58
cognitive skills, 99–100
Coleman, James, 56
Coleman report, 56, 57, 97
collective action, 137, 140
Committee for Economic Development, 13
Common Core State Standards, 19, 21, 34, 90, 101–102, 131
common school reforms, 59
competition, 55
Conant, James, 91–92, 116
Congressional Budget Office (CBO), 130–131

Congressional Education
Organization (CEO), 122,
130–131, 144
Consortium of Social Science
Associations (COSSA), 135
consultants, 81
coordination, 33–36
corporate R&D, 81
corporations, 113, 117
correlational data, 61
Council of Chief State School
Officers, 122, 131, 145
Council on Foreign Relations (CRF),
102–103
credibility, 10, 88, 108, 121, 130, 139
Cremin, Lawrence, 89
cross-sectional studies, 60–61
crowding effects, 80–88, 98, 106

data collection organizations, 81
David and Lucile Packard
Foundation, 17, 24
democratic governance, 90–91
Department of Education, 3, 9, 60,
63, 88
doctoral degrees, 66–67
donors
benefits for, 118–120
motivations of, 37–38, 110, 113,
114–115
tax advantages for, 113–114
dual-use technology, 75
Duke Endowment, 19

economic competitiveness, 99–100,
102, 103, 105
Economic Policy Institute, 103–104
economics, of charity, 28–31, 41–45,
114–116
Edison, Thomas, 50, 51

education
decentralization in, 116
evaluation in, 95–106
federal role in, 123–124
Gates Foundation spending on,
18–19, 43, 142
government funding of, 9–10, 24,
35, 47, 55–71, 109, 132–138
innovations in, 92, 116
local control of, 116–117, 124, 127
private foundation spending on,
18–28
states' role in, 125, 127–128
STEM, 62–64
educational inequalities, 56–57, 97
education and human resources
(EHR) directorate, 62–63, 68,
134
education degrees, 66
education policy, 34
advice industry and, 89–108
information to inform, 128–131
politics of, 89–93
private foundations and, 1–3
test-based accountability and,
124–126
education production functions,
57–58
education reforms
accountability and, 58–59
common school, 59
evaluation of, 26, 43–45, 117
failures of, 25–26, 43
market-based, 125–126
standards-based, 61, 101–102,
126–128
education research, 55
crowding effects in, 98
debate over, 58–59, 65, 90
evaluation of, 27

education research *(Cont.)*
  federal funding of, 9–10, 47, 55–71,
    109, 132–138
  history of, 55–58, 60–62
  methods, 57–58, 60–61, 69–71
  objective, 143
  policy options, 11–12
  private funding of, 18–19, 26–27,
    43, 142
  as public good, 136–137
  quality of, 58, 93–94, 95
  scientifically based, 61
  spending on, 52–53
education science, 55–58
Education Sciences Reform Act
    (ESRA), 57, 60, 61
Elementary and Secondary Education
    Act (ESEA), 61, 109, 110,
    123–124, 128
environmental legislation, 38
Environmental Protection Agency,
    38–39
Equality of Education Opportunity
    (EEO), 56, 57
ethics, of charity, 118–120
Europe, philanthropy in, 28–29
evaluation, 135
  of advice industry, 138–141
  bias in, 27
  independent, 27
  of programs, 26, 27, 43–45, 117
evaluation companies, 81
Every Student Succeeds Act (ESSA),
    110, 122–124, 126–128
evidence-informed advice, 8
externalities, 42–43

family foundations, 28, 40
  See also private foundations
Family Health International (FHI),
    82

federal government. *See* government
federal grants, 67–69
federalism, 28, 30, 55, 120–121
FHI-360, 82
Field Foundation, 32
First International Mathematics
    Study (FIMS), 98
First International Science Study
    (FISS), 98
Fleishman, John, 28, 30
Ford Foundation, 17, 19, 21–22, 24,
    31, 32
foreign financing, 106–108, 143
foreign students, 106
Foundation Center, 138
France, charitable giving in, 28–29
Franklin, Benjamin, 76–77
Friedman, Milton, 125
funding
  of charter schools, 24
  competition for, 67–70, 86
  of education, 18–28, 35
  of education research, 9–10, 26–27,
    47, 55–71, 109, 132–138
  foreign, 106–108, 143
  government, 3–4, 7–10, 35, 47–71,
    109–111, 132–138
  monitoring of, 132–138, 145
  private, 7, 18–28, 54
  of scientific research, 3–5, 7, 9–10,
    47–71, 73, 109–111, 132–138
  sources, and credibility, 10
  think tanks and, 10–11, 84, 86–88
F.W. Olin Foundation, 19

Gamoran, Adam, 56
Gates, Bill and Melinda, 37, 115
Gates Foundation. *See* Bill & Melinda
    Gates Foundation
GE Foundation, 19
Germany, 99

global positioning systems (GPS),
74–75
government
advice industry and, 80–81, 87–88
alignment between philanthropy
and, 33–36
budget constraints on, 8, 9
education funding by, 9–10, 24, 35,
46, 55–71, 109, 132–138
funding from, 7–10
information sources for, 128–131
role of, 3–4, 36, 48–49, 52, 54, 55,
73, 123–124
science funding by, 47–71, 109–
111, 132–138
spending by, 35–36
use of science by, 73–80
Government Accountability Office,
27, 130
graduate degrees, 66–67
Graham, Lindsey, 114
grant money, 67–69
Green, Michael, 110
Gregg, Judd, 34

Hanushek, Eric, 99–100
Harvey, Hal, 142
Henig, Jeff, 76, 84
Heritage Foundation, 101–102
Herter, Albert, 75
Hess, Frederick, 30, 126
Hewlett Foundation, 26–27
high-stakes accountability, 61
Holland, Paul, 70
Horace Mann League, 104
Howard Hughes Medical Institution
(HHMI), 37

ideology, 13, 21, 95, 118, 141
incentive effects, 114–116, 137
income inequality, 114

individual charity, 40–41
individualism, 116
Individuals with Disabilities
Education Act, 60
information, vertical integration of,
128–131
information overload, 122
infrastructure, spending on, 35–36
innovation, 92, 116
Institute of Education Sciences (IES),
57, 59–60, 62, 68–69, 134
Institute of International Education,
106
intellectual property law, 51
International Association for the
Evaluation of Educational
Achievement, 98
international comparative
assessment, 95–106
iron ships, 74–75

Jennings, Jack, 123
Jim Joseph Foundation, 26
John D. and Catherine T. MacArthur
Foundation, 17
John Templeton Foundation, 19

Kellogg Foundation, 19
Kennedy, Ted, 34, 124
Killewald, Alexandra, 99
Klein, Joel, 103
knowledge
demand for, 5
organization of, 122–131, 144–145
Kyoto Protocol, 136

Lagemann, Ellen Condliffe, 3, 35,
55–56
Lauder Institute, 81, 84, 140
learning time, 23
Lilly Endowment, 17, 19, 20

Lincoln, Abraham, 73–75, 77
Linn, Robert, 127
Long, Daniel, 56
longitudinal studies, 60–61
Loveless, Tom, 101

Madison, James, 30
market-based reforms, 23, 125–126
McPherson, Mike, 3
Medvetz, Thomas, 13
membership dues, 39–40
Menand, Louis, 79
Mervis, Jeffrey, 133
Miller, George, 34
minority students, academic
    achievement of, 56
mission agencies, 63
Mississippi Common Fund Trust, 19
model schools, 25
Moynihan, Daniel Patrick, 73

National Academies of Sciences,
    Engineering, and Medicine
    (NASEM), 80, 100, 112, 121–
    122, 132
    monitoring by, 137–138, 145
National Academy of Education
    (NAEd), 6, 7, 57, 121–122, 138,
    145
National Academy of Sciences (NAS),
    6, 7, 12–13, 100, 132
    advice from, 78–80
    establishment of, 74–75, 77–78
    work of, 75–76
national advocacy organizations, 24
National Assessment of Educational
    Progress, 57
National Board for Education
    Sciences, 60
National Bureau of Economic
    Research, 84

National Cancer Institute, 64
National Center for Education and
    the Economy (NCEE), 102
National Center for Education
    Statistics, 88
National Council of La Raza, 18
national defense spending, 52
National Governance Association,
    122, 131
National Institute of Child Health
    and Human Development
    (NICHD), 64, 68, 134
National Institute of Deafness
    and Other Communicative
    Disorders (NIDCD), 64, 68
National Institute of Education, 57
National Institutes of Health (NIH),
    3, 63–64, 114, 133
National Research Council (NRC),
    78, 79–80
National Science Foundation (NSF),
    3, 4, 9
    budget of, 62, 133–135
    education spending by, 64–65
    establishment of, 49, 75
    grant awards by, 67–68
    opposition to, 48–49
    work of, 75–76
national standards, 23
National Superintendents
    Roundtable, 104
A Nation at Risk, 96–97, 99, 102, 103
neuroscience, 58
Next Generation Science Standards,
    19
Nixon, Richard, 31–32
No Child Left Behind (NCLB), 34, 61,
    122, 124–128

Obama, Barack, 79, 80, 109, 126
Obama administration, 23, 101–102

objectivity, 10–13, 88, 107, 128, 143
Office of Educational Research and
    Improvement (OERI), 57, 60
Office of Technology Assessment
    (OTA), 6, 7, 13, 94, 123, 128–131,
    133
Olson, Mancur, 38
Open Educational Resources, 21
Open Society Foundations, 17, 24
Organization for Economic
    Cooperation and Development
    (OECD), 98, 104

Paris Agreement, 109, 135–138
partisanship, 7, 9, 13, 87, 95, 118, 133,
    141
Pasteur, Louis, 50–51
Pasteur's Quadrant (Stokes), 50–51
patent law, 51
peer review, 6, 135, 139
performance pay, 23
Perry, Mark, 101
personal values, 12
philanthro-capitalism, 110, 114
philanthropy, 15–45
    advocacy-driven, 9
    alignment between government
        and, 33–36
    challenges for, 142–143
    demand for, 42–43
    economics of, 28–31, 41–45,
        114–116
    educational, 18–28
    ethics of, 118–120
    in Europe, 28–29
    hostility toward, 113, 142–143
    individual, 40–41
    monitoring of, 132–138
    motivations for, 37–38, 113–115
    motivations of, 110
    physiology of, 118–120

politics of, 28–31
psychology of, 118–120
as public good, 36–41
strategic, 8, 110
trends in, 15–20
physiology, of charity, 118–120
pilot testing, 43, 121
Pilot Twelve-Country Study, 98
pluralism, 30–31
policy options, 11–12, 109–147
    for advice industry, 138–141, 146
    information to inform, 128–131
    knowledge organization, 122–131,
        144–145
    research funding, 132–138, 145
    tax code changes, 112–122, 144
political culture, 41
political science, 133–135
politicians, 9–10, 81, 111, 143
politics
    of charity, 28–31
    education and, 89–93
    of science funding, 48–49
    tax code and, 116
Pritchett, Henry, 3
private foundations, 8
    See also specific foundations
    accountability of, 31–33, 43, 121
    coordination by, 33–36
    criticism of, 42–43, 58, 113–114,
        142–143
    educational policy and, 1–3
    education spending by, 18–28
    growth in, 16
    historical perspective on, 3, 15–16
    power and influence of, 30, 88
    role of, 4, 28, 87
    small, 40
    theory and practice of, 20–28
    trends in, 8–9, 15–20
private schools, enrollment in, 35

private sector, R&D and, 54
privatization, 23
profit maximization, 115
Programme for International Student
  Assessment (PISA), 98–106
Programme for the International
  Assessment of Adult
  Competencies (PIAAC), 98
Progress in International Reading
  Literacy Study (PIRLS), 98
Progressive movement, 76, 77
psychology, of charity, 118–120
public good(s), 8, 9, 11, 29, 113
  charity and altruism as, 36–41
  education research as, 136–137
  science as, 50–55, 75–76
public policy, 109–147
  See also policy options
  advice industry and, 89–95
  climate, 135–138
  education, 34, 89–95
  politics of, 89–93
  private foundations and, 33–36
  research and, 5
  on science, 47–48, 51–52, 54–55,
    76–80
  think tanks and, 7–8, 87–88
public-private partnership, 41, 43, 143
public schools
  donations to, 42
  enrollment in, 35
  funding of, 24
qualitative research, 12, 60–61
quantitative research, 12

race, 56
Race to the Top, 34, 142
RAND Corporation, 6, 7, 82, 84, 100
randomized controlled experiments,
  60, 61, 69, 70
rationality, 76

Ravitch, Diane, 1–2, 3, 15, 23, 126
Reagan, Ronald, 96, 133
Reckhow, Sarah, 24–25, 33–34
reflective benefits, 119
Reich, Rob, 30–31, 117
religious organizations, 39–40
research and development (R&D)
  See also education research;
    scientific research
  basic vs. applied, 50–51, 53–54, 73
  changes in, 8
  corporate, 81
  economics of, 52
  funding of, 3–5, 7, 9–10, 52–53, 73,
    110–111
  in health and education, 59–60
  neutrality in, 7
  objective, 10–11, 43–45, 128
  political challenges to, 4, 9–10
  private sector and, 54
  as public good, 11
  public policy and, 5
  qualitative, 12, 60–61
  quantitative, 12
  social science, 7, 8, 55–71, 98
  university-based, 6, 53–54
researchers
  career pressures on, 67
  competition among, 67
  education, 65–66
  growth in number of, 9
  pressures on, 10
research organizations, 10–11
Rice, Condoleeza, 103
Rising Above the Gathering Storm,
  100
Robert Wood Johnson Foundation,
  17
Robert W. Woodruff Foundation,
  20
Rockefeller Foundation, 16, 30

Roosevelt, Franklin, 47, 73
Russell Sage Foundation, 15–16

Schelling, Thomas, 95
Schmidt, William, 99
Schneider, Mark, 100
scholarly research, 6, 11
school choice, 125
school desegregation, 56
science
    of education, 55–58
    funding of, 4–5, 9–10, 109, 110–111
    political attitudes toward, 143
    as public good, 50–55, 75–76
    public policy and, 76–80
    status of, 55
    translational, 54
    use of, by government, 73–80
science, technology, engineering,
        and mathematics (STEM)
        education, 62–64
Science and Public Policy, 49
science policy, 47–48, 51–52, 54–55,
        77
Science: The Endless Frontier, 47–48
scientifically based research, 61
scientific research
    federal funding of, 47–71, 132–138
    objective, 143
    output from, 53–54
    progress and, 56–57
    scholarly, 6, 11
scientism, 55
Second International Mathematics
        Study (SIMS), 98
self-interest, 118–119, 136
separation of powers, 30
Silicon Valley Community
        Foundation, 19
small schools, 25, 43
Smith, Harold, 48, 54–55

Smith, Lamar, 135
Snyder, Jeffrey, 24
social science research
    changes in, 8
    crowding effects in, 98
    funding of, 55–71
    neutrality in, 7
social sciences
    doctoral degrees in, 66–67
    graduate programs in, 9
Spencer Foundation, 26, 40
spot contracts, 129
SRI International, 83, 84
standards-based reform, 61, 101–102,
        126–128
Steelman, John, 49
Stewart, Potter, 32–33
Stokes, Donald, 50–51
Strategic Defense Initiative (SDI), 133
strategic philanthropy, 8, 110
Study of Early Child Care and Youth
        Development, 64
Summers, Lawrence, 101
sunshine laws, 80
Surowiecki, James, 113–114, 117
Susan Thompson Buffett Foundation,
        17
Sweden, charitable giving in, 29

tax code, 28–31, 37, 38, 40, 41–45,
        112–122, 144
teachers
    academic performance and, 105
    effectiveness of, 18
    performance pay for, 23
teacher unions, 33
Teaching and Learning International
        Survey (TALIS), 98
TeachingWorks, 116
Tea Party, 49
technology, dual-use, 75

Technology Assessment Board
    (TAB), 13
tenure, 67
terrorism, 109
test-based accountability, 18, 23, 34,
    122–123, 124–126
think tanks, 6–11, 78–80
    See also advice industry
    annual expenditures of, 85
    educational, 89–95
    foreign financing of, 106–108, 143
    funding of, 10–11, 84, 86, 87–88
    growth and diversity of, 80–88
    objectivity of, 13
    performance indicators for,
        138–141, 146
    public policy and, 7–8, 87–88
    role of, 7–8, 100
Third International Math and Science
    Study (TIMSS), 98, 99
Thomas Fordham Institute, 103
Tocqueville, Alexis de, 30
Toobin, Jeffrey, 32
tragedy of the commons, 111
translational science, 54
transparency, 121
Truman, Harry, 47, 48, 73
Tucker, Marc, 102, 103

United Nations Framework
    Convention on Climate Change
    (UNFCCC), 136–137

United States, charitable giving in,
    28, 29–31
universities, 6, 10, 11, 42, 81
    fiscal pressures on, 11
    foreign students in, 106
    pressures on scholars in, 67
    role of, 53–54
Urban Institute (UI), 83, 84
US Department of Education. *See*
    Department of Education

values, 12

Wallace Foundation, 19, 26
Walton Family Foundation, 15, 18,
    20, 22, 24
war, 74–75
War Revenue Act, 37
Washington, DC, 116
wealth concentration, 9, 15–16, 112
WestEd, 83
Whitehurst, Grover, 69
William, Dylan, 101
William and Flora Hewlett
    Foundation, 17, 21
William T. Grant Foundation, 27, 40
W.K. Kellogg Foundation, 17
World Giving Index (WGI), 28

Xie, Yu, 99

Zuckerberg, Mark, 109, 110, 113, 115